# Transition report update

## May 2006

## Contents

# Foreword by the Chief Economist

# The outlook is positive, although risks to macroeconomic stability remain.

The objective of this *Transition Report Update* is to review macroeconomic developments in the transition region in 2005 and provide an outlook for 2006. Traditionally, the *Update* has reported on capital flows in the region. This year we take a closer look at the flow of remittances from workers living abroad.

Remittances have become an important source of external capital for many transition countries, particularly in the Western Balkans and the poorest countries of the Commonwealth of Independent States. One country, Russia, acts as both an important source as well as a recipient of remittances.

As Chapter 1 of the *Update* shows, the exact magnitude of remittance flows is difficult to measure, as many transfers are made through informal channels. Recorded remittances alone, however, have reached almost US$ 500 per capita in Bosnia and Herzegovina and Serbia and Montenegro. In five countries – Albania, Bosnia and Herzegovina, Moldova, Serbia and Montenegro and Tajikistan – they are worth more than 10 per cent of GDP. In over a third of the transition region remittance flows exceed foreign direct investment (FDI). What is more, remittances fluctuate less, from year to year, than FDI.

Remittance income is primarily used for consumption and is partly responsible for the import boom observed in countries like Albania, Bosnia and Herzegovina and Moldova. However, a survey undertaken for this *Update* in five high-remittance countries shows that a small but important share of remittances is also used to finance investment and enterprise creation.

Remittances probably play a more important role in small enterprise development than is commonly assumed. Only about a quarter of the entrepreneurs interviewed received remittances, but almost half of them have used the funds for business purposes – primarily to finance start-ups, but also for capital expenditure and working capital. Enterprises with access to remittances typically financed 40 per cent of their start-up costs from this source. Remittances also help businesses to raise other sources of finance. Firms with access to remittances are able to cover a higher share of their financing needs through bank loans.

The main macroeconomic developments in the transition region in 2005 are discussed in Chapter 2 of the *Update*, complemented by country-by-country assessments at the end of the report. The general picture is positive, although some risks to macroeconomic stability remain. Transition economies continue to perform strongly, both in absolute terms and relative to most other major regions in the world. The preliminary growth estimate for the region for 2005 is 5.6 per cent. For 2006 we expect a modest weakening of performance to 5.3 per cent. Over the medium term the transition economies are expected to grow by around 4–5 per cent per year on average.

There are a number of risks to the macroeconomic outlook. In central Europe levels of external debt are generally high. These are mostly private and concentrated among foreign-owned enterprises and financial institutions, and any downturn in the economy could cause difficulties in maintaining confidence and sustainability. Political risks remain significant in parts of south-eastern Europe and the Commonwealth of Independent States (CIS). The resource-rich countries of the CIS, including Russia, should continue to benefit from high commodity prices. However, the continuation of growth and stability in these countries will require both a careful management of resource revenues and a renewed push on structural reforms.

As integration of the transition countries into the world economy increases, so does their vulnerability to global economic trends. As highlighted in last year's *Transition Report Update*, capital flows to transition countries are sensitive to the difference between local and international interest rates (the opportunity cost of investing in the region). With interest rates in western economies picking up, particularly in the United States, we may see a decrease in investor interest in the region. To remain competitive, the transition countries will need to offer strong growth prospects and an increasingly attractive business environment.

The *Transition Report Update* was prepared by the EBRD's Office of the Chief Economist (OCE) under my general guidance. The editorial team was led by Sam Fankhauser and consisted of Vanessa Mitchell-Thomson, Alan Rousso and Peter Sanfey. The chapter on remittances was drafted by Francesca Pissarides and

Peter Sanfey, with contributions from Svetlana Tashchilova. The macroeconomic overview and its summary charts and tables were put together by Libor Krkoska and Katrin Robeck. The country assessments were prepared by the OCE country economists. The country data tables were produced by Tatiana Lysenko under the guidance of Elisabetta Falcetti. Michelle Bacca, Angela Golding and Laura Sanchez provided administrative support. Anthony Martin and Angela Hill of the EBRD's Publishing Unit prepared the text for publication and managed the publication process. Editorial support was provided by Richard German. Steven Still of the EBRD's Design Unit managed the design and print production. The work on remittances was partially funded by the Swiss State Secretariat for Economic Affairs. This funding is gratefully acknowledged.

The assessments and views expressed in this *Update* are not necessarily those of the EBRD. The responsibility for the content rests with myself on behalf of OCE. The "cut-off" date for most of the information in the *Update* is mid-March 2006.

**Erik Berglof**
Chief Economist and Special Counsellor to the President

*5 April 2006*

# Remittances as a source of finance in transition countries

1

One of the biggest changes brought about by transition has been the increase in opportunities for individuals to live and work abroad. Potential mobility is greatest for the new European Union (EU) member states of central Europe, despite labour movement restrictions imposed by most of the older EU countries. The most substantial labour outflows from the transition region, however, have come from south-eastern Europe (especially the Western Balkans) and the Caucasus. This migration has resulted in a significant increase in remittances from workers living abroad. Although remittances mostly fund consumption, a small, but nevertheless important, amount finances investment and enterprise creation.

This chapter examines the size of remittance flows to transition countries and their role in boosting enterprise development. There are three reasons why the study of remittances is particularly relevant for transition. First, remittances are a relatively new phenomenon for many countries in the transition region. Some of the countries with the highest remittance inflows (relative to GDP) were receiving negligible amounts little more than a decade ago.[1] Secondly, under some circumstances, migration and remittance flows can facilitate the transition to a market economy – for example, by lowering the rate of unemployment in the recipient country and by allowing policy makers to pursue a more rapid course of transition.[2] Lastly, remittances can contribute to investment in small businesses, helping to revive the spirit of entrepreneurship that was often discouraged or even suppressed under previous regimes.

The focus of this chapter is on the potential use of remittances in the home country. Lack of access to finance is frequently cited by enterprises throughout the transition region as one of the main obstacles to starting, operating or expanding a business.[3] The enterprise sector of labour-exporting transition countries is typically dominated by micro, small and medium-sized businesses (micro enterprises with less than 10 employees forming the largest number). These businesses normally face the greatest difficulty in accessing external sources of finance, such as bank loans. Therefore, they rely on internal funds, such as own savings or retained earnings, and loans or gifts from family and friends. Importantly, this chapter addresses the extent to which current levels of entrepreneurship and investment are financed by remittances in the high labour-exporting transition countries.

The chapter is divided into two sections. The first provides an overview of total remittance flows to transition countries. In 2004 (the latest year for which comprehensive data are available) remittances totalled US$ 19.1 billion, or 1.3 per cent of overall GDP in the region. The true figure, however, is likely to have been much higher, as many remittances are sent as cash or goods through informal channels and are not recorded in the official statistics. The aggregate figure also conceals a wide variation across the countries of the region, with remittances ranging between 0.4 and 27 per cent of GDP. In addition, Russia is an important source of remittances to other countries in the region.[4]

Section 1 shows that remittances are relatively stable over time, although apparently large increases can occur when statistical coverage improves or more inflows are channelled through financial institutions. For some countries, remittance flows are larger and more stable than foreign direct investment (FDI), and may therefore serve as a more important and reliable source of finance.

The second section of the chapter considers remittances as a source of investment finance, based on the results of a survey of over 600 micro and small businesses in five transition countries where annual remittance inflows are large. These enterprises, which had all participated in the 2005 EBRD/World Bank Business Environment and Enterprise Performance Survey (BEEPS), were re-interviewed about the extent to which remittances had financed the start-up, operation or expansion of their business. The survey indicated that a significant share of the remittances received by enterprise owners was used to finance business investment and, in particular, start-ups. The survey also showed that the banking system plays an important role in the transfer of remittances, and that there is little correlation between the receipt of remittances and perceptions of the difficulty of accessing finance.

# 1. Remittances to transition countries

The study of remittances has attracted wide attention in recent years from the development community.[5] Increasingly, the important role that remittances play as an instrument for poverty alleviation and business development is being recognised.

## Chart 1

### Remittances as a percentage of GDP in transition countries, 2004

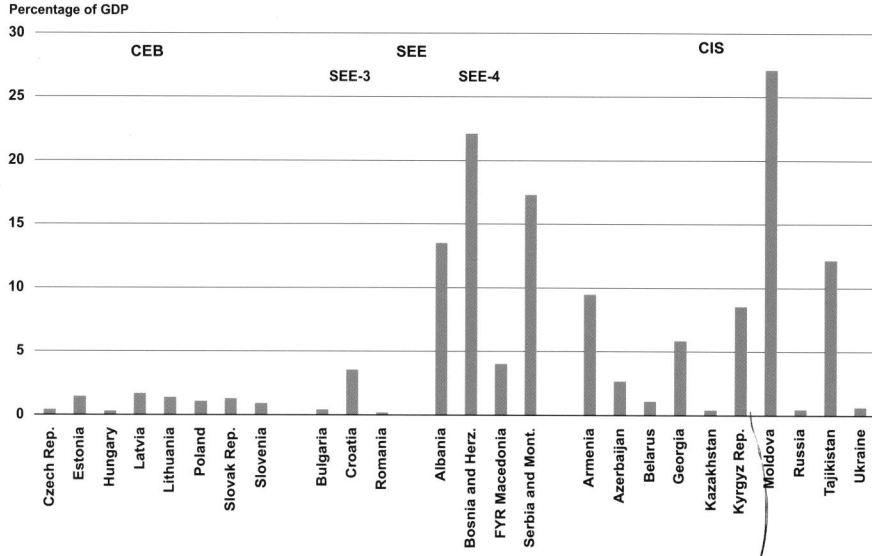

Sources: EBRD and IMF *Balance of Payments Yearbook* (2005).

Notes: Remittances are defined as the sum of three component parts in the balance of payments: workers' remittances, compensation received by employees and migrants' transfers. Unless otherwise stated, data on remittances have been taken from the IMF *Balance of Payments Yearbook*.

For Albania data on remittances for 2004 were taken from the National Bank of Albania. For Serbia and Montenegro data on private remittances were taken from recent IMF country reports. These estimates are much higher than those reported by the National Bank of Serbia in their annual report of 2004. For the Slovak Republic data on compensation of employees for 2004 were taken from the National Bank of the Slovak Republic.

No reliable data were available for Turkmenistan and Uzbekistan.

Data on compensation of employees in some countries (for example, Bosnia and Herzegovina) include the earnings of local employees of foreign embassies and international institutions, in line with the IMF *Balance of Payments manual*. However, these items are not remittances by themselves and arguably should not be included in remittance statistics.

Many countries fail to report any data for migrants' transfers. Bulgaria, the Czech Republic and Ukraine report no data on workers' remittances. The Kyrgyz Republic reports no data on compensation of employees.

The World Bank has estimated that total *recorded* remittances to developing countries reached US$ 160.4 billion in 2004, compared with US$ 31.2 billion in 1990. It has also speculated that the total figure could be up to 50 per cent higher if *unrecorded* remittances were included.[6]

Defining and measuring remittances can be difficult and sometimes controversial. In this chapter remittances are defined as the sum of three components in the balance of payments:[7]

■ workers' remittances – transfers by migrants employed and residing, typically for at least a year, in another country

■ compensation received by employees – wages, salaries and other benefits (cash or in-kind) received by non-resident workers, for work performed on behalf of residents of other countries, whilst living abroad

■ migrants' transfers – financial items or change in net worth arising from the change of residence from one country to another.

The primary source of the data is the IMF *Balance of Payments Yearbook*. The first two categories appear on the current account of the balance of payments, while the third (typically smaller) is included in the capital account.

According to the latest estimates, total gross remittance flows to transition countries amounted to US$ 19.1 billion in 2004. However, the total figure masks wide variations across the region. Chart 1 shows the remittances for each country as a percentage of GDP. Moldova had the highest ratio of remittances to GDP at 27.1 per cent, followed by Bosnia and Herzegovina (22.1 per cent), Serbia and Montenegro (17.3 per cent), Albania (13.5 per cent), and Tajikistan (12.2 per cent). Other countries with sizeable inflows included Armenia, Georgia and the Kyrgyz Republic. In contrast to the above countries of the Western Balkans (SEE-4) and Commonwealth of Independent States (CIS), recorded remittances were less than 2 per cent of GDP in the countries of central eastern Europe and the Baltic states (CEB) and in Bulgaria and Romania (both of which are scheduled to join the EU in 2007).

The volume of remittances to the transition region has grown steadily in recent years. Between 2001 and 2004, total inflows in (nominal) US dollar terms rose by 84 per cent, compared with a total increase in GDP (also in dollar terms) of 74 per cent. This contrasts with the commonly held view that remittances are counter-cyclical and rise in periods of economic hardship in the home countries.[8] Chart 2 shows this trend by region during 2001–04. The growth of remittances has been greatest in the non-oil-producing CIS countries, where the ratio to GDP has risen from 1.4 to 2.4 per cent. In the other transition regions the ratio has remained virtually unchanged.

Some of the largest increases in remittance inflows have occurred in countries recording rapid GDP growth in recent years, such as Armenia, Moldova and Tajikistan. In Moldova annual GDP growth has been above 6 per cent in every year since 2000. In Armenia and Tajikistan it has exceeded 8 per cent annually. It is therefore hard to argue that increased inflows are motivated by migrants' concern for the economic well-being of their relatives at home. Instead, it is more likely that the quality of remittance data and its coverage have improved.[9] Also, the upturn in the Russian economy since the crisis in 1998 has enhanced the working conditions and salaries of migrant workers there, and so remittances back to their home countries have increased. The relative buoyancy of remittances also reflects easier transfer through the banking system.

The importance of remittances for some transition countries is further illustrated by comparing the size of inflows with two other sources of foreign exchange inflows – net FDI and export revenue. Charts 3 and 4 show the top 10 countries in the region ranked by the ratio of remittances to net FDI and export revenue respectively. For Albania, Bosnia and Herzegovina, Moldova and Serbia and Montenegro, remittances exceeded net FDI in 2004 by between three and five times. Indeed, the ranking of these countries is identical to that for the remittance-to-GDP ratio discussed earlier. The same four countries also stand out in terms of the ratio of remittances to export revenue, although the relative ranking differs. Albania received 74 per cent more in remittances in 2004 than it did in export revenue. For Bosnia and Herzegovina, revenue from remittances also exceeded that of exports.

Remittances also constitute a relatively stable source of inflows, especially in comparison to FDI. Chart 5 compares

## Chart 2

### Remittances by region as a percentage of GDP, 2001–04

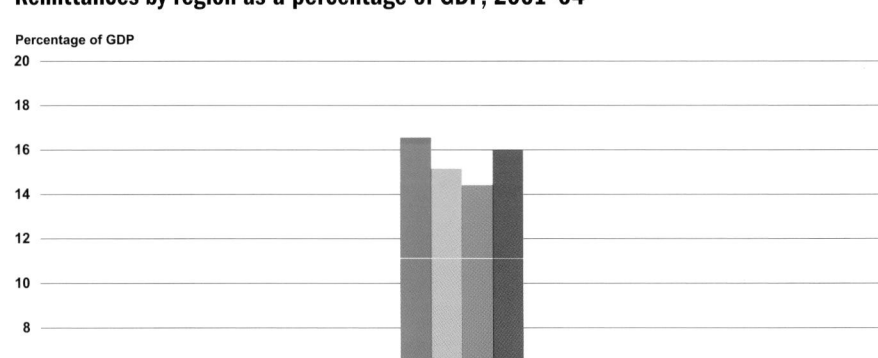

Percentage of GDP

■ 2001    ■ 2002    ■ 2003    ■ 2004

Sources: EBRD and IMF *Balance of Payments Yearbook* (2005).

Notes: Data on remittances have been taken from the IMF *Balance of Payments Yearbook*, unless otherwise stated (see Chart 1). Azerbaijan reports no data for compensation of employees in 2001–02, and in the Slovak Republic data on compensation of employees for 2001 were taken from the National Bank of the Slovak Republic.

Oil-producing countries in the CIS include Azerbaijan, Kazakhstan and Russia. The non-oil-producing countries include Armenia, Belarus, Georgia, the Kyrgyz Republic, Moldova, Tajikistan and Ukraine.

No reliable data were available for Turkmenistan and Uzbekistan.

## Chart 3

### Ratio of remittances to net FDI in selected transition countries, 2004

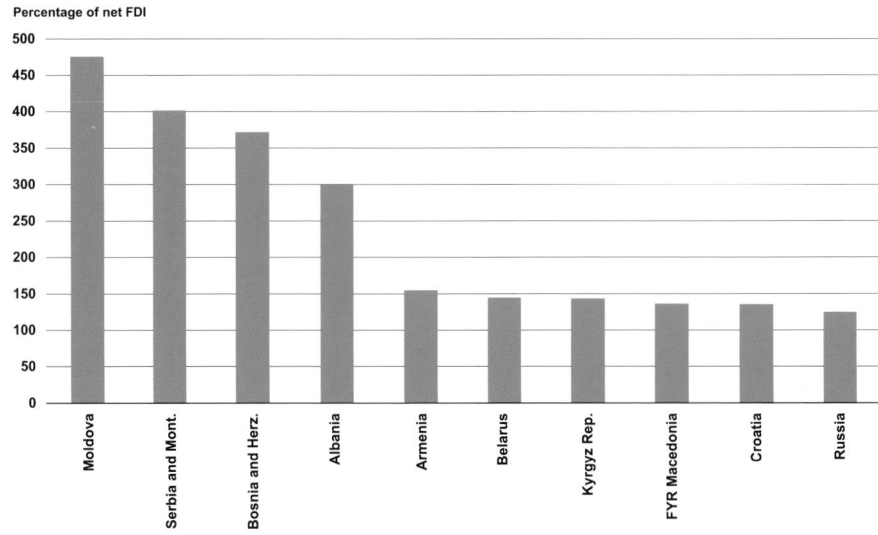

Percentage of net FDI

Sources: EBRD and IMF *Balance of Payments Yearbook* (2005).

Note: Data on remittances have been taken from the IMF *Balance of Payments Yearbook*, unless otherwise stated (see Chart 1).

the volatility of remittances and FDI over time. It tracks, for selected countries, the degree of variation for both series, evaluated from 1999–2004. The chart indicates that remittances are indeed more stable than FDI (which often hinges on one or two large privatisation deals, especially in those countries where remittances are of more importance).

There is also a link between remittances and trade deficits. Countries with high

remittance inflows tend to have large trade deficits – close to 20 per cent of GDP on average – while those with low inflows have average deficits of around 5 per cent of GDP. This supports the view that remittances mainly finance the consumption of imports (see Box 1 for the relationship between consumption patterns and remittances in Serbia). Nevertheless, as the next section argues, remittances can also be put to productive use.

## Chart 4

### Ratio of remittances to export revenue in selected transition countries, 2004

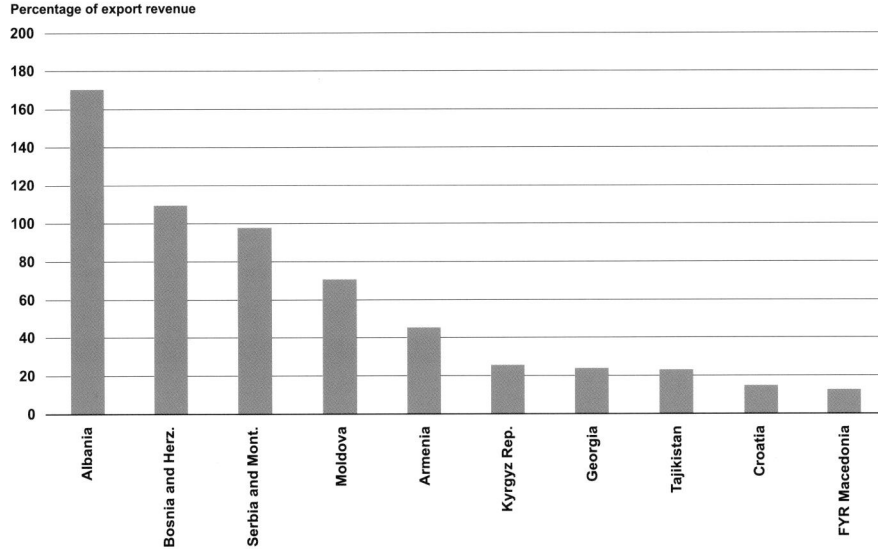

Percentage of export revenue

Sources: EBRD and IMF *Balance of Payments Yearbook* (2005).
Note: Data on remittances have been taken from the IMF *Balance of Payments Yearbook*, unless otherwise stated (see Chart 1).

## Chart 5

### Variability of remittances and net FDI in selected transition countries, 1999–2004

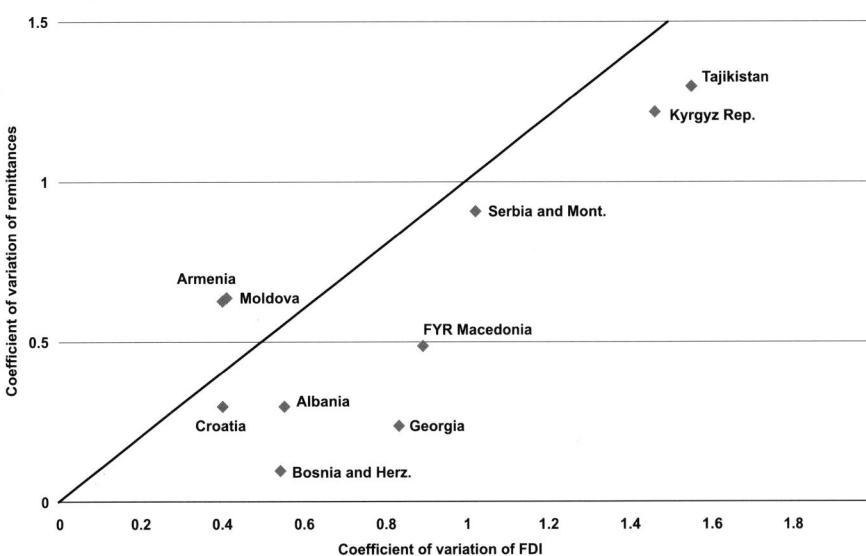

Sources: EBRD and IMF *Balance of Payments Yearbook* (2005).
Notes: Data on remittances have been taken from the IMF *Balance of Payments Yearbook*, unless otherwise stated (see Charts 1 and 2). Ukraine reports no data on workers' remittances in 1999 and 2000 and Azerbaijan reports no data on compensation of employees from 1999–2002.
The coefficient of variation is defined as the ratio of the standard deviation to the mean. It allows the variability of two different series to be compared on a common scale. Countries below the 45-degree line have greater variability in net FDI than remittances over the period.

# 2. Remittances as a source of microfinance

Financial intermediaries, such as banks, have grown rapidly in the transition countries in recent years.[10] However, enterprises in the region still rely on their own sources of funds to start up and carry out business to a larger extent than their counterparts in mature market economies. According to data from the 2005 BEEPS, enterprises in the transition countries finance 76 per cent of new investment with internal funds and loans from family and friends, compared with 65 per cent in mature market economies. (Remittances are not identified as a separate source of

finance, but may be considered part of the category of loans from family and friends.) The rest is funded through the financial sector (formal and informal), government subsidies and trade credit.

As noted earlier, remittance inflows are mainly used to finance consumption and are particularly important in this respect to poorer families in the transition region. However, in countries with a weak financial sector, remittances can also finance new or existing businesses. Recent research in developing countries has shown how remittances can help alleviate a lack of credit and can compensate for an undeveloped financial sector.[11] If the financial sector cannot meet the demand for credit, entrepreneurs – particularly those who lack a credit history, collateral and retained earnings – can use remittances to start up, operate and expand their businesses.

## Remittances and business development

To ascertain whether remittances play the same role across the transition region, a survey of more than 600 micro and small enterprises was carried out in January 2006. Enterprises in five countries with high remittance inflows relative to GDP – Albania, Bosnia and Herzegovina, Georgia, Moldova, and Serbia and Montenegro – were surveyed.[12] All of the enterprises had also participated in the 2005 BEEPS, allowing a comparison of the respective data. Table 1 shows the country distribution of the enterprises in the sample, their response rate and the number that received remittances.

The main purpose of the survey was to identify the extent to which micro and small enterprises use remittances to finance their start-up costs, investment and working capital needs. Table 1 shows that 130 of the 476 company owners (27.3 per cent) who provided valid responses had received remittances from abroad. There was little difference between micro (28 per cent) and small (27 per cent) enterprises, but responses varied across countries. The percentage of Moldovan entrepreneurs receiving remittances was much higher (40 per cent) than in the other countries (typically around 25 per cent). This was not surprising, however, given that Moldova has the highest ratio of remittances to GDP within the transition region.

## Box 1

### Consumption and remittances – the case of Serbia

Within the transition region, Serbia receives one of the highest levels of remittances (see Chart 1). But what effect do these remittances have on household consumption? A recent survey in Serbia highlights the link between remittances and consumer behaviour.[i] The survey identified both sources of income in households and detailed patterns of spending.

Individuals were asked about possible sources of non-labour income, including "help and presents from friends and family abroad". This category corresponds, more or less, to one of the components of remittances defined in this chapter. A total of 128 households, or about 5 per cent of the sample, had received remittances during the previous three months. The amounts ranged from 600 dinar (€9 at the then exchange rate) to 83,300 dinar (€1,283), with an average amount of 16,035 dinar (€247).

The most interesting finding of the survey was that remittances generally go to those families with an above-average financial situation. This can be seen in two ways. First, 39 per cent of respondents which received remittances rated their financial situation as "bad" or "very bad", compared with 52.5 per cent of those who did not receive remittances.

Meanwhile, 18 per cent of families receiving remittances described their condition as "good", compared with 11.5 per cent of those without. This result may be because recipients of remittances take the additional funds into account when assessing their financial situation. Secondly, those who receive remittances have on average a monthly income that is 15 per cent higher than those who do not, even when the amount of remittances is excluded. If they are included, the income of remittance-receiving households is 34 per cent higher. This suggests that remittances may lead to increased income disparities.[ii]

Another important conclusion was that, even though families which receive remittances consume more than those which do not, they also manage (on average) to save part of their total income. Monthly consumption, related to income, is 92 per cent for households receiving remittances and 107 per cent for non-remittance families.

The most prominent difference between the two groups relates to spending on items such as clothing and footwear – more than 60 per cent higher in remittance-receiving households. In contrast, there is little difference between the two groups in terms of possession of durables, such as refrigerators or televisions.

i  Living Standards Measurement Study (LSMS) household survey for Serbia, 2003.

ii These results will be presented in more detail in a forthcoming EBRD working paper.

Entrepreneurs who had received remittances were asked if they had used any part of the funds to finance their business activities. They were also asked to specify the percentage of their start-up costs, investment and working capital needs financed through remittances. Some 43 per cent of those entrepreneurs who received remittances had used them for one or more of these purposes. The responses were again equally balanced between micro and small enterprises, but with wide variations between countries (ranging from 84 per cent of the sample in Albania to 30 per cent in Georgia).

According to the survey, 93 per cent of entrepreneurs who used remittances for business development did so to establish their enterprises. Remittances also financed a significant proportion of investment and working capital needs, but to a lesser extent. Although the small size of the survey sample rules out any detailed formal statistical analysis, the results in Table 2 are informative. Perhaps the most significant finding concerns the importance of remittances for business creation; 40 per cent of start-up costs have been covered by remittances in the five countries overall. This suggests that remittances may be an underestimated channel through which migration supports enterprise creation. Most studies on this subject to date have considered wealth accumulated by returning migrants as the principal source of such support.[13]

### Table 1

### Micro and small enterprises participating in the remittances survey

| | Micro and small enterprises participating in BEEPS 2005 | Micro and small enterprises also participating in remittances survey | Respondents providing valid answers | Respondents receiving remittances |
|---|---|---|---|---|
| **Albania** | 151 | 132 | 103 | 25 |
| **Bosnia and Herzegovina** | 122 | 106 | 81 | 20 |
| **Georgia** | 149 | 126 | 81 | 20 |
| **Moldova** | 138 | 115 | 93 | 37 |
| **Serbia and Montenegro** | 195 | 160 | 118 | 28 |
| **Total** | 755 | 639 | 476 | 130 |

Source: EBRD.

Notes: Micro and small enterprises are defined as businesses with 2–49 employees.

The EBRD/World Bank Business Environment and Enterprise Performance Survey (BEEPS) was undertaken in spring 2005. This survey assessed the evolving business environment and performance of firms in the transition region. The remittances survey was carried out in January 2006.

Another interesting finding is that small enterprises have relied more heavily on remittances to cover start-up costs than micro firms. As small enterprises are generally older than micro firms, this may indicate that the importance of remittances for starting a business has decreased over time.

Table 3 shows that, in general, the share of remittances in start-up and investment costs were higher for older firms than for more recently established companies. This suggests that other sources of finance have gradually become available to take the place of remittances. The development of the banking sector and the significantly increased per capita income in recent years in all five countries provide further support to this hypothesis.

Although the BEEPS and remittance survey results imply that entrepreneurs who received remittances found it easier to access external sources of finance than those without remittances, the difference was small and not statistically significant.[14] The finding suggests that remittances are seen by entrepreneurs as an internal rather than external source of finance, more like equity than debt.

This interpretation is reinforced by two further observations. First, remittances are not a substitute for bank loans. On the contrary, recipients of remittances are able to finance working capital and investment needs through a higher share of bank loans than companies that do not receive remittances.[15] The availability of remittances – seen as equity or subordinated debt by lenders – strengthens the balance sheet of enterprises and may have a positive impact on the probability of obtaining a bank loan. Secondly, remittances are a substitute for internal funds/retained earnings in the financing of business activities.

## Remittances and bank transfers

The survey also explored the degree to which remittances were transferred through banks. Overall, more than half of the entrepreneurs who received remittances (76 out of 130) obtained them through a bank transfer. There was a wide variation across the sample countries, apparently unrelated to the degree of financial intermediation.[16]

It is more likely that country differences can be explained by the proximity of migrants. The closer the host country, the more likely migrants will bring remittances back with them as cash during visits home.

Familiarity with the host country may also be a factor. For example, in Georgia, all remittances were transferred through banks as the well-established migrant workforce is comfortable with the local banking system. In contrast, only 12 per cent of the sample in Albania used the banking system to transfer money. This can be explained partly by the fact that the majority of migrants had invested in a number of informal financial pyramid schemes which collapsed in 1997, wiping out the value of remittances and savings. This further reduced confidence in the banking sector, which has only recovered in recent years, and may be responsible for the low percentage of remittance transfers through banks.

Almost half of the entrepreneurs who used remittances to finance their business (26 out of 56) had the funds transferred through banks, which typically charged administrative fees of between 1 and 2 per cent to release the money. This response was virtually the same in all five countries, implying only minor technical obstacles for recipients to obtain money from abroad through banks.[17] Recipients do not necessarily need a bank account (although account holders pay a reduced fee on international money transfers), administrative fees are low, and money transfers are quickly accessible once funds have reached the recipient bank.

In some cases, regulations to prevent corruption and money-laundering force disclosure of the identity of recipients of even small amounts. This can act as a deterrent to using the formal banking sector for foreign exchange transactions. More importantly, however, incentives to keep funds with the recipient banks are limited. In many countries, deposit rates on accounts denominated in foreign currency are very low, due to the high reserve requirements (for example, 38 per cent in Serbia and Montenegro) and lack of competition in the banking system.

---

### Table 2

### Median share of business costs financed by remittances, in per cent

| | Firm size | Start-up costs | Investment | Working capital |
|---|---|---|---|---|
| **Albania** | Micro | 33 | 40 | 20 |
| | Small | 45 | 35 | 10 |
| | Total | 40 | 40 | 10 |
| **Bosnia and Herzegovina** | Micro | 10 | 80 | 10 |
| | Small | 30 | 30 | 30 |
| | Total | 30 | 30 | 30 |
| **Georgia** | Micro | 15 | 5 | 35 |
| | Small | 100 | 0 | 100 |
| | Total | 20 | 0 | 70 |
| **Moldova** | Micro | 50 | 30 | 20 |
| | Small | 60 | 20 | 10 |
| | Total | 50 | 20 | 20 |
| **Serbia and Montenegro** | Micro | 10 | 15 | 15 |
| | Small | 35 | 10 | 5 |
| | Total | 30 | 10 | 10 |
| **All countries** | | 40 | 20 | 12.5 |

Source: EBRD.

Notes: Data refer to the 130 enterprises participating in the remittances survey which received funds from family or friends working abroad. Micro enterprises are defined as those with 2–9 employees. Small enterprises are defined as those with 10–49 employees.

---

### Table 3

### Median share of business costs financed by remittances, by age of business and in per cent

| | Age of business (in years) | Start-up costs | Investment | Working capital |
|---|---|---|---|---|
| **Albania** | 0–4 | 32.5 | 45 | 10 |
| | 5–9 | 32.5 | 30 | 20 |
| | >10 | 45 | 35 | 0 |
| **Bosnia and Herzegovina** | 0–4 | — | — | — |
| | 5–9 | 30 | 30 | 30 |
| | >10 | — | — | — |
| **Georgia** | 0–4 | 10 | 5 | 85 |
| | 5–9 | 100 | 0 | 0 |
| | >10 | — | — | — |
| **Moldova** | 0–4 | 60 | 20 | 10 |
| | 5–9 | 50 | 20 | 20 |
| | >10 | 55 | 20 | 20 |
| **Serbia and Montenegro** | 0–4 | 10 | 10 | 10 |
| | 5–9 | 10 | 10 | 15 |
| | >10 | 50 | 25 | 0 |
| **All countries** | 0–4 | 20 | 20 | 10 |
| | 5–9 | 30 | 20 | 20 |
| | >10 | 50 | 25 | 10 |

Source: EBRD.

Note: Data refer to the 130 enterprises participating in the remittances survey which received funds from family or friends working abroad.

# 3. Conclusion

Several important features of remittances to transition countries are evident. First, remittance levels are significant – ranging from below 1 per cent of GDP in a number of countries to 27 per cent of GDP in Moldova. These figures would probably be much higher if unrecorded remittances were included. Secondly, remittances are a stable source of income (more so than FDI). Thirdly, remittances may be playing a more important role in small enterprise creation and expansion than has been previously assumed. In countries where the financial sector does not work efficiently, enterprises tend to rely more on their own sources of funding (internal funds) and on loans from family and friends to start up and operate businesses. Remittances are an important component of support from family and friends, just as savings from returning migrants boost internal funds.

The enterprise survey shows that remittances help to alleviate a lack of credit for business start-ups and for micro and small firm activity more generally. Nearly half of the entrepreneurs in the sample who benefited from remittances used these funds to start or further develop their own businesses. However, the share of remittances used to finance a business is greater for older enterprises than for younger firms, suggesting that other financial sources are becoming more accessible as transition progresses.

Other findings confirm that enterprises benefiting from remittances have better access to bank loans than others, and that a relatively large proportion of remittances are transferred through banks (although these may not be linked to business financing).

Remittance flows are a vital source of income for many transition countries. Nevertheless, their role to date has received little attention. Remittances are important, not just as a stable source of foreign exchange but also as much-needed finance for small businesses. However, the statistical coverage of remittances needs to be improved. To enhance their role and effectiveness in fostering transition, remittances need to be channelled through the formal financial sector, therefore widening access to finance more generally. Also, migrants need to be encouraged to think about how they can stimulate business creation and development in their home countries.

## Endnotes

1   Prior to the break-up of Yugoslavia and the Soviet Union, transfers between the constituent republics of these countries were considered internal transfers rather than remittances.

2   Migration and remittances may also retard the speed of transition if, for example, the most able people leave the country and the subsequent reduction in labour supply in the home country puts upward pressure on wages. See Mancellari et al. (1996) and Rapoport and Docquier (2005).

3   See the results from the latest EBRD/World Bank Business Environment and Enterprise Performance Survey (BEEPS), as summarised in the Transition Report 2005 (EBRD, 2005).

4   Figures from the latest IMF Balance of Payments Yearbook show a total outflow of remittances (as defined in the text) from Russia of more than US$5.5 billion, compared with an inflow of US$2.7 billion.

5   Recent examples include World Bank (2003 and 2006) and IMF (2005a). A useful overview of theoretical issues is contained in Rapoport and Docquier (2005).

6   See World Bank (2006).

7   This definition is consistent with recent work by the World Bank (see World Bank, 2006).

8   A recent paper by Sayan (2006), using time series evidence for 12 developing countries, fails to find much evidence in support of the counter-cyclical hypothesis.

9   See IMF (2005b, 2005c) and Kireyev (2006).

10   For a discussion of this phenomenon and the associated macroeconomic implications, see the Transition Report 2005.

11   See Giuliano and Ruiz-Arranz (2005).

12   Micro and small enterprises are defined as firms with 2–9 employees and 10–49 employees, respectively.

13   See Rapoport and Docquier (2005).

14   The mean value of the scores allocated to access to finance is 2.42 for the recipients of remittances and 2.48 for the enterprises which did not receive remittances. Scores range from 1= no obstacle to 4= major obstacle.

15   Bank loans accounted for an average of 12.6 per cent of working capital needs and 23.5 per cent of investment for recipients of remittances, compared with 10.7 per cent and 13 per cent respectively for firms which did not receive remittances.

16   The correlation between the share of remittances transferred through banks and the share of domestic credit to the private sector in GDP was low at 0.15.

17   The senders may, however, face more serious obstacles as they have to pay administration fees (and exchange rate commissions) that are often well in excess of those paid by the recipient.

## References

EBRD (2005), Transition Report 2005: Business in transition.

P. Giuliano and M. Ruiz-Arranz (2005), "Remittances, financial development and growth", IMF Working Paper No. WP/05/234, Washington D.C.

IMF (2005a), World economic outlook: globalization and external imbalances, April 2005, IMF, Washington D.C.

IMF (2005b), Republic of Tajikistan: Selected issues and statistical appendix, April 2005, IMF Country Report No. 05/131, Washington D.C.

IMF (2005c), Republic of Moldova: Selected issues, February 2005, IMF Country Report No. 05/54, Washington D.C.

IMF (2006), Serbia and Montenegro: Sixth Review, February 2006, IMF Country Report No. 06/58, Washington D.C.

A. Kireyev (2006), "The macroeconomics of remittances: the case of Tajikistan", IMF Working Paper No. WP/06/2, Washington D.C.

A. Mancellari, H. Papapanagos and P. Sanfey (1996), "Job creation and temporary emigration: the case of Albania", The Economics of Transition, vol. 4(2), pp. 471–490.

H. Rapoport and F. Docquier (2005), "The economics of migrants' remittances", Discussion Paper No. 1531, Institute for the Study of Labor, Bonn.

S. Sayan (2006), "Business cycles and workers' remittances: how do migrant workers respond to cyclical movements of GDP at home?" IMF Working Paper No. WP/06/52, Washington D.C.

World Bank (2003), Global development finance: striving for stability in development finance, Washington D.C.

World Bank (2006), Global economic prospects. Economic implications of remittances and migration, Washington D.C.

# Macroeconomic performance, outlook and risks

2

The transition countries continue to perform robustly, compared with most other major regions of the world. Macroeconomic stability has been maintained and inflation rates are, on average, at single-digit levels. Only a few early transition and natural resource-exporting countries have inflation rates above 10 per cent. In the latter group of countries, this is due to strong domestic spending pressures and weak monetary policies dealing with foreign exchange inflows.

In the medium term, the transition countries are expected to grow by 4–5 per cent each year on average. The economic performance of the new European Union (EU) member states will be driven by increased integration with world markets. Some other countries, including Russia, will continue to benefit from high commodity prices. However, the extent of the benefit will depend on responsible policies to maintain macroeconomic stability and on progress with reforms. Labour costs will continue to rise, but generally in line with increases in productivity.

The positive outlook assumes the maintenance of macroeconomic and political stability and steady progress with transition reforms. However, several key risks remain. The increased integration of the region, especially central eastern Europe and the Baltic states (CEB), into the world economy brings an increased vulnerability to negative shocks and potential loss of confidence in emerging markets. In parts of south-eastern Europe (SEE) and the Commonwealth of Independent States (CIS), political uncertainties remain a danger. In natural resource-rich CIS countries, the continuation of growth and stability requires careful management of volatile commodity prices. CIS countries not exporting oil or gas face a broader range of economic and political risks than other transition countries.

# 1. Output and employment

## 1.1. GDP growth

Average real GDP growth in transition countries declined to an estimated 5.6 per cent in 2005 from 6.7 per cent in 2004. This was due mainly to a slowdown in several large countries, including Poland, Romania and Ukraine. However, the transition region is catching up with the major advanced western economies, and growth rates compare favourably with most other emerging world markets except developing Asia. A small upturn is expected in CEB and SEE in 2006. The new EU member states and candidate countries are benefiting from their integration with the European single market, and the Western Balkans are also gaining advantages from their closer relationship with the EU. Growth in the CIS continued to out-perform other transition sub-regions in 2005, from a lower base, mostly as a result of high commodity prices. However, the rate of growth in the CIS is declining sharply and is likely to fall further in 2006, reflecting the limited investment to date in productive capacity.

## 1.2. Sources of GDP growth

GDP growth in CEB has been driven by investment and exports from mostly foreign-owned enterprises. Strong inflows of foreign direct investment (FDI) have been channelled particularly into manufacturers of cars and car components and electronic and optical equipment in recent years. The start of production at recently completed facilities in CEB has contributed to a significant increase in growth performance. This performance is likely to be sustained in the near future. In Romania and Ukraine, private consumption (particularly of imported goods) remains the impetus behind GDP growth. This has been financed by generous wage and pension increases, as well as strong credit expansion. Export growth rates in both countries, and also investment in Ukraine, decelerated sharply in 2005. In Russia growth has been driven by household consumption, underpinned by increases in private incomes and credit to the private sector. However, there has been a marked slowdown in the natural resources sector (reflected in slower export growth), due to capacity constraints and ineffective government policies.

## 1.3. Labour

Low labour force participation and high unemployment rates are common across the transition countries. Only Kazakhstan and Russia report a higher share of the working age population in the labour force, compared with the average for the EU-15 countries. In both Kazakhstan and Russia, job creation has been driven by high commodity prices. Relatively low life expectancy in these two countries also contributes to a lower working age population close to the retirement age. In CEB, Estonia and the Czech Republic have relatively high employment rates, supported by strong job creation by foreign-owned enterprises. Poland has a particularly high unemployment rate, exceeding 15 per cent of the labour force. A large proportion of the Polish working age population also remains outside of the labour force. Although wide-ranging social benefits across much of the transition region provide a necessary safety net, they may deter unemployed people and those not economically active from seeking new jobs.

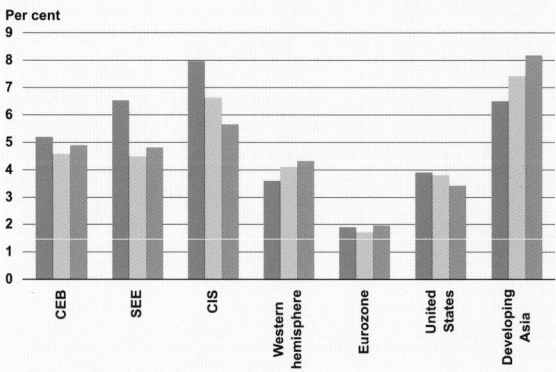

### Chart 1.1

**International comparison of growth, 2004–06**

Per cent

■ GDP growth 2004    ■ GDP growth 2005 (estimate)
■ GDP growth 2006 (projection)

Sources: EBRD and IMF *World Economic Outlook*.

Note: Data for CEB, SEE and CIS are taken from the EBRD. Data for the eurozone, developing Asia, the United States and the western hemisphere are taken from the *World Economic Outlook* (April 2006).

Developing Asia includes China, India and the newly industrialised Asian economies. The western hemisphere includes Central and Latin America. Regional aggregates are weighted averages.

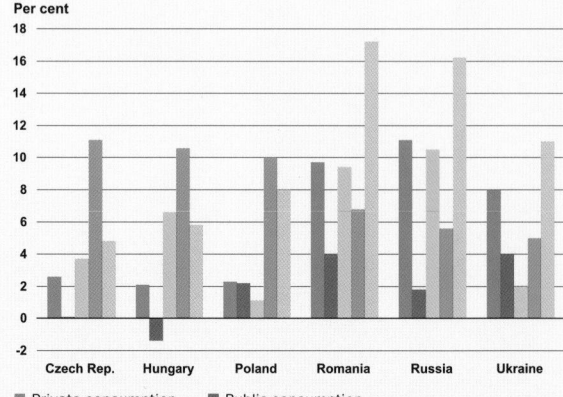

### Chart 1.2

**Sources of real growth in selected transition countries, 2005**

Per cent

■ Private consumption    ■ Public consumption
■ Gross fixed capital formation    ■ Exports of goods and services
■ Imports of goods and services

Source: EBRD.

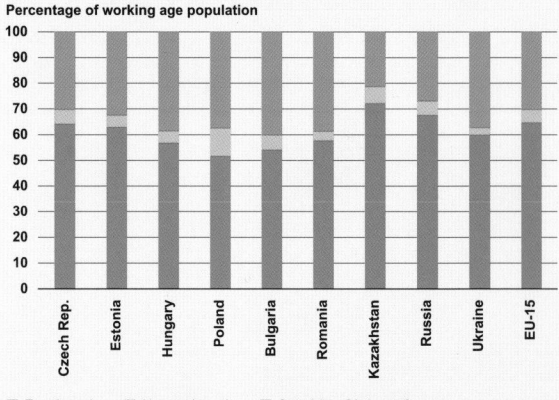

### Chart 1.3

**Composition of working age population in selected transition countries, 2005**

Percentage of working age population

■ Employed    ■ Unemployed    ■ Outside of labour force

Sources: Eurostat and EBRD.

Note: Data for EU member states and candidate countries taken from Eurostat. All other country data taken from national statistical offices.

# 2. Economic policies

## 2.1. Inflation

Most transition countries recorded an inflation rate below 10 per cent in 2005. Some – for example, Bosnia and Herzegovina, Bulgaria, the Baltic states and FYR Macedonia – have successfully used currency boards or a fixed exchange rate arrangement to underpin monetary policy. Others – such as the Czech Republic, Poland and the Slovak Republic – have adopted inflation targeting to achieve price stability. In CEB price increases in non-tradable goods and changes in indirect taxes following EU accession in 2004 have had an upward impact on overall inflation (although the effect has been modest). The average inflation rate in these countries remains, however, above rates in mature market economies. There is also a small group of transition countries where annual average inflation is above 10 per cent. These include Belarus, Turkmenistan and Uzbekistan (where transition reforms are lagging behind), Azerbaijan and Russia (two major oil producers), as well as Moldova, Serbia and Montenegro and Ukraine. All transition countries have experienced inflation pressures from increasing energy prices.

## 2.2. Fiscal policy

Many countries in CEB and SEE face continuing difficulties in balancing public spending with government revenues. This reflects the relatively high level of social expenditures, substantial enterprise subsidies, and large infrastructure investments. Hungary and Poland also face large interest payments on public debt, and would therefore benefit from the lower interest rates in the eurozone once they adopt the euro. The fiscal situation in some countries is further aggravated by the need to finance recently implemented pension system reforms. Nevertheless, Bulgaria and Estonia, both of which conduct a strict fiscal policy combined with a currency board arrangement, have reported significant primary fiscal surpluses. Commodity exporters in the CIS have generally reported substantial budget surpluses, with Azerbaijan, Kazakhstan and Russia saving most of the revenues in stabilisation funds. In Ukraine large increases in wages and social transfers, coupled with the slowing economy, have led to a relatively high primary fiscal deficit in 2005.

## 2.3. Maastricht criteria

Macroeconomic policy in the new EU member states is guided by the aim of adopting the euro in the future. This requires that they meet the Maastricht criteria on eurozone membership, measured by the five indicators presented in Table 2.1. The target date for entry varies across CEB. The three Baltic states, the Slovak Republic and Slovenia have already joined the Exchange Rate Mechanism II (ERM II) and intend to adopt the euro as soon as possible. By the end of 2005, however, only Slovenia had satisfied all five criteria. The larger CEB countries especially need to tighten their fiscal policies as the costs of pension reforms are only gradually included in the headline fiscal deficits. In the Baltic states inflation exceeded the reference value. Energy prices account for a large share of consumer expenditure in these countries, and their economies have been growing fast with prices of non-tradable goods increasing substantially.

### Chart 2.1
**Annual average inflation**

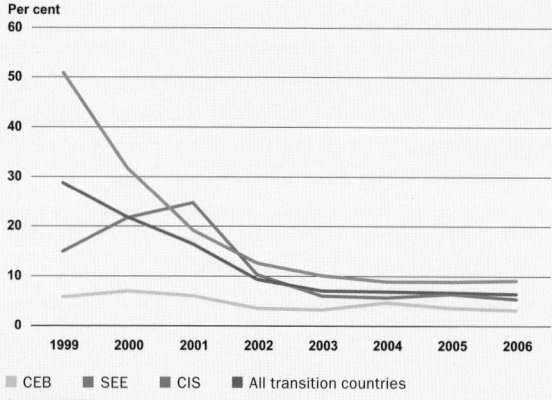

Source: EBRD.
Note: Data for 2005 and 2006 are EBRD estimates and projections.

### Chart 2.2
**Composition of fiscal balance in selected transition countries, 2005**

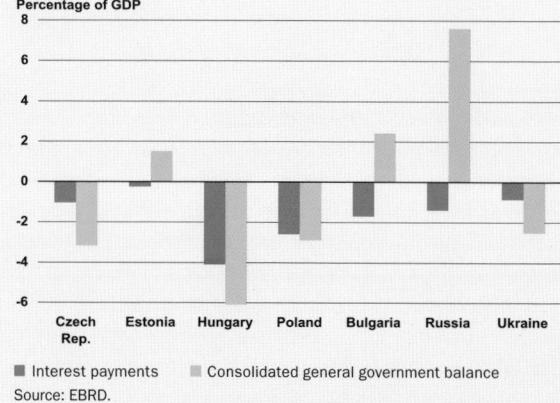

Source: EBRD.

### Table 2.1
**Maastricht criteria for new EU member states, 2005**

| | Inflation | Fiscal balance | Public debt | Interest rates | Exchange rate |
|---|---|---|---|---|---|
| Reference value | 2.5 | –3.0 | 60.0 | 5.3 | +/– 15% |
| Czech Rep. | 1.9 | –3.2 | 25.8 | 3.6 | 10.8 |
| Estonia | 4.1 | 1.5 | 5.1 | 6.3 | 0.0 |
| Hungary | 3.6 | –6.1 | 58.9 | 7.0 | 8.3 |
| Latvia | 6.7 | –1.2 | 12.6 | 5.9 | 6.7 |
| Lithuania | 2.7 | –2.0 | 17.5 | 4.7 | 0.0 |
| Poland | 2.1 | –2.9 | 47.4 | 4.9 | 19.0 |
| Slovak Rep. | 2.5 | –3.0 | 45.2 | 3.6 | 7.3 |
| Slovenia | 2.5 | –1.9 | 30.0 | 3.8 | 1.2 |

Source: EBRD.
Note: EU member states wishing to adopt the euro as their currency must meet five of the so-called Maastricht criteria:

▌ the average rate of inflation should be no more than 1.5 percentage points above the rate of the three EU countries with the lowest inflation one year before the examination

▌ the budget deficit must be below 3 per cent of GDP

▌ the government debt should not exceed 60 per cent of GDP

▌ the long-term interest rate should be no more than 2 percentage points above the rate of the three EU countries with the lowest inflation one year before the examination

▌ the country must have participated in ERM II for a period of at least two years prior to the convergence examination without severe tensions and the exchange rate against the euro should have stayed within set fluctuation margins.

The table presents the annual average inflation rate, fiscal balance and public debt as a share of GDP, the 10-year government bond yield at the end of year, and the difference between the maximum and minimum monthly exchange rate over the past two years as a share of the average exchange rate.

# 3. External sector

## 3.1. Current account

Many CEB countries run significant current account deficits. These not only reflect large trade deficits but also reinvested earnings by foreign-owned enterprises, which are shown both as outflows on the income balance in the current account and inflows of FDI in the capital account. Trade deficits in CEB have declined steeply over time, except for the Baltic states, as newly established production facilities have started exporting. Many countries in SEE – and also countries in the CIS which do not export oil and gas (with the exception of Belarus and Ukraine) – have established sizeable trade deficits, sometimes exceeding 20 per cent of GDP. In the Western Balkans and early transition countries in the CIS, trade deficits have mostly been covered by net current transfers, including remittances and international aid. Remittance inflows in several transition countries have exceeded 10 per cent of GDP, and reached as high as 27 per cent (in Moldova in 2004) – see Chapter 1. Official development assistance in the Western Balkans and parts of the CIS constitutes up to 5 per cent of GDP. Current account balances in oil and gas-exporting CIS countries are driven by commodity exports and, as a consequence, these countries have sizeable trade surpluses.

## 3.2. Foreign direct investment

CEB has benefited from a substantial increase in greenfield FDI since EU accession. However, overall net flows have been strongly influenced by a small number of large privatisations. Some CEB countries also have significant FDI outflows as local companies, many foreign-owned, invest abroad. A similar boost to greenfield FDI inflows can be expected in the short term in Bulgaria, Croatia and Romania as major investors may relocate there from CEB. Major oil and gas projects have attracted significant inflows of FDI to natural resource-rich CIS countries, although there was a sharp fall in net FDI in 2005 in Azerbaijan and Kazakhstan due to the withdrawal of some foreign investors and increased investment by local companies abroad. The Western Balkans and CIS countries not exporting oil or gas still receive only limited inflows of FDI in absolute terms, a large part of which is related to privatisations or acquisitions. Overall, net FDI inflows to transition countries are larger than inflows into China when expressed as a share of GDP.

## 3.3. External debt

In the majority of transition countries, total external public and private debt exceeds 40 per cent of GDP. Private debt accounts for the greatest proportion of external debt in these countries, with the exception of Serbia and Montenegro and the Kyrgyz Republic. Several smaller transition countries, such as Estonia and Latvia, have very high levels of private external debt, which is related to foreign ownership of the financial sector and the significant level of cross-border inter-company loans. Advanced transition countries benefit from investment grade ratings, while large local companies have access to international markets. Oil and gas-exporting countries also regularly access international capital markets. Less advanced transition countries, however, still rely mostly on multilateral and bilateral debt, and some of them continue to restructure their obligations to achieve debt sustainability. In the Kyrgyz Republic public debt accounts for about 90 per cent of total external debt, even after further rescheduling by the Paris Club in 2005. More debt relief may be required for the level to become sustainable.

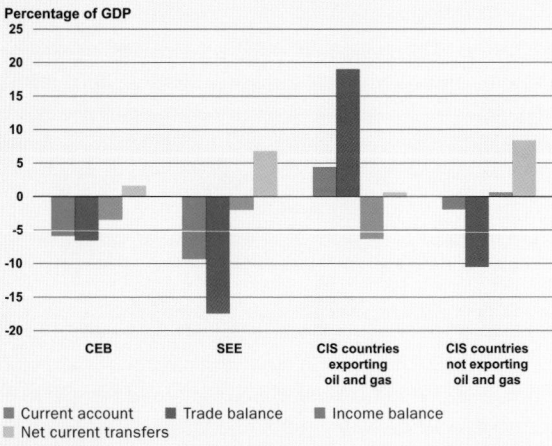

Chart 3.1

**Composition of current account, 2005**

Percentage of GDP

■ Current account    ■ Trade balance    ■ Income balance
■ Net current transfers

Source: EBRD.

Notes: Countries in the CIS which export oil and gas include Azerbaijan, Kazakhstan, Russia and Turkmenistan. Countries in the CIS which do not export oil and gas include Armenia, Belarus, Georgia, the Kyrgyz Republic, Moldova, Tajikistan, Ukraine and Uzbekistan.

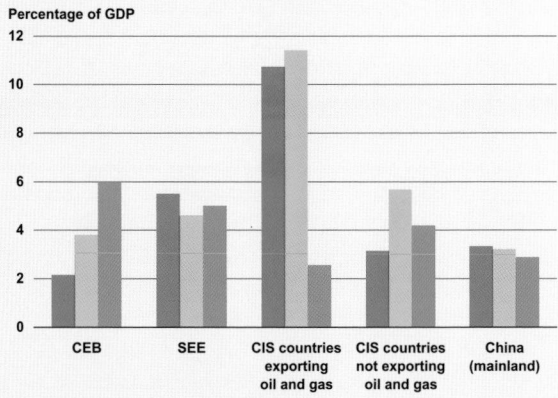

Chart 3.2

**Foreign direct investment, 2003–05**

Percentage of GDP

■ 2003    ■ 2004    ■ 2005

Sources: EBRD and IMF World Economic Outlook.

Notes: Countries in the CIS which export oil and gas include Azerbaijan, Kazakhstan, Russia and Turkmenistan. Countries in the CIS which do not export oil and gas include Armenia, Belarus, Georgia, the Kyrgyz Republic, Moldova, Tajikistan, Ukraine and Uzbekistan.

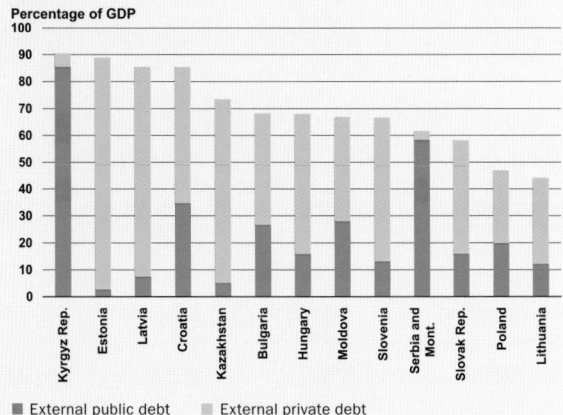

Chart 3.3

**Public and private external debt in selected transition countries, 2005**

Percentage of GDP

■ External public debt    ■ External private debt

Source: EBRD.

# 4. Outlook

## 4.1. GDP growth

In the next five years, transition countries are expected to grow annually by about 4.5 per cent on average, with the CIS achieving the highest growth rates of over 6 per cent a year. These forecasts are based partly on the fact that many transition countries are still at relatively low income levels and have strong potential for catch-up growth. Other influential factors are the availability of cheap skilled labour across the region, progress in structural and institutional reforms, high investment rates driven by private sector development and infrastructure upgrades, and natural resource endowment in a few CIS countries. This outlook (or base case scenario) assumes the maintenance of macroeconomic and political stability, steady progress in transition and no major external shocks. The growth forecasts are also subject to significant risks (see Section 5).

## 4.2. Per capita income

Per capita income in transition countries is expected to increase significantly over the next 10 years, exceeding growth rates in developed market economies by several percentage points each year on average. As a result, per capita income should converge towards the levels of developed countries. Only CEB countries, however, are expected to reach the current EU minimum within that period. If the outlook assumptions hold, this could happen by 2011, although there is likely to be significant variation among the performance of individual countries. The transition countries in SEE (except Croatia) and the CIS are not expected to approach this level of income in the foreseeable future, although their GDP growth rates are likely to continue exceeding those of CEB countries.

## 4.3. Labour costs

In the past five years, labour costs have increased significantly across the transition region. In nominal terms, however, even the most advanced countries have substantially lower labour costs than developed countries. For the region as a whole, strong growth in real labour costs (expressed in US dollars) of about 8–10 per cent a year on average is expected over the medium term. The high wage growth forecast for the CIS compared with CEB and SEE reflects the very low base. Wage increases are expected to be generally in line with productivity increases, implying no loss of competitiveness. However, some producers in labour-intensive industries, such as textiles and footwear, in advanced transition countries may find it increasingly difficult to remain competitive in relation to south-east Asian countries. Any failure to maintain macroeconomic and political stability or keep labour costs in line with productivity will most likely lead, as a result of weaker currencies in such a case, to a substantially lower growth of real US dollar labour costs.

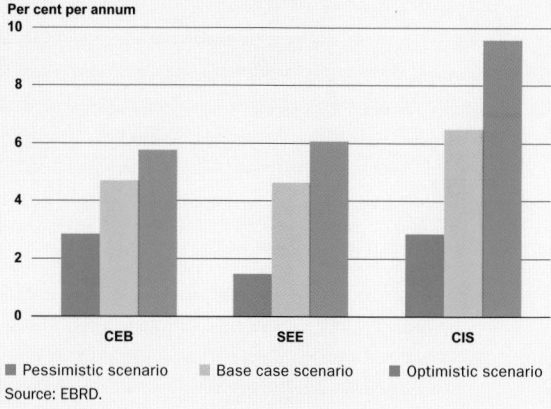

Chart 4.1

**GDP growth projections, 2006–10**

Per cent per annum

■ Pessimistic scenario ■ Base case scenario ■ Optimistic scenario
Source: EBRD.

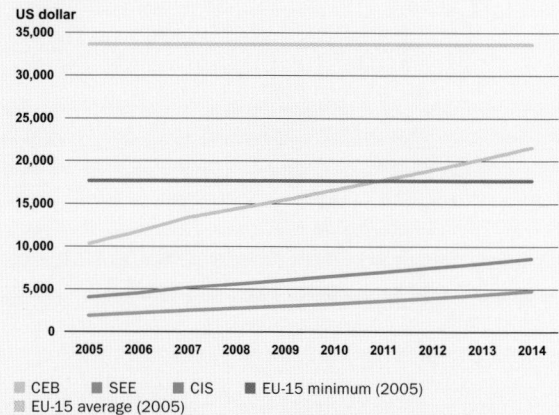

Chart 4.2

**GDP per capita projections in transition countries, 2005–14**

US dollar

■ CEB ■ SEE ■ CIS ■ EU-15 minimum (2005)
■ EU-15 average (2005)
Sources: EBRD and Eurostat.
Note: Data for CEB, SEE and CIS are taken from the EBRD. Data for EU-15 are taken from Eurostat.

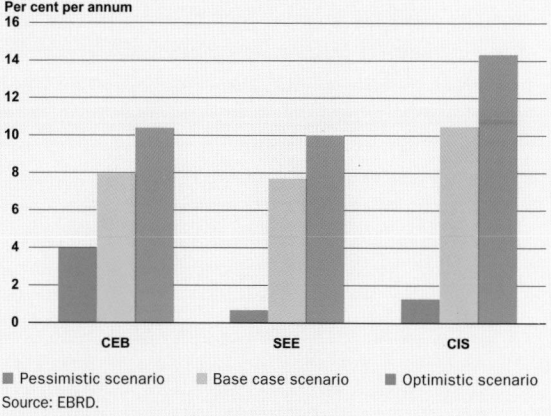

Chart 4.3

**Projected growth in labour costs, 2006–10**

Per cent per annum

■ Pessimistic scenario ■ Base case scenario ■ Optimistic scenario
Source: EBRD.
Note: Real labour costs are calculated in US dollars.

# 5. Risks

## 5.1. Economic risks

The outlook for transition countries is subject to significant risks. Any loss of confidence in emerging markets would have an impact in the region and could cause a significant drop in growth and FDI. Countries with weaker fundamentals would be more vulnerable to these global risks. In CEB the major risk factors are high fiscal deficits and, in some cases, a limited commitment to implementing necessary public sector reforms. The high level of private external debt is another factor that needs to be monitored carefully. In SEE high trade deficits emphasise the reliance of several countries on remittance and official assistance flows. Risks associated with monetary policy or the exchange rate regime in SEE are relatively low due to strong exchange rate controls in a number of countries. The public and external account balances in oil and gas-exporting CIS countries benefit from strong commodity prices, but these may decline in the long term and vulnerabilities may increase. CIS countries not exporting oil and gas, which are on average the poorest in the region, are subject to higher economic risks than other transition countries.

## 5.2. Political and business environment risks

Political and business environment risks are relatively modest in CEB, but higher on average in SEE and the CIS. In the Western Balkans significant political risks persist due to several unresolved issues (the future status of Kosovo, the possible break-up of the State Union of Serbia and Montenegro). Business environment risks are also high in this part of SEE due to weak regulatory structures and legal institutions. In the CIS countries, there are uncertainties over political succession mechanisms in many countries and unresolved social tensions in the Kyrgyz Republic and Uzbekistan. Frozen conflicts in the western CIS and Caucasus region also heighten political risks. Commitment to reform of state institutions is weak across much of the CIS and the business environment is particularly poor in the natural resource-rich countries.

## 5.3 Energy dependency

High commodity prices have so far been a source of strong growth in several transition countries, including Russia. This growth has benefited many CIS countries not exporting oil and gas, for which Russia is the main export market and to which Russia provides gas at below market price rates. However, the low diversification of energy sources, coupled with Russia's policy of increasing its gas export prices towards international levels, could become a source of increased economic uncertainty. Transportation constraints, due to the lack of investment in new pipelines, have also increased risks to energy security. To mitigate these risks, a few countries, most notably the Czech Republic and the Slovak Republic, are increasing their energy storage capacities. Some other CEB and SEE countries, such as Romania, have significant gas supplies of their own, accounting for 35–70 per cent of domestic consumption. Ukraine is also one of the few transition countries where gas imports from Russia account for less than 50 per cent of gas consumption. However, even Ukraine is reliant on gas transit through Russia since it imports most of its gas from Turkmenistan. Georgia has recently reached an agreement with Iran to purchase additional natural gas to diversify its energy sources.

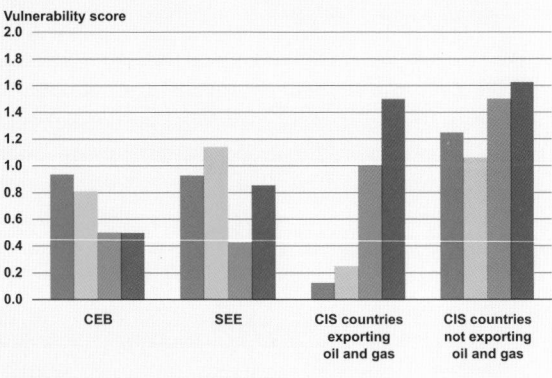

**Chart 5.1**

### Macroeconomic and financial sector vulnerability

Vulnerability score

- ■ Public sector    ■ External sector
- ■ Monetary conditions and exchange rate regime    ■ Financial sector

Source: EBRD.

Notes: The vulnerability score is calculated by assessing risks to the main areas of the economy. Scores range from 0 (not vulnerable) to 2 (seriously vulnerable).

Countries in the CIS which export oil and gas include Azerbaijan, Kazakhstan, Russia and Turkmenistan. Countries in the CIS which do not export oil and gas include Armenia, Belarus, Georgia, the Kyrgyz Republic, Moldova, Tajikistan, Ukraine and Uzbekistan.

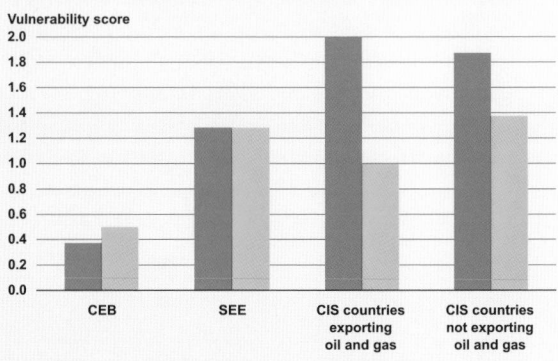

**Chart 5.2**

### Business environment and political vulnerability

Vulnerability score

- ■ Business environment    ■ Political and policy stability

Source: EBRD.

Notes: The vulnerability score is calculated by assessing risks to the business and political environment. Scores range from 0 (not vulnerable) to 2 (seriously vulnerable).

Countries in the CIS which export oil and gas include Azerbaijan, Kazakhstan, Russia and Turkmenistan. Countries in the CIS which do not export oil and gas include Armenia, Belarus, Georgia, the Kyrgyz Republic, Moldova, Tajikistan, Ukraine and Uzbekistan.

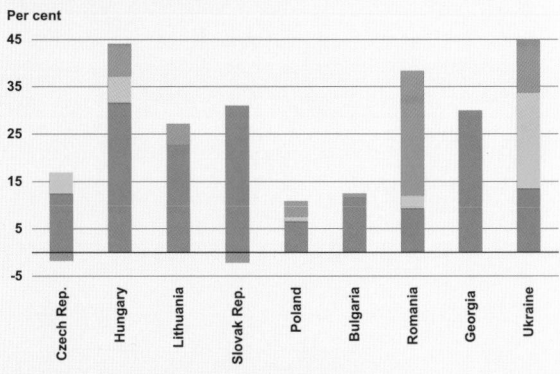

**Chart 5.3**

### Sources of natural gas as a share of total end-users' energy consumption, 2004

Per cent

- ■ Natural gas imported from Russia    ■ Other imports
- ■ Domestic gas production or stored gas

Sources: BP Statistical Review of World Energy, Georgian Gas International Cooperation and International Energy Agency (Ukraine).

Notes: Data for Ukraine refer to 2005. Natural gas imports in the Czech Republic and the Slovak Republic exceeded consumption due to increases in stored gas.

# Annex:
# Macroeconomic performance tables

Table A1

## Growth in real GDP in central and eastern Europe and the CIS

| | 1994 | 1995 | 1996 | 1997 | 1998 | 1999 | 2000 | 2001 | 2002 | 2003 | 2004 | 2005 Estimate | 2006 Projection | Estimated level of real GDP in 2005 |
|---|---|---|---|---|---|---|---|---|---|---|---|---|---|---|
| **Central eastern Europe and the Baltic states** | | | | | *(in per cent)* | | | | | | | | | *(1989=100)* |
| Czech Republic | 2.2 | 5.9 | 4.2 | -0.7 | -1.1 | 1.2 | 3.9 | 2.6 | 1.5 | 3.2 | 4.7 | 6.0 | 5.5 | 121 |
| Estonia | -1.6 | 4.5 | 4.4 | 11.1 | 4.4 | 0.3 | 7.9 | 6.5 | 7.2 | 6.7 | 7.8 | 9.6 | 6.8 | 123 |
| Hungary | 2.9 | 1.5 | 1.3 | 4.6 | 4.9 | 4.2 | 5.2 | 4.3 | 3.8 | 3.4 | 4.6 | 4.1 | 4.2 | 127 |
| Latvia | 2.2 | -0.9 | 3.8 | 8.3 | 4.7 | 3.3 | 6.9 | 8.0 | 6.4 | 7.2 | 8.3 | 10.2 | 7.7 | 99 |
| Lithuania | -9.8 | 3.3 | 4.7 | 7.0 | 7.3 | -1.7 | 4.7 | 6.4 | 6.8 | 10.5 | 7.0 | 7.5 | 6.2 | 98 |
| Poland | 5.2 | 7.0 | 6.2 | 7.1 | 5.0 | 4.5 | 4.2 | 1.1 | 1.4 | 3.8 | 5.3 | 3.2 | 4.5 | 148 |
| Slovak Republic | 6.2 | 5.8 | 6.1 | 4.6 | 4.2 | 1.5 | 2.0 | 3.8 | 4.6 | 4.5 | 5.5 | 6.0 | 6.0 | 128 |
| Slovenia | 5.8 | 4.9 | 3.6 | 4.8 | 3.6 | 5.6 | 4.1 | 2.7 | 3.5 | 2.7 | 4.2 | 3.9 | 4.0 | 131 |
| *Average[1]* | *3.9* | *5.5* | *4.8* | *5.0* | *3.8* | *3.5* | *4.3* | *2.5* | *2.4* | *4.0* | *5.2* | *4.6* | *4.9* | *133* |
| **South-eastern Europe** | | | | | | | | | | | | | | |
| **SEE-3** | | | | | | | | | | | | | | |
| Bulgaria | 1.8 | 2.9 | -9.4 | -5.6 | 4.0 | 2.3 | 5.4 | 4.0 | 4.8 | 4.5 | 5.6 | 5.8 | 5.5 | 94 |
| Croatia | 5.9 | 6.8 | 6.0 | 6.5 | 2.5 | -0.9 | 2.9 | 4.4 | 5.2 | 4.3 | 3.8 | 4.0 | 3.8 | 98 |
| Romania | 3.9 | 7.1 | 4.0 | -6.1 | -4.8 | -1.2 | 1.8 | 5.3 | 4.9 | 5.2 | 8.3 | 4.0 | 5.0 | 104 |
| **SEE-4** | | | | | | | | | | | | | | |
| Albania | 8.3 | 13.3 | 9.1 | -10.2 | 12.7 | 10.1 | 7.3 | 7.2 | 3.4 | 6.0 | 5.9 | 5.5 | 5.0 | 138 |
| Bosnia and Herzegovina | na | 20.8 | 86.0 | 37.0 | 15.6 | 9.6 | 5.5 | 4.3 | 5.3 | 3.0 | 6.0 | 5.0 | 5.0 | na |
| FYR Macedonia | -1.8 | -1.1 | 1.2 | 1.4 | 3.4 | 4.3 | 4.5 | -4.5 | 0.9 | 2.8 | 4.1 | 3.6 | 4.0 | 88 |
| Serbia and Montenegro | 2.5 | 6.1 | 7.8 | 10.1 | 1.9 | -18.0 | 5.0 | 5.5 | 3.8 | 2.7 | 7.2 | 5.0 | 5.0 | 58 |
| *Average[1]* | *3.9* | *6.0* | *2.2* | *1.1* | *0.6* | *-2.3* | *3.6* | *4.6* | *4.6* | *4.4* | *6.5* | *4.5* | *4.8* | *97* |
| **Commonwealth of Independent States** | | | | | | | | | | | | | | |
| Armenia | 5.4 | 6.9 | 5.9 | 3.3 | 7.3 | 3.3 | 5.9 | 9.6 | 13.2 | 13.9 | 10.1 | 13.9 | 8.5 | 111 |
| Azerbaijan | -19.7 | -11.8 | 0.8 | 6.0 | 10.0 | 11.0 | 6.2 | 6.5 | 8.1 | 11.5 | 10.2 | 26.4 | 25.0 | 92 |
| Belarus | -11.7 | -10.4 | 2.8 | 11.4 | 8.4 | 3.4 | 5.8 | 4.7 | 5.0 | 7.0 | 11.4 | 9.2 | 7.0 | 123 |
| Georgia | -11.4 | 2.4 | 10.5 | 10.6 | 2.9 | 3.0 | 1.9 | 4.7 | 5.5 | 11.1 | 6.2 | 8.5 | 6.5 | 48 |
| Kazakhstan | -12.6 | -8.2 | 0.5 | 1.7 | -1.9 | 2.7 | 9.8 | 13.5 | 9.8 | 9.3 | 9.4 | 9.4 | 8.5 | 113 |
| Kyrgyz Republic | -20.1 | -5.4 | 7.1 | 9.9 | 2.1 | 3.7 | 5.4 | 5.3 | 0.0 | 6.7 | 7.1 | -0.6 | 5.2 | 84 |
| Moldova | -30.9 | -1.4 | -5.9 | 1.6 | -6.5 | -3.4 | 2.1 | 6.1 | 7.8 | 6.6 | 7.3 | 7.1 | 5.5 | 47 |
| Russia | -12.7 | -4.0 | -3.6 | 1.4 | -5.3 | 6.4 | 10.0 | 5.1 | 4.7 | 7.3 | 7.1 | 6.4 | 5.5 | 88 |
| Tajikistan | -18.9 | -12.5 | -4.4 | 1.7 | 5.3 | 3.7 | 8.3 | 10.2 | 9.1 | 10.2 | 10.6 | 6.7 | 7.0 | 74 |
| Turkmenistan | -17.3 | -7.2 | -6.7 | -11.3 | 6.7 | 16.5 | 18.6 | 20.4 | 15.8 | 17.1 | 17.2 | 9.6 | 10.6 | 163 |
| Ukraine | -22.9 | -12.2 | -10.0 | -3.0 | -1.9 | -0.2 | 5.9 | 9.2 | 5.2 | 9.4 | 12.1 | 2.6 | 1.2 | 59 |
| Uzbekistan | -4.2 | -0.9 | 1.6 | 2.5 | 4.3 | 4.3 | 3.8 | 4.1 | 3.1 | 1.5 | 7.4 | 7.0 | 4.0 | na |
| *Average[1]* | *-13.5* | *-5.0* | *-3.6* | *1.4* | *-3.9* | *5.3* | *9.0* | *6.1* | *5.2* | *7.7* | *8.0* | *6.6* | *5.7* | *82* |
| **All transition countries** | | | | | | | | | | | | | | |
| *Average[1]* | *-5.2* | *0.1* | *0.2* | *2.7* | *-0.8* | *3.6* | *6.0* | *4.3* | *4.0* | *5.8* | *6.7* | *5.6* | *5.3* | *94* |

Note: Data for 1994-2004 represent the most recent official estimates of outturns as reflected in publications from the national authorities, the IMF, the World Bank and Eurostat. Data for 2005 are preliminary actuals, mostly official government estimates. Data for 2006 represent EBRD projections.

[1] Weighted averages. The weights used for the growth rates are EBRD estimates of nominal dollar-GDP lagged by one year; those used for the index in the last column are EBRD estimates of GDP converted at PPP US$ exchange rates in 1989.

Table A2

## Inflation in central and eastern Europe and the CIS

(change in annual average retail/consumer price level, in per cent)

| | 1994 | 1995 | 1996 | 1997 | 1998 | 1999 | 2000 | 2001 | 2002 | 2003 | 2004 | 2005 Estimate | 2006 Projection |
|---|---|---|---|---|---|---|---|---|---|---|---|---|---|
| **Central eastern Europe and the Baltic states** | | | | | | | | | | | | | |
| Czech Republic | 9.9 | 9.6 | 8.9 | 8.4 | 10.6 | 2.1 | 4.0 | 4.7 | 1.8 | 0.2 | 2.8 | 1.9 | 1.9 |
| Estonia | 47.7 | 29.0 | 23.1 | 11.2 | 8.1 | 3.3 | 4.0 | 5.8 | 3.6 | 1.3 | 3.0 | 4.1 | 3.5 |
| Hungary | 18.8 | 28.2 | 23.6 | 18.3 | 14.3 | 10.0 | 9.8 | 9.2 | 5.3 | 4.7 | 6.8 | 3.6 | 1.9 |
| Latvia | 35.9 | 25.0 | 17.6 | 8.4 | 4.7 | 2.4 | 2.6 | 2.5 | 1.9 | 2.9 | 6.2 | 6.7 | 6.0 |
| Lithuania | 72.1 | 39.6 | 24.6 | 8.9 | 5.1 | 0.8 | 1.0 | 1.5 | 0.3 | -1.2 | 1.2 | 2.7 | 2.8 |
| Poland | 32.2 | 27.8 | 19.9 | 14.9 | 11.8 | 7.3 | 10.1 | 5.5 | 1.9 | 0.8 | 3.5 | 2.1 | 0.8 |
| Slovak Republic | 13.4 | 9.9 | 5.8 | 6.1 | 6.7 | 10.6 | 12.0 | 7.3 | 3.0 | 8.5 | 7.5 | 2.5 | 3.0 |
| Slovenia | 21.0 | 12.6 | 9.7 | 9.1 | 7.9 | 6.1 | 8.9 | 8.4 | 7.5 | 5.6 | 3.6 | 2.5 | 2.5 |
| *Median[1]* | *26.6* | *26.4* | *18.8* | *9.0* | *8.0* | *4.7* | *6.5* | *5.7* | *2.5* | *2.1* | *3.6* | *2.6* | *2.7* |
| *Mean[1]* | *31.4* | *22.7* | *16.7* | *10.7* | *8.7* | *5.3* | *6.6* | *5.6* | *3.2* | *2.9* | *4.3* | *3.3* | *2.8* |
| **South-eastern Europe** | | | | | | | | | | | | | |
| **SEE-3** | | | | | | | | | | | | | |
| Bulgaria | 96.3 | 62.0 | 123.0 | 1,082.0 | 22.2 | 0.7 | 9.9 | 7.4 | 5.9 | 2.3 | 6.1 | 5.0 | 3.5 |
| Croatia | 97.6 | 2.0 | 3.5 | 3.6 | 5.7 | 4.2 | 6.2 | 4.9 | 2.2 | 1.8 | 2.1 | 3.3 | 3.0 |
| Romania | 136.7 | 32.3 | 38.8 | 154.8 | 59.1 | 45.8 | 45.7 | 34.5 | 22.5 | 15.3 | 11.9 | 9.5 | 7.5 |
| **SEE-4** | | | | | | | | | | | | | |
| Albania | 22.6 | 7.8 | 12.7 | 33.2 | 20.6 | 0.4 | 0.1 | 3.1 | 5.2 | 2.4 | 2.9 | 2.3 | 3.0 |
| FYR Macedonia | 126.5 | 16.4 | 2.3 | 2.6 | -0.1 | -0.7 | 5.8 | 5.3 | 2.4 | 1.1 | -0.3 | 0.1 | 2.0 |
| Serbia and Montenegro | 3.3 | 78.6 | 94.3 | 21.3 | 29.5 | 37.1 | 60.4 | 91.1 | 21.2 | 11.3 | 9.5 | 16.3 | 11.4 |
| *Median[1]* | *97.0* | *24.4* | *25.8* | *27.3* | *21.4* | *2.5* | *8.1* | *6.4* | *5.6* | *2.4* | *4.5* | *4.2* | *3.3* |
| *Mean[1]* | *80.5* | *33.2* | *45.8* | *216.3* | *22.8* | *14.6* | *21.4* | *24.4* | *9.9* | *5.7* | *5.4* | *6.1* | *5.1* |
| **Commonwealth of Independent States** | | | | | | | | | | | | | |
| Armenia | 4,962.0 | 175.8 | 18.7 | 14.0 | 8.7 | 0.7 | -0.8 | 3.2 | 1.2 | 4.7 | 6.9 | 0.6 | 0.7 |
| Azerbaijan | 1,664.0 | 412.0 | 19.7 | 3.5 | -0.8 | -8.5 | 1.8 | 1.5 | 2.8 | 2.2 | 6.8 | 10.3 | 13.0 |
| Belarus | 2,221.0 | 709.3 | 52.7 | 63.9 | 72.9 | 293.7 | 168.6 | 61.1 | 42.5 | 28.4 | 18.1 | 10.3 | 8.5 |
| Georgia | 15,606.5 | 162.7 | 39.4 | 7.1 | 3.6 | 19.2 | 4.1 | 4.6 | 5.7 | 4.9 | 5.7 | 8.4 | 5.5 |
| Kazakhstan | 1,892.0 | 176.3 | 39.1 | 17.4 | 7.1 | 8.3 | 13.2 | 8.4 | 5.9 | 6.4 | 6.9 | 7.6 | 7.7 |
| Kyrgyz Republic | 180.7 | 43.5 | 31.9 | 23.4 | 10.5 | 35.9 | 18.7 | 6.9 | 2.0 | 3.1 | 4.1 | 4.3 | 5.0 |
| Moldova | 487.0 | 30.2 | 23.5 | 11.8 | 7.7 | 39.3 | 31.1 | 9.6 | 5.2 | 11.6 | 12.5 | 12.0 | 10.2 |
| Russia | 311.4 | 197.7 | 47.8 | 14.7 | 27.6 | 86.1 | 20.8 | 21.6 | 15.7 | 13.7 | 11.0 | 11.3 | 10.5 |
| Tajikistan | 350.0 | 609.0 | 418.0 | 88.0 | 43.2 | 27.6 | 32.9 | 38.6 | 12.2 | 16.3 | 7.1 | 7.0 | 6.4 |
| Turkmenistan | 1,748.0 | 1,005.3 | 992.4 | 83.7 | 16.8 | 24.2 | 8.3 | 11.6 | 8.8 | 5.6 | 5.9 | 10.6 | 9.2 |
| Ukraine | 891.0 | 377.0 | 80.0 | 15.9 | 10.6 | 22.7 | 28.2 | 12.0 | 0.8 | 5.2 | 9.0 | 13.5 | 11.3 |
| Uzbekistan | 1,568.3 | 304.6 | 43.1 | 70.9 | 29.0 | 57.3 | 49.2 | 47.5 | 44.3 | 14.8 | 8.8 | 7.0 | 17.5 |
| *Median[1]* | *1,616.2* | *251.2* | *41.3* | *16.7* | *10.6* | *25.9* | *19.8* | *10.6* | *5.8* | *6.0* | *7.0* | *9.4* | *8.9* |
| *Mean[1]* | *2,656.8* | *350.3* | *150.5* | *34.5* | *19.7* | *50.5* | *31.3* | *18.9* | *12.3* | *9.7* | *8.6* | *8.6* | *8.8* |
| **All transition countries** | | | | | | | | | | | | | |
| ***Median[1]*** | ***131.6*** | ***41.6*** | ***24.1*** | ***14.8*** | ***10.6*** | ***9.2*** | ***9.9*** | ***7.4*** | ***5.2*** | ***4.8*** | ***6.5*** | ***5.9*** | ***5.3*** |
| ***Mean[1]*** | ***1,254.5*** | ***176.3*** | ***85.2*** | ***69.1*** | ***17.0*** | ***28.3*** | ***21.4*** | ***16.1*** | ***8.9*** | ***6.7*** | ***6.5*** | ***6.4*** | ***6.1*** |

Note: Data for 1994-2004 represent the most recent official estimates of outturns as reflected in publications from the national authorities, the IMF, the World Bank and Eurostat. Data for 2005 are preliminary actuals, mostly official government estimates. Data for 2006 represent EBRD projections. Estimates for inflation in Bosnia and Herzegovina are provided in the country assessments at the back of this report.

[1] The median is the middle value after all inflation rates have been arranged in order of size. The mean (unweighted average) tends to exceed the median, due to outliers caused by very high inflation rates in certain countries.

Table A3

## General government balances in central and eastern Europe and the CIS

| | 1994 | 1995 | 1996 | 1997 | 1998 | 1999 | 2000 | 2001 | 2002 | 2003 | 2004 | 2005 Estimate | 2006 Projection |
|---|---|---|---|---|---|---|---|---|---|---|---|---|---|
| **Central eastern Europe and the Baltic states** | | | | | | | *(in per cent of GDP)* | | | | | | |
| Czech Republic | -1.2 | -1.1 | -1.6 | -2.4 | -4.2 | -3.6 | -3.7 | -5.9 | -6.8 | -12.4 | -3.0 | -3.2 | -3.9 |
| Estonia | 1.2 | -1.2 | -1.5 | 1.9 | -0.3 | -3.7 | -0.6 | 0.3 | 1.5 | 2.6 | 1.7 | 1.5 | 0.0 |
| Hungary | -7.5 | -6.7 | -5.0 | -6.8 | -8.0 | -5.6 | -3.0 | -3.5 | -8.4 | -6.4 | -5.4 | -6.1 | -6.2 |
| Latvia | -3.9 | -3.6 | -1.7 | 0.7 | -0.7 | -4.9 | -2.8 | -2.1 | -2.3 | -1.2 | -1.0 | -1.2 | -1.5 |
| Lithuania | -4.8 | -4.2 | -4.4 | -1.1 | -3.0 | -5.6 | -2.5 | -2.0 | -1.4 | -1.2 | -1.4 | -2.0 | -1.8 |
| Poland | -2.8 | -3.1 | -3.3 | -4.4 | -3.9 | -3.1 | -2.3 | -3.7 | -3.2 | -4.7 | -3.8 | -2.9 | -3.2 |
| Slovak Republic | -1.4 | 0.4 | -1.3 | -5.2 | -5.0 | -7.1 | -12.3 | -6.0 | -5.7 | -3.7 | -3.3 | -3.0 | -3.5 |
| Slovenia | -0.2 | -0.2 | -0.2 | -1.6 | -2.2 | -2.1 | -3.4 | -2.8 | -2.4 | -2.0 | -2.0 | -1.9 | -1.7 |
| *Average [1]* | *-2.6* | *-2.5* | *-2.4* | *-2.4* | *-3.4* | *-4.5* | *-3.8* | *-3.2* | *-3.6* | *-3.6* | *-2.3* | *-2.4* | *-2.7* |
| **South-eastern Europe** | | | | | | | | | | | | | |
| *SEE-3* | | | | | | | | | | | | | |
| Bulgaria | -5.7 | -5.6 | -10.3 | -0.3 | 1.7 | 0.4 | -0.5 | 1.4 | -0.2 | 0.6 | 1.3 | 2.4 | 3.0 |
| Croatia | 1.2 | -1.4 | -1.0 | -1.9 | -1.0 | -8.2 | -6.5 | -6.7 | -5.0 | -6.3 | -4.9 | -4.4 | -4.2 |
| Romania | -2.2 | -2.5 | -3.9 | -4.5 | -4.4 | -2.1 | -3.8 | -3.5 | -2.0 | -2.0 | -1.4 | -0.8 | -1.4 |
| *SEE-4* | | | | | | | | | | | | | |
| Albania | -12.6 | -10.1 | -10.8 | -13.6 | -12.0 | -12.2 | -9.2 | -8.5 | -7.2 | -4.4 | -5.0 | -3.3 | -4.1 |
| Bosnia and Herzegovina | na | -0.3 | -4.4 | -0.5 | -5.2 | -4.8 | -3.1 | -2.5 | -4.1 | -1.7 | -1.9 | 0.1 | 0.3 |
| FYR Macedonia | -2.7 | -1.0 | -1.4 | -0.4 | -1.7 | 0.0 | 2.5 | -6.3 | -5.6 | -0.1 | 0.7 | 0.3 | -0.6 |
| Serbia and Montenegro | na | na | na | na | na | na | -0.9 | -1.3 | -4.5 | -3.3 | -0.3 | 0.9 | 2.3 |
| *Average [1]* | *-4.4* | *-3.5* | *-5.3* | *-3.5* | *-3.8* | *-4.5* | *-3.1* | *-3.9* | *-4.1* | *-2.5* | *-1.6* | *-0.7* | *-0.7* |
| **Commonwealth of Independent States** | | | | | | | | | | | | | |
| Armenia | -16.5 | -9.0 | -8.5 | -5.8 | -4.9 | -7.2 | -6.4 | -3.8 | -0.4 | -1.1 | -1.7 | -1.0 | -2.9 |
| Azerbaijan | -11.2 | -3.1 | -2.4 | -4.0 | -3.9 | -4.7 | -0.6 | -0.4 | -0.5 | -1.2 | 0.8 | -1.1 | -1.1 |
| Belarus | -3.5 | -2.7 | -1.5 | -0.7 | -1.0 | -2.0 | -0.1 | -1.9 | -1.8 | -1.4 | 0.0 | -0.8 | -1.5 |
| Georgia | -7.4 | -5.3 | -7.3 | -6.7 | -5.4 | -6.7 | -4.0 | -2.0 | -2.0 | -2.5 | 2.3 | -1.5 | -1.1 |
| Kazakhstan | -7.4 | -3.4 | -5.3 | -7.0 | -8.0 | -5.2 | -1.0 | 2.7 | 1.4 | 2.9 | 2.7 | 0.7 | 3.1 |
| Kyrgyz Republic | -11.6 | -17.3 | -9.5 | -9.2 | -9.5 | -12.7 | -11.4 | -5.6 | -5.3 | -5.2 | -4.1 | -4.8 | -3.7 |
| Moldova | -10.6 | -6.7 | -8.0 | -10.5 | -7.4 | -6.2 | -1.8 | -0.3 | -2.2 | 1.0 | 0.2 | 2.1 | -0.9 |
| Russia | -10.4 | -6.6 | -9.4 | -8.5 | -8.1 | -3.1 | 3.2 | 2.9 | 0.6 | 1.1 | 2.9 | 7.6 | na |
| Tajikistan | -10.1 | -6.1 | -5.8 | -3.8 | -3.8 | -3.1 | -5.6 | -3.2 | -2.5 | -1.8 | -2.7 | -3.6 | -3.5 |
| Turkmenistan | 1.7 | 0.4 | 0.3 | -0.2 | -2.6 | 0.0 | -0.3 | 0.6 | 0.2 | -1.3 | 0.0 | 0.0 | 0.0 |
| Ukraine | -8.7 | -4.7 | -3.2 | -5.4 | -2.5 | -2.3 | -1.1 | -0.9 | 0.1 | -0.7 | -4.5 | -2.5 | -3.4 |
| Uzbekistan | -4.4 | -4.1 | -7.3 | -2.2 | -3.3 | -2.6 | -2.2 | -2.1 | -1.5 | -0.8 | 0.4 | -3.7 | na |
| *Average [1]* | *-8.3* | *-5.7* | *-5.7* | *-5.3* | *-5.0* | *-4.7* | *-2.6* | *-1.2* | *-1.2* | *-0.9* | *-0.3* | *-0.7* | *-1.5* |
| **All transition countries** | | | | | | | | | | | | | |
| **Average [1]** | **-5.7** | **-4.2** | **-4.6** | **-4.0** | **-4.2** | **-4.6** | **-3.1** | **-2.5** | **-2.6** | **-2.1** | **-1.2** | **-1.2** | **-1.7** |

Note: Data for 1994-2004 represent the most recent official estimates of outturns as
reflected in publications from the national authorities, the IMF, the World Bank
and Eurostat. Data for 2005 are preliminary actuals, mostly official government
estimates. Data for 2006 represent EBRD projections.

[1] Unweighted average for the region.

Table A4

## Current account balance in central and eastern Europe and the CIS

| | 1994 | 1995 | 1996 | 1997 | 1998 | 1999 | 2000 | 2001 | 2002 | 2003 | 2004 | 2005 Estimate | 2006 Projection |
|---|---|---|---|---|---|---|---|---|---|---|---|---|---|
| **Central eastern Europe and the Baltic states** | | | | | *(in per cent of GDP)* | | | | | | | | |
| Czech Republic | -1.9 | -2.5 | -6.7 | -6.3 | -2.1 | -2.5 | -4.9 | -5.4 | -5.6 | -6.3 | -6.0 | -2.1 | -2.6 |
| Estonia | -6.9 | -4.2 | -8.6 | -11.4 | -8.6 | -4.4 | -5.4 | -5.7 | -10.2 | -12.1 | -12.7 | -11.1 | -11.5 |
| Hungary | -9.4 | -3.7 | -4.0 | -4.5 | -7.2 | -7.8 | -8.5 | -6.1 | -7.1 | -8.7 | -8.8 | -7.6 | -7.8 |
| Latvia | 5.0 | -0.3 | -5.0 | -5.6 | -9.8 | -9.1 | -4.8 | -7.6 | -6.8 | -8.2 | -13.0 | -11.0 | -10.4 |
| Lithuania | -2.2 | -9.6 | -9.0 | -10.0 | -11.7 | -11.0 | -5.9 | -4.7 | -5.2 | -6.9 | -7.7 | -7.2 | -7.0 |
| Poland | 1.0 | 0.6 | -2.1 | -3.7 | -4.0 | -7.4 | -5.8 | -2.8 | -2.5 | -2.1 | -4.1 | -1.6 | -1.8 |
| Slovak Republic | 4.3 | 2.0 | -10.1 | -9.2 | -9.3 | -5.3 | -3.3 | -9.0 | -8.0 | -0.8 | -3.5 | -6.0 | -3.4 |
| Slovenia | 4.0 | -0.4 | 0.3 | 0.3 | -0.6 | -3.3 | -2.8 | 0.1 | 1.8 | 0.0 | -2.1 | -0.3 | na |
| *Average [1]* | *-0.8* | *-2.3* | *-5.7* | *-6.3* | *-6.7* | *-6.4* | *-5.2* | *-5.2* | *-5.5* | *-5.6* | *-7.2* | *-5.9* | *-6.4* |
| **South-eastern Europe** | | | | | | | | | | | | | |
| *SEE-3* | | | | | | | | | | | | | |
| Bulgaria | -0.3 | -1.5 | 1.7 | 10.0 | -0.5 | -5.0 | -5.6 | -7.3 | -5.3 | -9.3 | -8.5 | -14.9 | -7.4 |
| Croatia | 5.9 | -7.7 | -5.5 | -11.6 | -6.7 | -7.0 | -2.5 | -3.7 | -8.4 | -7.2 | -5.5 | -5.7 | -5.8 |
| Romania | -1.4 | -5.0 | -7.3 | -6.1 | -6.9 | -3.6 | -3.6 | -5.8 | -3.4 | -6.0 | -7.5 | -9.3 | -10.6 |
| *SEE-4* | | | | | | | | | | | | | |
| Albania | -14.3 | -7.1 | -8.1 | -12.6 | -6.8 | -7.7 | -7.4 | -6.4 | -9.7 | -8.2 | -6.1 | -7.1 | -6.9 |
| Bosnia and Herzegovina | na | na | -27.3 | -30.0 | -27.0 | -17.9 | -13.1 | -16.1 | -21.7 | -17.8 | -17.3 | -17.8 | -16.4 |
| FYR Macedonia | -7.8 | -6.7 | -7.7 | -7.7 | -7.5 | -0.9 | -1.9 | -7.1 | -9.5 | -3.2 | -7.8 | -1.3 | -5.0 |
| Serbia and Montenegro | na | na | -9.8 | -6.5 | -4.2 | -4.4 | -4.7 | -4.6 | -8.9 | -9.6 | -12.5 | -8.8 | -10.4 |
| *Average [1]* | *-3.6* | *-5.6* | *-9.1* | *-9.2* | *-8.5* | *-6.6* | *-5.5* | *-7.3* | *-9.6* | *-8.8* | *-9.3* | *-9.3* | *-8.9* |
| **Commonwealth of Independent States** | | | | | | | | | | | | | |
| Armenia | -16.0 | -17.0 | -18.2 | -18.0 | -22.1 | -16.6 | -14.5 | -10.0 | -6.3 | -6.8 | -4.5 | -4.2 | -3.8 |
| Azerbaijan | -10.3 | -13.2 | -25.8 | -23.1 | -30.7 | -13.1 | -3.5 | -0.9 | -12.3 | -27.8 | -29.8 | -5.1 | 21.7 |
| Belarus | -9.1 | -4.3 | -3.6 | -6.1 | -6.7 | -1.6 | -3.2 | -3.2 | -2.1 | -2.4 | -4.5 | 2.1 | 2.4 |
| Georgia | -22.3 | -7.5 | -9.1 | -10.6 | -8.9 | -7.7 | -4.5 | -6.6 | -5.8 | -7.4 | -8.3 | -7.4 | -7.3 |
| Kazakhstan | -7.6 | -1.3 | -3.6 | -3.6 | -5.5 | -1.4 | 2.0 | -6.3 | -4.2 | -0.9 | 1.3 | 2.1 | -2.9 |
| Kyrgyz Republic | -7.6 | -15.7 | -23.3 | -7.8 | -22.2 | -14.7 | -5.7 | -1.6 | -3.1 | -4.2 | -3.4 | -5.2 | -2.1 |
| Moldova | -8.4 | -8.0 | -11.1 | -14.2 | -19.7 | -5.8 | -7.6 | -1.7 | -4.0 | -6.6 | -4.4 | -7.3 | -6.0 |
| Russia | 2.8 | 2.2 | 2.8 | 0.0 | 0.1 | 12.6 | 18.0 | 11.1 | 8.4 | 8.3 | 10.3 | 12.3 | na |
| Tajikistan | -20.6 | -15.2 | -7.8 | -4.0 | -7.3 | -0.9 | -6.0 | -5.0 | -3.6 | -1.3 | -4.0 | -3.7 | -4.7 |
| Turkmenistan | 4.0 | 0.9 | 0.1 | -25.3 | -36.7 | -24.3 | 13.6 | 3.2 | 13.0 | 5.2 | 1.2 | 8.2 | 14.3 |
| Ukraine | -3.2 | -3.1 | -2.7 | -2.7 | -3.1 | 5.2 | 4.7 | 3.7 | 7.5 | 5.8 | 10.5 | 1.6 | -1.7 |
| Uzbekistan | 2.1 | -0.2 | -7.8 | -5.4 | -0.9 | -2.0 | 2.4 | -1.5 | 3.0 | 8.9 | 9.8 | 8.3 | na |
| *Average [1]* | *-8.0* | *-6.9* | *-9.2* | *-10.1* | *-13.6* | *-5.9* | *-0.4* | *-1.6* | *-0.8* | *-2.4* | *-2.2* | *0.1* | *1.0* |
| **All transition countries** | | | | | | | | | | | | | |
| ***Average [1]*** | ***-4.8*** | ***-5.1*** | ***-8.1*** | ***-8.7*** | ***-10.2*** | ***-6.2*** | ***-3.1*** | ***-4.1*** | ***-4.4*** | ***-5.0*** | ***-5.5*** | ***-4.1*** | ***-4.0*** |

Note: Data for 1994-2004 represent the most recent official estimates of outturns as reflected in publications from the national authorities, the IMF, the World Bank and Eurostat. Data for 2005 are preliminary actuals, mostly official government estimates. Data for 2006 represent EBRD projections.

[1] Unweighted average for the region.

Table A5

# GDP growth forecasts for 2006
(in per cent)

| | Average[1] | Range[2] | EBRD | European Union (Nov 2005) | IMF (Apr 2006) | OECD (Nov 2005) | United Nations DESA[4] (Jan 2006) | CSFB[5] (Feb 2006) | Dun & Bradstreet (Jan 2006) | Economist Intelligence Unit (Jan 2006) | Global Insight Inc.[6] (Jan 2006) | IWH[7] (Feb 2006) | JP Morgan (Feb 2006) | Kopint-Datorg[8] (Jan 2006) | Vienna Institute[9] (Feb 2006) |
|---|---|---|---|---|---|---|---|---|---|---|---|---|---|---|---|
| **Central eastern Europe and the Baltic states** | | | | | | | | | | | | | | | |
| Czech Republic | 4.6 | 1.1 | 5.5 | 4.4 | 4.4 | 4.5 | 4.5 | na | 4.6 | 4.4 | 4.5 | 4.5 | 4.8 | 5.1 | 4.5 |
| Estonia | 7.1 | 1.7 | 6.8 | 7.2 | 7.9 | na | 6.8 | na | 6.2 | 7.3 | 7.5 | 7.5 | na | 7.0 | 7.2 |
| Hungary | 4.2 | 0.8 | 4.2 | 3.9 | 4.4 | 4.5 | 4.2 | 4.4 | 3.7 | 4.4 | 4.0 | 4.0 | 4.5 | 4.3 | 4.2 |
| Latvia | 7.9 | 2.2 | 7.7 | 7.7 | 9.0 | na | 8.0 | na | 6.8 | 7.7 | 8.4 | 8.0 | na | 7.5 | 7.7 |
| Lithuania | 6.4 | 1.6 | 6.2 | 6.2 | 6.5 | na | 6.4 | na | 5.9 | 6.0 | 6.2 | 7.5 | na | 6.4 | 6.2 |
| Poland | 4.2 | 0.9 | 4.5 | 4.3 | 4.2 | 3.7 | 3.8 | 4.5 | 4.6 | 4.0 | 4.5 | 4.5 | 4.2 | 4.3 | 3.8 |
| Slovak Republic | 5.8 | 0.9 | 6.0 | 5.5 | 6.3 | 5.6 | 5.4 | na | 5.6 | 5.6 | 5.6 | 5.8 | 5.9 | 5.9 | 6.0 |
| Slovenia | 4.0 | 0.4 | 4.0 | 4.0 | 4.0 | na | 3.8 | na | 4.2 | 4.0 | 4.2 | 4.2 | na | 3.8 | 3.9 |
| *Average* | *5.5* | *1.2* | *5.6* | *5.4* | *5.8* | *4.6* | *5.4* | *4.5* | *5.2* | *5.4* | *5.6* | *5.8* | *4.9* | *5.5* | *5.4* |
| *Weighted average[3]* | *4.6* | *1.0* | *4.9* | *4.5* | *4.7* | *na* | *4.4* | *na* | *4.6* | *4.5* | *4.7* | *4.7* | *na* | *4.7* | *4.4* |
| **South-eastern Europe** | | | | | | | | | | | | | | | |
| *SEE-3* | | | | | | | | | | | | | | | |
| Bulgaria | 5.3 | 1.7 | 5.5 | 5.5 | 5.5 | na | 4.8 | 5.3 | 5.4 | 4.3 | 4.5 | 5.6 | 5.5 | 6.0 | 5.3 |
| Croatia | 4.0 | 0.6 | 3.8 | 4.0 | 4.1 | na | 4.2 | 4.1 | 4.1 | 4.0 | 3.7 | na | na | 4.3 | 3.7 |
| Romania | 5.2 | 1.7 | 5.0 | 5.3 | 5.2 | na | 4.8 | 4.5 | 5.5 | 4.5 | 6.2 | 5.8 | 5.4 | 5.8 | 4.5 |
| *SEE-4* | | | | | | | | | | | | | | | |
| Albania | 5.3 | 1.0 | 5.0 | na | 5.0 | na | 5.6 | na | 6.0 | 5.0 | 5.3 | na | na | na | 5.5 |
| Bosnia and Herzegovina | 5.7 | 0.9 | 5.0 | na | na | na | 5.8 | na | 5.7 | 5.6 | 5.9 | na | na | na | 6.0 |
| FYR Macedonia | 3.9 | 0.7 | 4.0 | na | 4.0 | na | 3.9 | na | 4.0 | 4.0 | 3.3 | na | na | 4.0 | 4.0 |
| Serbia and Montenegro | 5.3 | 1.0 | 5.0 | na | na | na | 6.0 | 5.5 | 5.5 | 5.0 | 5.4 | 5.7 | 5.5 | 5.0 | na |
| *Average* | *5.0* | *1.1* | *4.8* | *na* | *4.8* | *na* | *5.0* | *4.9* | *5.2* | *4.6* | *4.9* | *5.7* | *5.5* | *5.3* | *4.8* |
| *Weighted average[3]* | *5.0* | *1.3* | *4.8* | *na* | *na* | *na* | *4.9* | *na* | *5.2* | *4.5* | *5.3* | *na* | *na* | *na* | *na* |
| **Commonwealth of Independent States** | | | | | | | | | | | | | | | |
| Armenia | 8.4 | 2.5 | 8.5 | na | 7.5 | na | 8.5 | na | na | 10.0 | 7.6 | na | na | na | na |
| Azerbaijan | 23.3 | 9.5 | 25.0 | na | 26.2 | na | 22.0 | na | 18.0 | 27.5 | 21.2 | na | na | na | na |
| Belarus | 6.7 | 2.5 | 7.0 | na | 5.5 | na | 8.0 | na | 6.0 | 6.0 | 7.4 | na | na | na | na |
| Georgia | 7.6 | 4.5 | 6.5 | na | 6.4 | na | 5.5 | na | 10.0 | 10.0 | 7.4 | na | na | na | na |
| Kazakhstan | 8.3 | 1.5 | 8.5 | na | 8.0 | na | 8.5 | na | 7.4 | 8.5 | 8.9 | na | na | na | na |
| Kyrgyz Republic | 4.0 | 2.5 | 5.2 | na | 5.0 | na | 4.0 | na | 4.3 | 3.0 | 2.7 | na | na | na | na |
| Moldova | 5.8 | 2.0 | 5.5 | na | 6.0 | na | 7.0 | na | na | 5.5 | 5.0 | na | na | na | na |
| Russia | 5.8 | 1.5 | 5.5 | na | 6.0 | 5.7 | 5.5 | 5.7 | 5.5 | 6.0 | 5.5 | 6.0 | 6.5 | 5.0 | 6.2 |
| Tajikistan | 6.9 | 1.7 | 7.0 | na | 8.0 | na | 7.0 | na | 6.3 | 7.0 | 6.3 | na | na | na | na |
| Turkmenistan | 9.4 | 12.3 | 10.6 | na | 6.5 | na | 5.0 | na | 8.0 | 9.0 | 17.3 | na | na | na | na |
| Ukraine | 2.7 | 5.0 | 1.2 | na | 2.3 | na | 2.4 | 1.0 | 5.0 | 3.8 | 4.5 | na | 2.0 | 0.0 | 5.0 |
| Uzbekistan | 5.7 | 3.2 | 4.0 | na | 7.2 | na | 5.0 | na | 6.0 | 6.3 | 5.5 | na | na | na | na |
| *Average* | *7.9* | *4.1* | *7.9* | *na* | *7.9* | *5.7* | *7.4* | *3.4* | *7.7* | *8.6* | *8.3* | *6.0* | *4.3* | *2.5* | *5.6* |
| *Weighted average[3]* | *6.0* | *2.1* | *5.7* | *na* | *6.1* | *na* | *5.7* | *na* | *na* | *6.3* | *6.0* | *na* | *na* | *na* | *na* |
| **All transition countries** | | | | | | | | | | | | | | | |
| *Average* | *6.4* | *2.4* | *6.4* | *5.3* | *6.6* | *4.8* | *6.2* | *4.4* | *6.2* | *6.6* | *6.6* | *5.8* | *4.9* | *5.0* | *5.2* |
| *Weighted average[3]* | *5.4* | *1.6* | *5.3* | *na* | *na* | *na* | *5.1* | *na* | *na* | *5.4* | *5.4* | *na* | *na* | *na* | *na* |

Note: The dates in brackets indicate the months in which the forecasts were reported or published by each institution. There may in some instances be substantial delays between preparation and publication of forecasts.

[1] The number at the bottom of this column is calculated as the mean of all the average forecasts shown in the column.
[2] Data show the difference between the highest and the lowest forecasts.
[3] Weighted average based on EBRD estimates of nominal US dollar GDP in each country in 2005.
[4] United Nations Department of Economic and Social Affairs (DESA).
[5] Credit Suisse First Boston.
[6] Formerly DRI-WEFA.
[7] Institute for Economic Research, Halle, Germany.
[8] Institute for Economic and Market Research Information, Hungary.
[9] Vienna Institute for International Economic Studies (WIIW).

Table A6

## Average annual inflation forecasts for 2006

(change in the average consumer price level, in per cent)

| | Average[1] | Range[2] | EBRD | European Union (Nov 2005) | IMF (Apr 2006) | OECD (Nov 2005) | United Nations DESA[3] (Jan 2006) | CSFB[4] (Feb 2006) | Dun & Bradstreet (Jan 2006) | Economist Intelligence Unit (Jan 2006) | Global Insight Inc.[5] (Jan 2006) | IWH[6] (Feb 2006) | JP Morgan (Feb 2006) | Kopint-Datorg[7] (Jan 2006) | Vienna Institute[8] (Feb 2006) |
|---|---|---|---|---|---|---|---|---|---|---|---|---|---|---|---|
| **Central eastern Europe and the Baltic states** | | | | | | | | | | | | | | | |
| Czech Republic | 2.6 | 1.0 | 1.9 | 2.9 | 2.8 | 2.8 | 2.5 | na | 2.0 | 2.5 | 2.8 | 2.5 | 2.6 | 2.5 | 2.8 |
| Estonia | 3.2 | 1.1 | 3.5 | 3.3 | 3.6 | na | 3.0 | na | 3.3 | 3.2 | 3.2 | 2.5 | na | 2.9 | 3.3 |
| Hungary | 2.0 | 1.7 | 1.9 | 2.0 | 2.0 | 2.0 | 2.0 | 1.5 | 3.2 | 1.7 | 1.7 | 2.0 | 1.5 | 1.9 | 2.0 |
| Latvia | 5.9 | 1.0 | 6.0 | 6.0 | 6.4 | na | 6.0 | na | 5.7 | 5.8 | 5.4 | 5.5 | na | 5.8 | 6.0 |
| Lithuania | 2.6 | 1.7 | 2.8 | 2.8 | 3.2 | na | 2.5 | na | 1.5 | 2.6 | 2.8 | 2.5 | na | 2.9 | 2.8 |
| Poland | 1.9 | 1.7 | 0.8 | 2.3 | 1.3 | 1.9 | 2.0 | 1.3 | 2.5 | 1.8 | 2.1 | 2.5 | 1.2 | 2.4 | 2.5 |
| Slovak Republic | 3.5 | 1.3 | 3.0 | 3.6 | 3.6 | 4.3 | 4.0 | na | 3.0 | 3.8 | 3.7 | 3.0 | 3.5 | 3.5 | 3.0 |
| Slovenia | 2.4 | 0.3 | 2.5 | 2.5 | 2.4 | na | 2.3 | na | 2.6 | 2.5 | 2.3 | 2.5 | na | 2.3 | 2.4 |
| *Average* | *3.0* | *1.2* | *2.8* | *3.2* | *3.2* | *2.8* | *3.0* | *1.4* | *3.0* | *3.0* | *3.0* | *2.9* | *2.2* | *3.0* | *3.1* |
| **South-eastern Europe** | | | | | | | | | | | | | | | |
| *SEE-3* | | | | | | | | | | | | | | | |
| Bulgaria | 5.3 | 3.4 | 3.5 | 5.5 | 6.9 | na | 5.5 | 6.5 | 3.6 | 5.8 | 6.2 | 5.5 | 5.1 | 3.9 | 6.0 |
| Croatia | 3.1 | 1.1 | 3.0 | 3.1 | 3.2 | na | 3.5 | 3.4 | 2.4 | 3.2 | 3.5 | na | na | 2.6 | 3.0 |
| Romania | 7.3 | 2.2 | 7.5 | 7.4 | 7.9 | na | 7.8 | 7.4 | 6.5 | 7.4 | 6.8 | 7.5 | 7.5 | 5.8 | 8.0 |
| *SEE-4* | | | | | | | | | | | | | | | |
| Albania | 2.7 | 1.3 | 3.0 | na | 2.5 | na | 2.5 | na | 2.1 | 2.6 | 3.4 | na | na | na | 2.5 |
| Bosnia and Herzegovina | 2.8 | 3.9 | 2.0 | na | na | na | 2.5 | na | 1.4 | 3.4 | 5.3 | na | na | na | 2.0 |
| FYR Macedonia | 1.9 | 1.4 | 2.0 | na | 1.8 | na | 1.5 | na | 2.8 | 1.4 | 1.6 | na | na | na | 2.0 |
| Serbia and Montenegro | 13.1 | 3.6 | 11.4 | na | na | na | 15.0 | 13.7 | 11.5 | 15.0 | 11.7 | na | na | 13.5 | na |
| *Average* | *5.2* | *2.4* | *4.6* | *5.3* | *4.5* | *na* | *5.5* | *7.8* | *4.3* | *5.5* | *5.5* | *6.5* | *6.3* | *6.5* | *3.9* |
| **Commonwealth of Independent States** | | | | | | | | | | | | | | | |
| Armenia | 2.0 | 2.3 | 0.7 | na | 3.0 | na | 3.0 | na | na | 1.7 | 1.8 | na | na | na | na |
| Azerbaijan | 9.4 | 5.6 | 13.0 | na | 8.6 | na | 9.5 | na | 7.8 | 7.4 | 10.0 | na | na | na | na |
| Belarus | 10.3 | 6.0 | 8.5 | na | 10.4 | na | 10.5 | na | 13.0 | 12.5 | 7.0 | na | na | na | na |
| Georgia | 6.7 | 2.7 | 5.5 | na | 5.3 | na | 8.0 | na | 6.8 | 7.7 | 6.7 | na | na | na | na |
| Kazakhstan | 7.1 | 1.6 | 7.7 | na | 7.5 | na | 7.5 | na | 6.1 | 7.0 | 6.8 | na | na | na | na |
| Kyrgyz Republic | 5.0 | 1.7 | 5.0 | na | 5.7 | na | 4.0 | na | 4.7 | 5.3 | 5.2 | na | na | na | na |
| Moldova | 10.4 | 3.8 | 10.2 | na | 9.4 | na | 12.0 | na | na | 12.0 | 8.2 | na | na | na | na |
| Russia | 10.1 | 1.2 | 10.5 | na | 10.4 | 10.7 | 9.5 | 10.4 | 9.5 | 9.9 | 10.1 | 10.0 | 10.2 | 9.5 | 10.0 |
| Tajikistan | 7.1 | 1.4 | 6.4 | na | 7.8 | na | 7.0 | na | 6.8 | 6.8 | 7.6 | na | na | na | na |
| Turkmenistan | 10.5 | 5.1 | 9.2 | na | 7.9 | na | 10.5 | na | 13.0 | 11.0 | 11.5 | na | na | na | na |
| Ukraine | 11.0 | 3.2 | 11.3 | na | 13.0 | na | 12.0 | 11.0 | 9.8 | 10.5 | 10.9 | na | 10.1 | 11.0 | 10.0 |
| Uzbekistan | 11.4 | 10.6 | 17.5 | na | 11.3 | na | 13.0 | na | 12.5 | 7.4 | 6.9 | na | na | na | na |
| *Average* | *8.4* | *3.8* | *8.8* | *na* | *8.4* | *10.7* | *8.9* | *10.7* | *9.0* | *8.3* | *7.7* | *10.0* | *10.2* | *10.3* | *10.0* |
| **All transition countries** | | | | | | | | | | | | | | | |
| *Average* | *6.0* | *2.7* | *5.9* | *3.8* | *5.9* | *4.3* | *6.3* | *6.9* | *5.8* | *6.0* | *5.7* | *4.2* | *5.2* | *5.0* | *4.3* |

Note: The dates in brackets indicate the months in which the forecasts were reported or published by each institution. There may in some instances be substantial delays between preparation and publication of forecasts.

1 The number at the bottom of this column is calculated as the mean of all the average forecasts shown in the column.
2 Data show the difference between the highest and the lowest forecast.
3 United Nations Department of Economic and Social Affairs (DESA).
4 Credit Suisse First Boston.
5 Formerly DRI-WEFA.
6 Institute for Economic Research, Halle, Germany.
7 Institute for Economic and Market Research Information, Hungary.
8 Vienna Institute for International Economic Studies (WIIW).

Table A7

## Foreign direct investment
(net inflows recorded in the balance of payments)

| | 1994 | 1995 | 1996 | 1997 | 1998 | 1999 | 2000 | 2001 | 2002 | 2003 | 2004 | 2005 Estimate | 2006 Projection | Cumulative FDI inflows 1989-2005 | Cumulative FDI inflows per capita 1989-2005 | FDI inflows per capita 2004 | FDI inflows per capita 2005 | FDI inflows 2004 | FDI inflows 2005 |
|---|---|---|---|---|---|---|---|---|---|---|---|---|---|---|---|---|---|---|---|
| | *(in US$ million)* | | | | | | | | | | | | | *(in US$ mln)* | *(US$)* | *(US$)* | | *(in per cent of GDP)* | |
| **Central eastern Europe and the Baltic states** | | | | | | | | | | | | | | | | | | | |
| Czech Republic | 749 | 2,526 | 1,276 | 1,275 | 3,591 | 6,234 | 4,943 | 5,476 | 8,276 | 1,895 | 3,960 | 10,135 | 4,500 | 51,882 | 5,076 | 387 | 992 | 4.0 | 8.1 |
| Estonia | 212 | 199 | 111 | 130 | 574 | 222 | 324 | 343 | 153 | 763 | 781 | 2,882 | 1,200 | 6,929 | 5,144 | 578 | 2,140 | 7.0 | 22.1 |
| Hungary | 1,097 | 4,772 | 3,335 | 3,715 | 3,070 | 3,060 | 2,151 | 3,573 | 2,722 | 479 | 3,542 | 3,500 | 3,500 | 40,771 | 4,045 | 351 | 347 | 3.5 | 3.0 |
| Latvia | 279 | 245 | 379 | 515 | 303 | 331 | 400 | 114 | 250 | 256 | 596 | 622 | 740 | 4,339 | 1,882 | 257 | 270 | 4.4 | 4.0 |
| Lithuania | 31 | 72 | 152 | 328 | 921 | 478 | 375 | 439 | 715 | 142 | 510 | 655 | 667 | 4,848 | 1,415 | 148 | 191 | 2.3 | 3.0 |
| Poland | 1,846 | 3,617 | 4,445 | 4,863 | 6,049 | 7,239 | 9,327 | 5,804 | 3,901 | 4,284 | 11,826 | 8,177 | 8,400 | 72,359 | 1,898 | 310 | 214 | 5.0 | 3.0 |
| Slovak Republic | 236 | 194 | 199 | 84 | 374 | 701 | 2,058 | 1,460 | 4,007 | 549 | 1,259 | 1,650 | 2,000 | 13,094 | 2,434 | 234 | 307 | 3.1 | 4.0 |
| Slovenia | 129 | 161 | 167 | 303 | 221 | 59 | 71 | 226 | 1,489 | -139 | 277 | 346 | 470 | 3,476 | 1,747 | 139 | 174 | 1.0 | 1.0 |
| *Total* | *4,580* | *11,785* | *10,063* | *11,212* | *15,102* | *18,324* | *19,649* | *17,435* | *21,512* | *8,229* | *22,751* | *27,968* | *21,477* | *197,698* | *2,713* | *312* | *384* | *3.8* | *6.0* |
| **South-eastern Europe** | | | | | | | | | | | | | | | | | | | |
| ***SEE-3*** | | | | | | | | | | | | | | | | | | | |
| Bulgaria | 105 | 98 | 138 | 507 | 537 | 802 | 998 | 803 | 876 | 2,070 | 1,232 | 1,991 | 2,107 | 10,300 | 1,327 | 159 | 257 | 5.1 | 7.6 |
| Croatia | 110 | 109 | 486 | 347 | 835 | 1,420 | 1,085 | 1,407 | 591 | 2,025 | 899 | 2,000 | 1,200 | 11,429 | 2,573 | 203 | 450 | 2.6 | 5.0 |
| Romania | 341 | 417 | 415 | 1,267 | 2,079 | 1,025 | 1,051 | 1,154 | 1,080 | 2,156 | 5,020 | 5,230 | 4,480 | 21,414 | 985 | 232 | 241 | 6.9 | 5.6 |
| ***SEE-4*** | | | | | | | | | | | | | | | | | | | |
| Albania | 65 | 89 | 97 | 42 | 45 | 51 | 143 | 204 | 135 | 178 | 343 | 288 | 339 | 1,745 | 545 | 107 | 90 | 5.0 | 3.0 |
| Bosnia and Herzegovina | 0 | 0 | 0 | 0 | 67 | 177 | 150 | 130 | 266 | 382 | 490 | 400 | 570 | 2,061 | 542 | 129 | 105 | 6.0 | 4.0 |
| FYR Macedonia | 24 | 10 | 11 | 30 | 128 | 32 | 175 | 441 | 78 | 96 | 156 | 97 | 200 | 1,277 | 639 | 78 | 48 | 2.9 | 2.0 |
| Serbia and Montenegro | na | na | 0 | 740 | 113 | 112 | 25 | 165 | 562 | 1,405 | 1,031 | 2,020 | 2,000 | 6,173 | 741 | 124 | 242 | 4.0 | 8.0 |
| *Total* | *646* | *723* | *1,147* | *2,932* | *3,804* | *3,619* | *3,627* | *4,304* | *3,588* | *8,313* | *9,172* | *12,026* | *10,896* | *54,400* | *1,061* | *179* | *235* | *4.6* | *5.0* |
| **Commonwealth of Independent States** | | | | | | | | | | | | | | | | | | | |
| Armenia | 8 | 25 | 18 | 52 | 221 | 122 | 104 | 70 | 111 | 121 | 217 | 255 | 152 | 1,325 | 408 | 68 | 79 | 6.0 | 5.0 |
| Azerbaijan | 22 | 330 | 627 | 1,115 | 1,023 | 510 | 149 | 299 | 1,048 | 2,353 | 2,351 | -728 | -2,124 | 9,100 | 1,102 | 285 | -88 | 27.0 | -6.0 |
| Belarus | 11 | 15 | 105 | 350 | 201 | 443 | 119 | 96 | 453 | 170 | 163 | 303 | 200 | 2,444 | 251 | 17 | 31 | 0.7 | 1.0 |
| Georgia | 8 | 6 | 54 | 236 | 221 | 62 | 153 | 80 | 122 | 335 | 503 | 415 | 390 | 2,196 | 475 | 109 | 90 | 10.0 | 6.0 |
| Kazakhstan | 660 | 964 | 1,137 | 1,320 | 1,143 | 1,468 | 1,278 | 2,861 | 2,164 | 2,213 | 5,383 | 1,000 | 2,500 | 22,963 | 1,520 | 357 | 66 | 13.2 | 2.0 |
| Kyrgyz Republic | 38 | 96 | 47 | 83 | 87 | 38 | -7 | -1 | 5 | 46 | 131 | 83 | 65 | 656 | 128 | 26 | 16 | 5.9 | 3.0 |
| Moldova | 12 | 25 | 23 | 78 | 75 | 38 | 127 | 102 | 132 | 71 | 148 | 175 | 150 | 1,037 | 306 | 44 | 52 | 5.7 | 6.0 |
| Russia | 408 | 1,460 | 1,656 | 1,681 | 1,492 | 1,102 | -463 | 216 | -72 | -1,769 | 2,132 | 7,000 | 8,500 | 14,843 | 103 | 15 | 49 | 0.0 | 1.0 |
| Tajikistan | 12 | 10 | 18 | 18 | 25 | 21 | 24 | 10 | 36 | 32 | 272 | 36 | 60 | 531 | 82 | 42 | 6 | 13.0 | 1.6 |
| Turkmenistan | 103 | 233 | 108 | 108 | 62 | 125 | 131 | 170 | 276 | 226 | 354 | 300 | 308 | 2,275 | 350 | 54 | 46 | 5.0 | 4.0 |
| Ukraine | 151 | 257 | 516 | 581 | 747 | 489 | 594 | 769 | 698 | 1,411 | 1,711 | 6,500 | 1,800 | 15,082 | 320 | 36 | 138 | 3.0 | 8.0 |
| Uzbekistan | 73 | -24 | 90 | 167 | 140 | 121 | 75 | 83 | 65 | 70 | 187 | 250 | 300 | 1,354 | 52 | 7 | 10 | 2.0 | 2.0 |
| *Total* | *1,505* | *3,397* | *4,398* | *5,789* | *5,437* | *4,540* | *2,283* | *4,753* | *5,038* | *5,279* | *13,552* | *15,589* | *12,301* | *73,804* | *264* | *48* | *56* | *7.6* | *2.8* |
| **All transition countries** | | | | | | | | | | | | | | | | | | | |
| **Total** | **6,731** | **15,905** | **15,608** | **19,934** | **24,343** | **26,482** | **25,560** | **26,492** | **30,138** | **21,821** | **45,475** | **55,582** | **44,674** | **325,902** | **807** | **112** | **138** | **5.7** | **4.3** |

Sources: IMF, central banks and EBRD estimates.

## Table A8

## Selected major privatisations in transition countries in 2005

| Company | Country | Sector | Number of employees | Date completed | Sale price (in US$ million)[1] | Debt taken on (in US$ million)[1] | Investment commitments (in US$ million)[1] | Method of privatisation | Privatised share (in per cent)[1] | Buyer's origin |
|---|---|---|---|---|---|---|---|---|---|---|
| Devechi Broiler | Azerbaijan | Food and food products | 700 | Mar 2005 | 0.59 | na | na | Auction | na | Azerbaijan |
| Sheki Ipek | Azerbaijan | Textile industry | 1,250 | Mar 2005 | 0.51 | 16.00 | 2.20 | Tender | 98.3 | Azerbaijan |
| Gekchai-Konserv | Azerbaijan | Food and food products | 200 | Nov 2005 | 0.33 | na | na | Auction | na | Azerbaijan |
| Minsktorgavtotrans | Belarus | Transport | 1,937 | Jun 2005 | 0.07 | na | na | Auction | 1.3 | Belarus |
| Shoe Factory Baranovich | Belarus | Consumer goods | 394 | Dec 2005 | 0.02 | na | na | Auction | na | Russia |
| Rudnik Krečnjaka i Tvornica Kreča Doboj | Bosnia and Herz. | Mining | 86 | Apr 2005 | 0.65 | 0.64 | 1.94 | Tender | 58.7 | Bosnia and Herz. |
| Livnick Banja Luka | Bosnia and Herz. | Metal and metal products | 386 | Jun 2005 | 0.06 | na | 6.67 | Tender | na | Slovenia |
| Pleven district heating plant | Bulgaria | Electricity, gas, water | 224 | May 2005 | 16.89 | na | 33.03 | Tender | 100.0 | Bulgaria |
| Burgas district heating plant | Bulgaria | Electricity, gas, water | 153 | Jul 2005 | 9.61 | na | 26.68 | Tender | 100.0 | Bulgaria |
| Gypsum Koshava | Bulgaria | Construction | 335 | Jun 2005 | 1.75 | na | na | Tender | 99.5 | Bulgaria |
| Dunarit Russe | Bulgaria | Chemical Products | 506 | Apr 2005 | 1.27 | na | 8.22 | Auction | 92.0 | Bulgaria |
| Adriatic Split | Croatia | Tourism | 101 | Jun 2005 | 28.60 | na | 31.96 | Tender | 87.8 | Croatia |
| IPK Kandit Osijek | Croatia | Food and food products | 545 | Jul 2005 | 10.19 | na | na | Auction | 100.0 | Croatia |
| Istra Pula | Croatia | Consumer goods | 130 | Sep 2005 | 5.26 | na | 26.59 | Tender | 67.6 | Croatia |
| Slobodna Dalmacija Split | Croatia | Publisher | 686 | Aug 2005 | 4.12 | na | 45.71 | Tender | 34.6 | Croatia |
| Vrbovec Vrbovec | Croatia | Agribusiness | 1,338 | Mar 2005 | 0.17 | 6.73 | 10.09 | Tender | 92.0 | Croatia |
| Český Telecom | Czech Rep. | Telecommunications | 8,794 | Jun 2005 | 3,455.60 | na | na | Tender | 51.1 | Spain |
| Unipetrol | Czech Rep. | Oil and gas | 11,500 | May 2005 | 541.58 | 150.57 | na | Tender | 63.0 | Poland |
| Severočeské doly | Czech Rep. | Mining | 3,724 | Dec 2005 | 378.09 | na | na | Tender | 93.1 [2] | Czech Rep. |
| Ocean Shipping Company Ltd | Georgia | Transport | na | Apr 2005 | 93.00 | na | na | Tender | na | Georgia |
| Madneuli | Georgia | Mining | 842 | Dec 2005 | 36.00 | 28.70 | na | Tender | 97.2 | UK |
| Electric-carriage repair | Georgia | Manufacturing | na | Jun 2005 | 6.00 | na | na | na | na | na |
| Georgian Telecom Ltd | Georgia | Telecommunications | na | Feb 2005 | 5.00 | na | na | Direct selection | 81.0 [3] | US |
| Elnavalmshenebeli | Georgia | Manufacturing | 1,300 | Mar 2005 | 4.15 | na | na | Tender | 51.0 | Russia |
| Budapest Airport | Hungary | Transport | 2,291 | Dec 2005 | 2,350.05 | na | 329.61 | Tender | 75.0 [4] | UK |
| Antenna Hungária | Hungary | Telecommunications | 735 | Oct 2005 | 232.73 | na | 60.71 | Tender | 75.0 [4] | Switzerland |
| Hungexpo | Hungary | Exhibitions and fairs | 200 | Dec 2005 | 40.47 | na | 25.30 | Tender | 77.0 | France |
| Kaztsink | Kazakhstan | Manufacturing | 15,552 | Dec 2005 | 110.93 | na | na | Tender | 22.6 [5] | Philippines |
| Vasil'kovskoe Soloto | Kazakhstan | Mining | 798 | Aug 2005 | 17.70 | na | na | Tender | 35.0 [6] | Netherlands |
| Kondensat | Kazakhstan | Manufacturing | 284 | Jul 2005 | 9.90 | na | na | Auction | 8.7 | Kazakhstan |
| Kadamzhaiskii Sur'myanyi Kombinat | Kyrgyz Rep. | Mining | 1,100 | May 2005 | 2.37 | 7.31 | 14.50 | Tender | na | Kazakhstan |
| Chakan GES | Kyrgyz Rep. | Electricity, gas, water | 144 | Jun 2005 | 0.61 | na | 0.24 | Tender | na | Kyrgyz Rep. |
| Naryngidroenrgostroi | Kyrgyz Rep. | Construction | 5480 | Jan 2005 | 0.17 | na | na | Auction | na | Kyrgyz Rep. |
| Erkin-Too | Kyrgyz Rep. | Manufacturing | na | Mar 2005 | 0.05 | na | 3.00 | Tender | na | Kyrgyz Rep. |
| Tokmaksoe AP KSM | Kyrgyz Rep. | Manufacturing | 280 | Aug 2005 | 0.01 | na | 2.07 | Auction | na | Kyrgyz Rep. |
| Lietuvos Avialinijos | Lithuania | Transport | 568 | Aug 2005 | 9.45 | 35.28 | 3.66 | Tender | 100.0 | Lithuania |
| Mažeikių elektinė | Lithuania | Electricity, gas, water | 315 | Oct 2005 | 6.52 | 5.60 | na | Tender | na | Lithuania |
| Spauda | Lithuania | Publisher | 226 | Mar 2005 | 3.85 | 2.82 | na | Tender | 68.7 | Lithuania |
| Berechet | Moldova | Agribusiness | 192 | Dec 2005 | 0.43 | na | na | Auction | 63.5 | Moldova |
| Fabrica de vin Cojusna | Moldova | Food and food products | 163 | Aug 2005 | 0.25 | na | 3.00 | Tender | 88.8 | Russia |
| Parcul de autobuze din Bălţi | Moldova | Transport | 322 | Sep 2005 | 0.10 | na | 2.07 | Tender | na | Moldova |
| Polmos Bialistok | Poland | Food and food products | 391 | Oct 2005 | 422.77 | na | 23.97 | Tender | 61.0 | US |
| Zespół Elektrocieplowni w Łodzi | Poland | Electricity, gas, water | 2,578 | Aug 2005 | 278.32 | na | 84.14 | Tender | 85.0 | France |
| Impexmetal | Poland | Trade | 142 | Jan 2005 | 59.54 | na | na | Auction | 31.5 | Poland |
| Banca Comerciala Romana | Romania | Banking | 22,000 | Dec 2005 | 2,828.11 | na | na | Tender | 61.9 | Austria |
| Atelierele Centrale Criscior | Romania | Manufacturing | 261 | Feb 2005 | 0.33 | na | 0.65 | Tender | na | Romania |
| Moldoplast Iaşi | Romania | Chemical products | 370 | Nov 2005 | 0.22 | na | 4.81 | Tender | 96.4 | Romania |
| Polief | Russia | Chemical products | na | Mar 2005 | 107.56 | na | na | Tender | 100.0 | Russia |
| Halogen | Russia | Chemical products | 2,615 | Feb 2005 | 29.39 | na | na | Auction | 50.8 | Russia |
| Sea Port St Petersburg | Russia | Transport | 418 | Nov 2005 | 28.41 | na | na | Auction | 48.8 | Russia |

# Table A8 continued

## Selected major privatisations in transition countries in 2005

| Company | Country | Sector | Number of employees | Date completed | Sale price (in US$ million) | Debt taken on (in US$ million)[1] | Investment commitments (in US$ million)[1] | Method of privatisation | Privatised share (in per cent)[1] | Buyer's origin |
|---|---|---|---|---|---|---|---|---|---|---|
| Slovenska Autobusova Doprava Bratislava | Slovak Rep. | Transport | 720 | Apr 2005 | 9.36 | na | na | Tender | 49.0 | Slovak Rep. |
| Slovenska Autobusova Doprava Trencin | Slovak Rep. | Transport | 984 | Apr 2005 | 2.51 | na | na | Tender | 49.0 | Slovak Rep. |
| Rubin | Serbia and Mont. | Food and food products | 1,020 | Mar 2005 | 254.61 | 9.04 | 14.37 | Tender | 70.0 | Serbia and Mont. |
| Jubanka | Serbia and Mont. | Banking | 1,319 | Jan 2005 | 192.25 | na | na | Tender | 89.0[7] | Greece |
| Telecom Montenegro | Serbia and Mont. | Telecommunications | na | Mar 2005 | 144.19 | na | na | Tender | 51.1 | Hungary |
| Kombinat Aluminijuma Podgorica | Serbia and Mont. | Manufacturing | 2,746 | Nov 2005 | 61.34 | na | 27.00 | Tender | 65.4 | Russia/Cyprus |
| Novosadska Banka | Serbia and Mont. | Banking | 878 | May 2005 | 92.59 | na | 44.27 | Tender | 83.3[8] | Austria |
| Continental Banka | Serbia and Mont. | Banking | 643 | Jul 2005 | 62.61 | na | na | Tender | 98.9 | Slovenia |
| PZP Beograd | Serbia and Mont. | Construction | 650 | Jun 2005 | 23.78 | 28.89 | 16.53 | Tender | 70.0 | Serbia and Mont. |
| ZHBK & CD | Tajikistan | Manufacturing | 178 | Oct 2005 | 1.28 | 0.06 | 1.93 | Tender | na | Tajikistan |
| ELTO | Tajikistan | Manufacturing | 231 | May 2005 | 0.62 | 0.25 | 0.64 | Tender | na | Tajikistan |
| Monolitstroy | Tajikistan | Manufacturing | 349 | Aug 2005 | 0.40 | 1.61 | 0.96 | Tender | na | Tajikistan |
| Kryvorizhstal | Ukraine | Metal and metal products | 50,891 | Oct 2005 | 4,724.83 | na | na | Auction | 93.0 | Germany |
| Krasnodonugol | Ukraine | Mining | 22,290 | May 2005 | 91.58 | na | na | Auction | 39.9 | Ukraine |
| Samarkand tea packing factory | Uzbekistan | Food and food products | 307 | Jan 2005 | 0.20 | 3.20 | 3.00 | Tender | 100.0 | US |
| Bukhara Gips | Uzbekistan | Construction | 335 | Sep 2005 | 1.50 | na | 6.30 | Tender | 30.8 | Germany |
| AkhangaranTsement | Uzbekistan | Construction | 1,910 | Jun 2005 | 7.00 | na | na | Tender | 50.0[9] | US |
| Samarkandskii Liftostroitel'nyi Zavod | Uzbekistan | Manufacturing | 392 | Aug 2005 | 1.00 | na | 23.00 | Tender | na | Iran |

Sources: EBRD privatisation survey, Bureau van Dijk/Zephyr and various news wires.

Note: The table lists up to five privatisations in each country and includes both initial and residual privatisations. Seven privatisations are listed for Serbia and Montenegro as the table includes privatisations in both Serbia and in Montenegro. National privatisation agencies or other pertinent authorities were asked to determine the three main privatisations in terms of privatisation revenue and the three most important privatisations in terms of company size (turnover or number of employees). Privatised companies with less than 50 employees were not considered. For this reason, no privatisations are listed for Armenia and FYR Macedonia. No major privatisations took place in Albania, Estonia, Latvia and Slovenia. Data for Turkmenistan were not available.

[1] na = not available.
[2] Acquisition increased from 37.31 per cent to 93.10 per cent.
[3] Acquisition increased from 30 per cent to 81 per cent.
[4] 75 per cent minus one share.
[5] An additional 6 per cent (two minority stakes - 1 per cent and 5 per cent) was sold via the stock exchange in August 2005.
[6] An additional 5 per cent was sold via the stock exchange in July 2005.
[7] This share was increased to 97.14 per cent in August 2005 and to 100 per cent by the end of 2005.
[8] This share was increased to 95.6 per cent in November 2005.
[9] Acquisition increased from 25 per cent to 50 per cent.

# Country assessments

The following assessments provide country-by-country information on macroeconomic developments in 2005 and the outlook for 2006. The "cut-off" date for the information is mid-March 2006.

The macroeconomic assessment for each country leads with two summary bullets, highlighting main developments and key risks. These are followed by four short analytical sections:

▮ Real economy

▮ Economic policies

▮ External sector

▮ Outlook and risks.

These assessments are complemented by four charts that summarise recent trends and changes in key policy variables.

The qualitative assessment for each country is followed by a table of selected macro-economic indicators. These indicators give a quantitative overview of developments, as well as the EBRD's forecasts for the current year on growth, inflation, the fiscal balance, the current account balance and foreign direct investment.

Data are drawn from a variety of sources, including national authorities, other international organisations and EBRD staff estimates. Wherever possible, data have been drawn from cross-country sources such as the IMF's International Financial Statistics to ensure maximum comparability. Nonetheless, data quality for some of the transition economies is still weak, and countries' statistical methods may differ. The most recent GDP and fiscal data for the Czech Republic, Estonia, Hungary, Latvia, Lithuania, Poland, the Slovak Republic and Slovenia have been recalculated according to Eurostat methodology (ESA95). Footnotes at the end of the table provide further detail on important statistical issues.

# Albania

## Economic performance and prospects

GDP growth has slowed slightly due to large-scale power cuts, but inflation remains low and the exchange rate stable.

High fiscal and current account deficits, along with infrastructure deficiencies, pose the main risks to macroeconomic stability.

## Real economy

Real GDP growth declined to 5.5 per cent in 2005, mainly due to power cuts late in the year. Private consumption was boosted by remittances, while infrastructure projects continued to drive economic development. (These projects were financed mainly by international financial institutions.) Official unemployment has reached around 15 per cent of the labour force of 1.1 million workers. However, 700,000 emigrants who are not included in this total work abroad, mainly in Greece and Italy.

## Economic policies

In 2005 average inflation, at 2.3 per cent, was within the 2–4 per cent target range set by the Bank of Albania (BOA). The BOA lowered its main repo rate to 5 per cent in March 2005. The real exchange rate appreciation against the euro declined to 3.2 per cent in 2005 from about 8 per cent in 2004. The exchange rate is subject to significant seasonal fluctuations due to remittance flows. Foreign exchange transactions are now mostly done through official channels rather than the informal, unregulated market.

The general government deficit was 3.3 per cent in 2005, down from 5.0 per cent in the previous year. While tax revenues grew in the first half of 2005, government expenditure also increased rapidly in the run-up to parliamentary elections in July. However, 2005 was the first year since the start of transition in which the current budget balance (excluding grants and capital expenditures) was positive. With the IMF's agreement, the new government has reduced registration fees and cut the income tax rate for small businesses.

## External sector

In 2005 high remittances continued to cover most of the trade deficit, estimated at over 20 per cent of GDP. The current account deficit exceeded 7 per cent of GDP. Albania also benefits from substantial official international assistance which, at between US$ 200 million and US$ 300 million a year, is equivalent to 3–4 per cent of GDP. Total external debt (mostly official and long-term) declined from 25 per cent of GDP in 2003 to 20 per cent by end-2005. The government has continued to restructure old inoperative bilateral debt, estimated at about US$ 102 million. All current obligations are being repaid on time.

## Outlook and risks

The economy is expected to continue growing by 5–7 per cent a year in the medium term. However, inadequate infrastructure remains a key risk factor. Political stability and a deepening of the relationship with the EU (following the initialling of a Stabilisation and Association Agreement in February 2006) will help maintain a favourable macroeconomic environment.

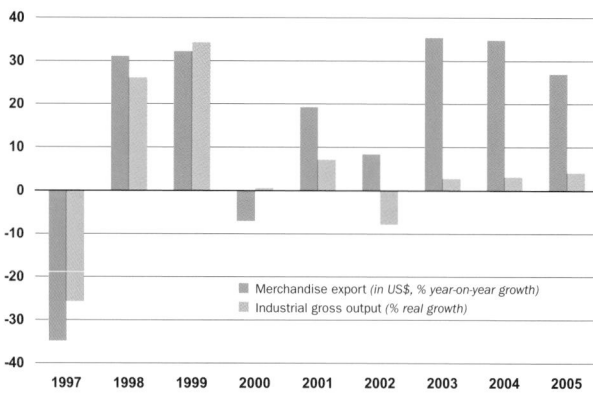

**Exports and industrial production growth year-on-year**

- Merchandise export *(in US$, % year-on-year growth)*
- Industrial gross output *(% real growth)*

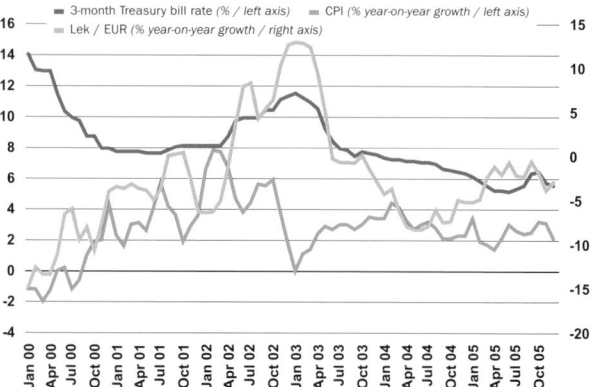

**Inflation, exchange rate developments and interest rates**

- 3-month Treasury bill rate *(% / left axis)*
- CPI *(% year-on-year growth / left axis)*
- Lek / EUR *(% year-on-year growth / right axis)*

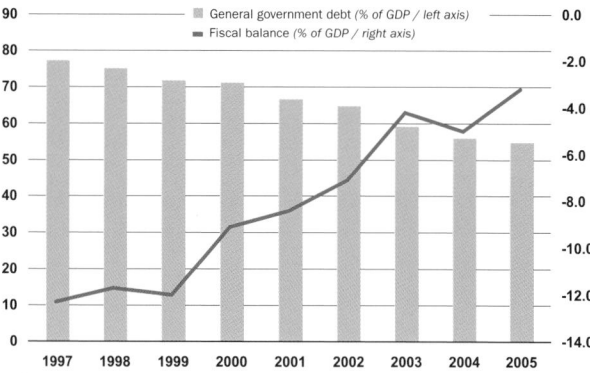

**Debt and fiscal balance**

- General government debt *(% of GDP / left axis)*
- Fiscal balance *(% of GDP / right axis)*

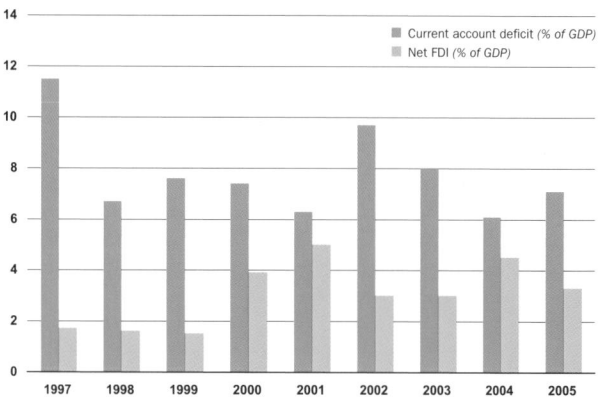

**Current account deficit and net FDI**

- Current account deficit *(% of GDP)*
- Net FDI *(% of GDP)*

| | 2000 | 2001 | 2002 | 2003 | 2004 | 2005 Estimate | 2006 Projection |
|---|---|---|---|---|---|---|---|
| **Output and expenditure** | | | | *(Percentage change in real terms)* | | | |
| GDP | 7.3 | 7.2 | 3.4 | 6.0 | 5.9 | 5.5 | 5.0 |
| Private consumption | 5.3 | na | na | na | na | na | na |
| Public consumption | 7.4 | na | na | na | na | na | na |
| Gross fixed capital formation [1] | 17.9 | na | na | na | na | na | na |
| Exports of goods and services | 5.8 | na | na | na | na | na | na |
| Imports of goods and services | 6.5 | na | na | na | na | na | na |
| Industrial gross output | 0.5 | 7.1 | -7.9 | 2.7 | 3.1 | 4.0 | na |
| Agricultural gross output | 4.5 | 2.2 | 2.1 | 3.0 | 3.8 | 3.0 | na |
| **Employment [2]** | | | | *(Percentage change)* | | | |
| Labour force (end-year) | -1.8 | -3.0 | -12.2 | -0.3 | -0.8 | 0.9 | na |
| Employment (end-year) | 0.2 | -13.8 | 0.0 | 0.7 | -0.4 | 0.9 | na |
| | | | | *(In per cent of labour force)* | | | |
| Unemployment (end-year) | 16.8 | 14.5 | 15.8 | 15.0 | 14.5 | 14.7 | na |
| **Prices and wages** | | | | *(Percentage change)* | | | |
| Consumer prices (annual average) | 0.1 | 3.1 | 5.2 | 2.4 | 2.9 | 2.3 | 3.0 |
| Consumer prices (end-year) | 4.2 | 3.5 | 1.7 | 3.3 | 2.2 | 2.0 | 3.0 |
| Producer prices (annual average) | 5.0 | -5.8 | 6.5 | 6.7 | 12.4 | 2.5 | na |
| Producer prices (end-year) | na | -4.0 | 11.2 | 5.0 | 12.3 | 2.4 | na |
| Gross average monthly earnings in economy (annual average) | 19.7 | 24.7 | 11.7 | 10.0 | 6.0 | 7.3 | na |
| **Government sector** | | | | *(In per cent of GDP)* | | | |
| General government balance | -9.2 | -8.5 | -7.2 | -4.4 | -5.0 | -3.3 | -4.1 |
| General government expenditure | 31.9 | 31.6 | 31.1 | 28.4 | 28.7 | 26.7 | na |
| General government debt | 71.3 | 66.8 | 64.8 | 60.6 | 55.6 | 54.8 | na |
| **Monetary sector [3]** | | | | *(Percentage change)* | | | |
| Broad money (M2, end-year) | 10.4 | 15.4 | 5.3 | 9.2 | 10.8 | 11.4 | na |
| Domestic credit (end-year) | 8.6 | 4.1 | 6.7 | 11.0 | 7.7 | 13.2 | na |
| | | | | *(In per cent of GDP)* | | | |
| Broad money (M2, end-year) | 49.8 | 51.9 | 51.0 | 50.4 | 49.9 | 50.6 | na |
| **Interest and exchange rates** | | | | *(In per cent per annum, end-year)* | | | |
| Refinancing rate [4] | 10.8 | 7.0 | 8.5 | 6.5 | 5.3 | 5.0 | na |
| Treasury bill rate (3-month maturity) | 10.8 | 8.0 | 11.2 | 7.4 | 6.2 | 5.5 | na |
| Deposit rate (1 year) | 6.9 | 6.9 | 8.0 | 5.5 | 4.5 | 3.0 | na |
| Lending rate (1 year) [5] | 21.2 | 15.3 | 14.6 | 11.8 | 11.0 | 12.0 | na |
| | | | | *(Leks per US dollar)* | | | |
| Exchange rate (end-year) | 142.8 | 135.9 | 134.0 | 106.4 | 92.6 | 98.1 | na |
| Exchange rate (annual average) | 143.9 | 143.6 | 140.2 | 121.3 | 102.8 | 98.1 | na |
| **External sector** | | | | *(In millions of US dollars)* | | | |
| Current account | -273 | -261 | -435 | -470 | -460 | -621 | -662 |
| Trade balance | -821 | -1,027 | -1,155 | -1,336 | -1,579 | -1,933 | -2,055 |
| Merchandise exports | 255 | 305 | 330 | 447 | 603 | 766 | 932 |
| Merchandise imports | 1,076 | 1,332 | 1,485 | 1,783 | 2,182 | 2,699 | 2,987 |
| Foreign direct investment, net | 143 | 204 | 135 | 178 | 343 | 288 | 339 |
| Gross reserves, excluding gold (end-year) | 608 | 737 | 860 | 1,026 | 1,374 | 1,459 | na |
| External debt stock | 1,640 | 1,200 | 1,180 | 1,420 | 1,673 | 1,747 | na |
| | | | | *(In months of imports of goods and services)* | | | |
| Gross reserves, excluding gold (end-year) | 4.8 | 4.9 | 5.0 | 4.8 | 5.1 | 4.4 | na |
| | | | | *(In per cent of exports of goods and services)* | | | |
| Debt service | 4.0 | 4.1 | 6.8 | 5.0 | 4.1 | 4.3 | na |
| **Memorandum items** | | | | *(Denominations as indicated)* | | | |
| Population (end-year, million) | 3.1 | 3.1 | 3.2 | 3.2 | 3.2 | 3.2 | na |
| GDP (in billions of leks) | 531 | 589 | 630 | 696 | 780 | 857 | 937 |
| GDP per capita (in US dollars) | 1,185 | 1,309 | 1,406 | 1,812 | 2,372 | 2,730 | na |
| Share of industry in GDP (in per cent) | 8.1 | 7.8 | 7.7 | 7.5 | 7.3 | 7.1 | na |
| Share of agriculture in GDP (in per cent) | 32.0 | 31.9 | 28.4 | 27.6 | 26.8 | 26.3 | na |
| Current account/GDP (in per cent) | -7.4 | -6.4 | -9.7 | -8.2 | -6.1 | -7.1 | -6.9 |
| External debt - reserves (in US$ million) | 1,032 | 463 | 320 | 394 | 299 | 288 | na |
| External debt/GDP (in per cent) | 44.4 | 29.3 | 26.3 | 24.7 | 22.0 | 20.0 | na |
| External debt/exports of goods (in per cent) | 232.4 | 142.9 | 128.9 | 121.7 | 104.2 | 86.7 | na |

[1] Includes changes in inventories.

[2] Figures do not include emigrant workers abroad who accounted for an estimated 27.4 per cent of the total labour force in 2000.

[3] Data up to and including 2001 are based on the previous reporting standard. The new reporting standard, in accordance with the 2000 Monetary and Financial Statistics Manual, excludes blocked deposits from broad money.

[4] From 2001 the figures show the repo rate of the central bank.

[5] The figures show the weighted average monthly rate for new credit in leks for maturities between six months and one year in December each year.

# Armenia

## Economic performance and prospects

■ Despite strong economic growth, the level of tax evasion remains high, tax collection is weak, and fiscal policy has been loosened.

■ Productivity gains are necessary to offset the economy's vulnerability to commodity prices and to avoid a slowdown in growth.

## Real economy

The economy grew by 13.9 per cent in real terms in 2005, exceeding the already high growth rates achieved in the previous four years. This was largely driven by the construction and services sectors, along with agriculture. Growth in industrial production was mainly due to an expanding base metals sector. Increased consumer spending was supported by higher incomes and growing remittances.

## Economic policies

Fiscal policy has loosened over the past few years, due mainly to substantial rises in social and infrastructure expenditures committed under poverty reduction targets. Despite significant nominal increases in tax revenues in 2005, the incidence of tax evasion and exemptions remains high and is reflected in the low and stable ratio of tax revenue to GDP (15.6 per cent). The Central Bank of Armenia (CBA) has announced a shift in monetary policy from monetary targeting to inflation targeting in 2006. Annual average inflation for 2005 was 0.6 per cent against an objective of 3 per cent.

## External sector

Exports and imports increased by almost 30 per cent in 2005. While diamond exports declined, other exports (particularly base metals) expanded. Import growth was largely fuelled by spending on foreign consumer goods and on products, materials and machines required for construction projects. The trade deficit remained high, but continued to be offset by substantial remittance flows. According to the CBA, total private transfers (mainly remittances from Russia), including those not captured by the balance of payments, are expected to have exceeded US$ 1 billion in 2005. The capital account recorded a 29 per cent increase in foreign direct investment over the first nine months of 2005. A modest increase in external debt, coupled with strong economic growth, led to a further decline in the ratio of external debt to GDP to 26.7 per cent.

## Outlook and risks

Economic growth can be maintained in the medium term, given tight macroeconomic policies and progress in structural reforms. New investments in infrastructure and other industries, and increased grant flows from the United States, should also stimulate development in the regions. However, the economy remains at risk from continued currency appreciation, vulnerability to commodity prices, the ongoing economic blockade by some neighbouring countries (leading to the loss of key markets and to high transport costs), and dependence on soft finance from donors and multilateral institutions.

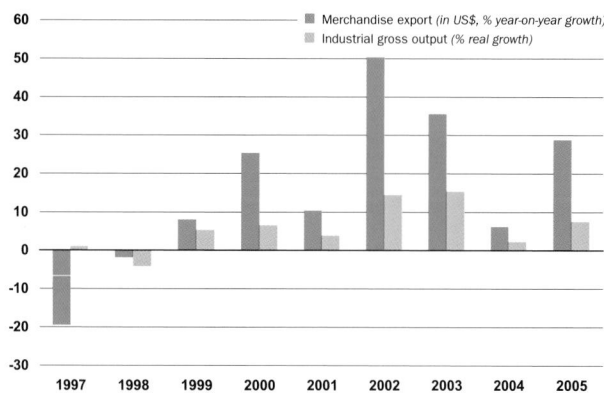

**Exports and industrial production growth year-on-year**

■ Merchandise export (in US$, % year-on-year growth)
■ Industrial gross output (% real growth)

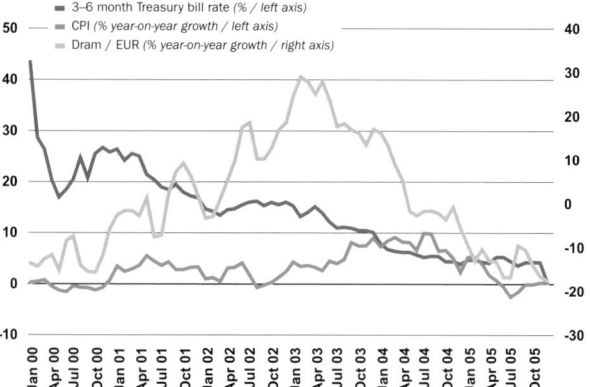

**Inflation, exchange rate developments and interest rates**

■ 3–6 month Treasury bill rate (% / left axis)
■ CPI (% year-on-year growth / left axis)
■ Dram / EUR (% year-on-year growth / right axis)

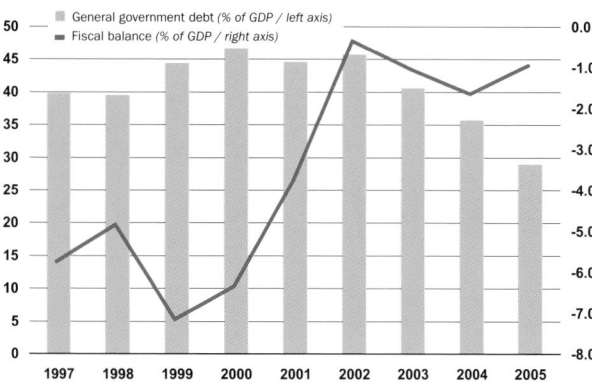

**Debt and fiscal balance**

■ General government debt (% of GDP / left axis)
■ Fiscal balance (% of GDP / right axis)

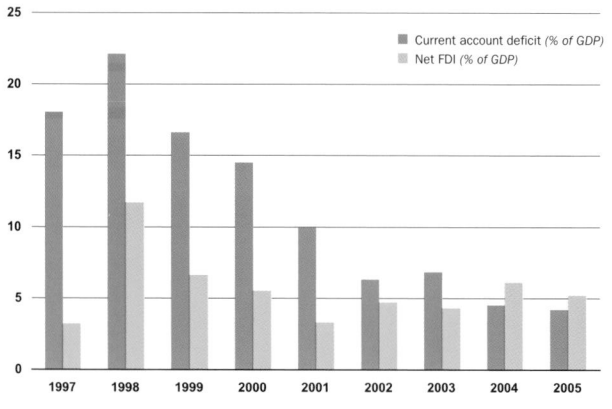

**Current account deficit and net FDI**

■ Current account deficit (% of GDP)
■ Net FDI (% of GDP)

| | 2000 | 2001 | 2002 | 2003 | 2004 | 2005 Estimate | 2006 Projection |
|---|---|---|---|---|---|---|---|
| **Output and expenditure** | *(Percentage change in real terms)* | | | | | | |
| GDP | 5.9 | 9.6 | 13.2 | 13.9 | 10.1 | 13.9 | 8.5 |
| Private consumption | 8.3 | 7.5 | 9.0 | 6.9 | 10.2 | na | na |
| Public consumption | 2.8 | 4.3 | 2.2 | 14.1 | 16.1 | na | na |
| Gross fixed capital formation | 16.2 | 5.3 | 33.1 | 33.7 | 12.4 | na | na |
| Exports of goods and services | 16.6 | 20.8 | 26.3 | 23.2 | 3.7 | na | na |
| Imports of goods and services | 5.1 | 1.2 | 9.0 | 31.0 | 3.0 | na | na |
| Industrial gross output | 6.5 | 3.8 | 14.4 | 15.3 | 2.1 | 7.5 | na |
| Agricultural gross output | -2.4 | 11.6 | 4.5 | 4.0 | 14.5 | 11.2 | na |
| **Employment** | *(Percentage change)* | | | | | | |
| Labour force (end-year) | -1.0 | -2.5 | -12.2 | -0.6 | -0.5 | -2.6 | na |
| Employment (end-year) | -1.6 | -1.0 | -12.5 | 0.5 | -0.1 | -0.5 | na |
| | *(In per cent of labour force)* | | | | | | |
| Unemployment (annual average) [1] | 11.7 | 10.4 | 10.8 | 10.1 | 9.4 | 7.4 | na |
| **Prices and wages** | *(Percentage change)* | | | | | | |
| Consumer prices (annual average) | -0.8 | 3.2 | 1.2 | 4.7 | 6.9 | 0.6 | 0.7 |
| Consumer prices (end-year) | 0.4 | 3.0 | 2.0 | 8.6 | 1.9 | -0.2 | 2.4 |
| Producer prices (annual average) | 0.8 | -0.4 | 2.5 | 5.9 | 21.7 | 7.9 | na |
| Producer prices (end-year) | 0.4 | -3.6 | 0.9 | 21.1 | 25.3 | -4.0 | na |
| Gross average monthly earnings in economy (annual average) | 15.0 | 10.7 | 12.2 | 21.7 | 22.8 | 29.5 | na |
| **Government sector [2]** | *(In per cent of GDP)* | | | | | | |
| General government balance | -6.4 | -3.8 | -0.4 | -1.1 | -1.7 | -1.0 | -2.9 |
| General government expenditure | 25.9 | 20.9 | 19.3 | 18.9 | 17.2 | 17.7 | na |
| General government debt | 46.8 | 44.6 | 45.7 | 40.6 | 35.7 | 29.0 | na |
| **Monetary sector** | *(Percentage change)* | | | | | | |
| Broad money (M2, end-year) | 39.7 | 4.3 | 34.0 | 10.4 | 22.3 | 27.2 | na |
| Domestic credit (end-year) | 10.7 | -9.8 | -8.1 | -9.6 | 41.1 | 38.2 | na |
| | *(In per cent of GDP)* | | | | | | |
| Broad money (M2, end-year) | 14.7 | 13.4 | 15.6 | 14.4 | 15.1 | 16.3 | na |
| **Interest and exchange rates** | *(In per cent per annum, end-year)* | | | | | | |
| Refinancing rate | 25.0 | 15.0 | 13.5 | 7.0 | 3.8 | 3.5 | na |
| Money market rate [3] | 18.6 | 19.4 | 12.3 | 7.5 | 3.1 | 4.3 | na |
| Deposit rate [4] | 18.1 | 14.9 | 9.5 | 6.9 | 4.4 | 6.5 | na |
| Lending rate [4] | 28.6 | 27.7 | 23.4 | 20.8 | 18.2 | 17.3 | na |
| | *(Drams per US dollar)* | | | | | | |
| Exchange rate (end-year) | 552.2 | 561.8 | 584.9 | 566.0 | 486.3 | 450.2 | na |
| Exchange rate (annual average) | 539.5 | 555.1 | 573.4 | 578.8 | 533.5 | 457.8 | na |
| **External sector** | *(In millions of US dollars)* | | | | | | |
| Current account | -277 | -212 | -149 | -191 | -162 | -204 | -213 |
| Trade balance | -463 | -431 | -369 | -434 | -458 | -590 | -607 |
| Merchandise exports | 310 | 342 | 514 | 696 | 738 | 950 | 1,033 |
| Merchandise imports | 773 | 773 | 883 | 1,130 | 1,196 | 1,540 | 1,640 |
| Foreign direct investment, net | 104 | 70 | 111 | 121 | 217 | 255 | 152 |
| Gross reserves, excluding gold (end-year) | 314 | 329 | 430 | 502 | 547 | 755 | na |
| External debt stock | 860 | 906 | 1,026 | 1,098 | 1,183 | 1,299 | na |
| | *(In months of imports of goods and services)* | | | | | | |
| Gross reserves, excluding gold (end-year) | 3.9 | 4.0 | 4.7 | 4.3 | 4.3 | 4.8 | na |
| | *(In per cent of exports of goods and services)* | | | | | | |
| Debt service | 10.7 | 9.7 | 10.1 | 11.4 | 7.2 | 4.8 | na |
| **Memorandum items** | *(Denominations as indicated)* | | | | | | |
| Population (end-year, million) | 3.3 | 3.2 | 3.2 | 3.2 | 3.2 | 3.2 | na |
| GDP (in billions of drams) | 1,031 | 1,176 | 1,362 | 1,625 | 1,896 | 2,228 | 2,401 |
| GDP per capita (in US dollars) | 582 | 659 | 740 | 874 | 1,106 | 1,499 | na |
| Share of industry in GDP (in per cent) | 21.9 | 20.5 | 18.9 | 19.9 | 19.7 | 18.7 | na |
| Share of agriculture in GDP (in per cent) | 27.0 | 24.9 | 23.4 | 21.3 | 22.5 | 18.8 | na |
| Current account/GDP (in per cent) | -14.5 | -10.0 | -6.3 | -6.8 | -4.5 | -4.2 | -3.8 |
| External debt - reserves (in US$ million) | 546 | 577 | 596 | 596 | 636 | 544 | na |
| External debt/GDP (in per cent) | 45.0 | 42.8 | 43.2 | 39.1 | 33.3 | 26.7 | na |
| External debt/exports of goods and services (in per cent) | 192.4 | 171.4 | 147.0 | 121.5 | 120.1 | 106.0 | na |

[1]  Registered unemployed.

[2]  Central government account only.

[3]  Average of one to three-month Treasury bills.

[4]  Weighted average rate for maturities of 15 days to less than one year.

# Azerbaijan

## Economic performance and prospects

■ Economic growth reached record levels in 2005, supported by a large increase in oil production and exports.

■ Tighter fiscal policy and more efficient state-owned enterprises are necessary to curb exchange rate appreciation pressures and support the development of the non-oil sector.

### Real economy

Real GDP growth reached a record 26.4 per cent in 2005, reflecting increases in oil production and exports, and large capital investments. The oil sector accounted for about 41 per cent of GDP in 2005, underpinning the growth of industry as a whole by about 33.5 per cent. Agricultural expansion was only about 7.1 per cent.

### Economic policies

Government revenues increased by 43.5 per cent during 2005 as tax revenues were boosted by high oil prices and production. However, higher expenditure, mainly on long-term infrastructure investment, caused the government budget to record a deficit of 1.1 per cent of GDP in 2005, compared with a surplus of 0.8 per cent in 2004. Money supply and credit also rose sharply, fuelling inflation. In response, the National Bank of Azerbaijan (NBA) abandoned the de facto fixed exchange rate to the US dollar in February 2005 and allowed the manat to appreciate in real terms (by 11 per cent against the dollar by end-2005). The NBA also increased its refinancing rate three times from May 2005 (twice by 0.5 per cent and once by 1 per cent). As a result, annual inflation fell from 13.9 per cent in April to 5.3 per cent in December.

### External sector

While exports surged in the second half of 2005, import growth, associated mostly with oil and gas development projects, slowed as major capital investments were completed. This led to a trade surplus of about 2.7 per cent of GDP in 2005, compared with a surplus of 1.9 per cent in 2004. Consequently, the current account was almost in balance in 2005, compared with a 30 per cent deficit in 2004. Foreign direct investment decreased significantly due to the fall in investment related to pipeline construction.

### Outlook and risks

The economic boom is expected to continue in the short term, with growth rates in excess of 20 per cent. Following the opening of the Baku-Tbilisi-Ceyhan and South Caucasus pipelines, increased oil and gas export capacity will support the current account surplus from 2006. However, the economy is vulnerable to a decline in oil prices, and the current high level of oil-related revenues may delay essential structural reforms. While economic diversification is necessary for sustained growth, the real exchange rate appreciation associated with large capital inflows and oil-revenue spending may undermine non-oil sector development.

**Exports and industrial production growth year-on-year**

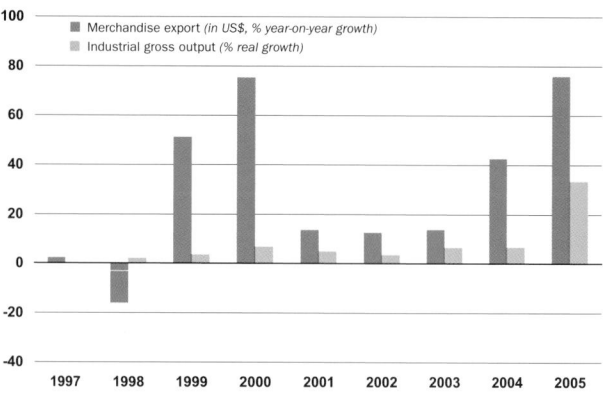

**Inflation, exchange rate developments and interest rates**

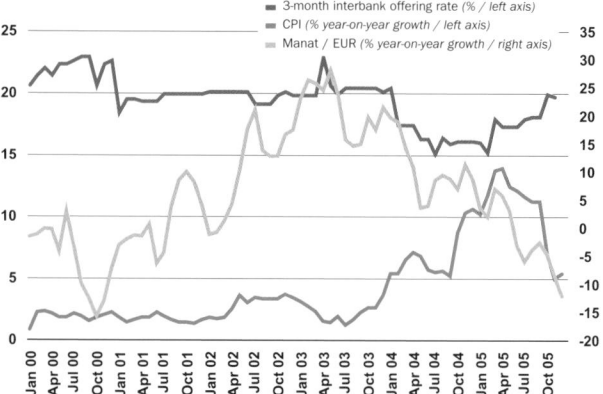

**Debt and fiscal balance**

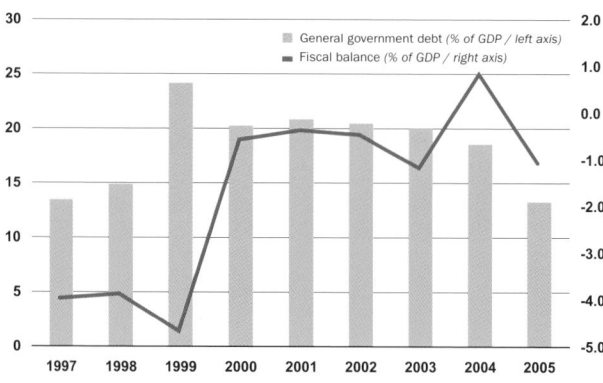

**Current account deficit and net FDI**

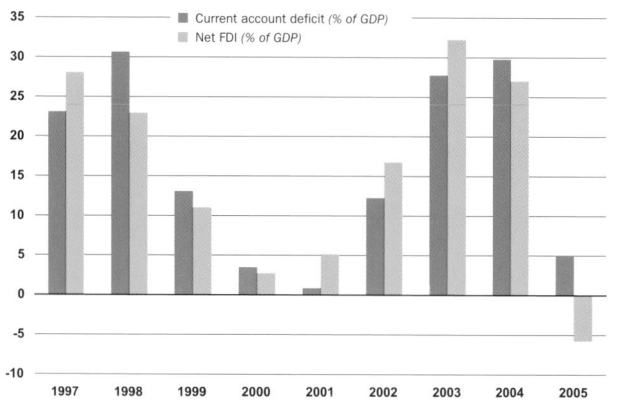

| | 2000 | 2001 | 2002 | 2003 | 2004 | 2005 Estimate | 2006 Projection |
|---|---|---|---|---|---|---|---|
| **Output and expenditure** | | | | *(Percentage change in real terms)* | | | |
| GDP | 6.2 | 6.5 | 8.1 | 11.5 | 10.2 | 26.4 | 25.0 |
| Private consumption | 12.1 | 9.9 | 6.2 | 19.2 | 13.2 | na | na |
| Public consumption | 2.2 | 4.9 | 5.2 | 18.2 | 11.2 | na | na |
| Gross fixed capital formation | 2.6 | 20.6 | 31.9 | 32.9 | 23.4 | na | na |
| Exports of goods and services | na | na | na | na | na | na | na |
| Imports of goods and services | na | na | na | na | na | na | na |
| Industrial gross output [1] | 6.9 | 5.1 | 3.6 | 6.6 | 6.7 | 33.5 | na |
| Agricultural gross output | 12.1 | 11.1 | 6.4 | 5.6 | 7.6 | 7.1 | na |
| **Employment** | | | | *(Percentage change)* | | | |
| Labour force (end-year) | 0.0 | 0.4 | 0.4 | 0.6 | 0.5 | na | na |
| Employment (end-year) | -0.1 | 0.3 | 0.3 | 0.5 | 0.5 | na | na |
| | | | | *(In per cent of labour force)* | | | |
| Unemployment (end-year) | 1.1 | 1.3 | 1.3 | 1.4 | 1.5 | na | na |
| **Prices and wages** | | | | *(Percentage change)* | | | |
| Consumer prices (annual average) | 1.8 | 1.5 | 2.8 | 2.2 | 6.8 | 10.3 | 13.0 |
| Consumer prices (end-year) | 2.2 | 1.5 | 3.3 | 3.6 | 10.5 | 5.3 | 8.0 |
| Producer prices (annual average) | 27.4 | 1.8 | -2.3 | 16.1 | 12.9 | na | na |
| Producer prices (end-year) | 14.5 | -4.4 | -5.2 | 11.2 | na | na | na |
| Gross average monthly earnings in economy (annual average) | 20.2 | 17.3 | 21.3 | 21.4 | 26.2 | 41.7 | na |
| **Government sector** | | | | *(In per cent of GDP)* | | | |
| General government balance [2] | -0.6 | -0.4 | -0.5 | -1.2 | 0.8 | -1.1 | -1.1 |
| General government expenditure | 20.8 | 18.7 | 27.7 | 28.3 | 26.0 | 23.5 | na |
| General government debt | 20.3 | 20.9 | 20.5 | 20.0 | 18.6 | 13.3 | na |
| **Monetary sector** | | | | *(Percentage change)* | | | |
| Broad money (M2, end-year) | 15.9 | 7.7 | 15.6 | 27.9 | 31.9 | 34.9 | na |
| Domestic credit (end-year) | 13.5 | -38.1 | 84.2 | 27.1 | 42.5 | 39.2 | na |
| | | | | *(In per cent of GDP)* | | | |
| Broad money (M2, end-year) | 6.9 | 6.6 | 6.7 | 7.3 | 8.0 | 7.6 | na |
| **Interest and exchange rates** | | | | *(In per cent per annum, end-year)* | | | |
| Refinance rate (6 months) | 10.0 | 10.0 | 7.0 | 7.0 | 7.0 | 7.0 | na |
| Interbank interest rate (3 months) [3] | 22.5 | 19.8 | 19.7 | 20.3 | 16.6 | na | na |
| Deposit rate | 12.9 | 8.5 | 8.7 | 9.5 | 9.2 | na | na |
| Lending rate | 19.7 | 19.7 | 17.4 | 15.5 | 15.7 | na | na |
| | | | | *(Manats per US dollar)* | | | |
| Exchange rate (end-year) | 4,565.0 | 4,775.0 | 4,893.0 | 4,923.0 | 4,903.0 | 4,593.0 | na |
| Exchange rate (annual average) | 4,474.2 | 4,656.6 | 4,860.8 | 4,910.7 | 4,913.5 | 4,727.1 | na |
| **External sector** | | | | *(In millions of US dollars)* | | | |
| Current account | -187 | -49 | -770 | -2,020 | -2,586 | -655 | 4,197 |
| Trade balance | 260 | 581 | 482 | -98 | 162 | 2,359 | 6,717 |
| Merchandise exports | 1,799 | 2,046 | 2,305 | 2,625 | 3,743 | 6,592 | 11,826 |
| Merchandise imports | 1,539 | 1,465 | 1,823 | 2,723 | 3,581 | 4,233 | 5,109 |
| Foreign direct investment, net | 149 | 299 | 1,048 | 2,353 | 2,351 | -728 | -2,124 |
| Gross reserves, excluding gold (end-year) [4] | 680 | 725 | 721 | 803 | 923 | 1,181 | na |
| External debt stock | 1,044 | 1,154 | 1,252 | 1,432 | 1,585 | 1,663 | na |
| | | | | *(In months of imports of goods and services)* | | | |
| Gross reserves, excluding gold (end-year) | 4.0 | 4.1 | 2.8 | 2.0 | 1.8 | na | na |
| | | | | *(In per cent of exports of goods and services)* | | | |
| Debt service | 4.6 | 4.9 | 4.4 | 5.2 | 3.6 | na | na |
| **Memorandum items** | | | | *(Denominations as indicated)* | | | |
| Population (end-year, million) | 8.0 | 8.1 | 8.2 | 8.3 | 8.3 | 8.3 | na |
| GDP (in billions of manats) | 23,591 | 26,578 | 30,312 | 35,733 | 42,651 | 60,380 | 87,969 |
| GDP per capita (in US dollars) [5] | 659 | 705 | 760 | 881 | 1,051 | 1,546 | na |
| Share of industry in GDP (in per cent) | 36.0 | 37.6 | 37.4 | 37.3 | 37.8 | na | na |
| Share of agriculture in GDP (in per cent) | 15.9 | 14.8 | 13.8 | 12.2 | 11.3 | na | na |
| Current account/GDP (in per cent) | -3.5 | -0.9 | -12.3 | -27.8 | -29.8 | -5.1 | 21.7 |
| External debt - reserves (in US$ million) | 364 | 429 | 531 | 629 | 662 | 482 | na |
| External debt/GDP (in per cent) | 19.8 | 20.2 | 20.1 | 19.7 | 18.3 | 13.0 | na |
| External debt/exports of goods and services (in per cent) | 50.7 | 49.4 | 46.9 | 46.8 | 37.4 | na | na |

[1] Until 2004 industrial output excludes crude oil production.
[2] General government consolidates all levels of government, except for municipalities and state-owned enterprises, and includes the State Oil Fund and other extra-budgetary funds.
[3] 90-day interbank offer rate in manats, nominal.

[4] By end-December 2005 there were additional foreign exchange assets of approximately US$ 1,394 million in the State Oil Fund.
[5] An improved method of calculating value-added in the oil sector has led to a sharp upward revision in nominal GDP and related variables for 2000, relative to previous estimates.

# Belarus

## Economic performance and prospects

■ Strong output growth continued in 2005, but concerns remain about directed credits and wage rises exceeding productivity increases in some sectors.

■ In the absence of structural reforms, the economy will remain dependent on Russia for export markets, cheaper gas supplies and official financing.

## Real economy

Real growth remained robust at an estimated 9.2 per cent in 2005, although down from 11 per cent in 2004. The economy benefited from strong growth in Russia and high oil prices. Belarus imports crude oil from Russia and then exports refined oil products. Higher oil prices therefore mean higher margins and profits for Belarussian refineries, as well as additional budget revenues. Industrial output and services expanded by over 10 per cent in 2005, but agricultural output increased by only 2.1 per cent.

## Economic policies

Fiscal revenues in 2005 were above projections due to higher than expected VAT receipts, profit tax and taxes on external trade. Extra revenue led to an increase in spending in the last quarter of the year. The official budget deficit was estimated at 0.8 per cent in 2005, below the government's target of 1.8 per cent. As inflation continued to slow (to an estimated 8 per cent by the end of 2005), the National Bank of Belarus lowered the discount rate six times during 2005 (from 17 per cent to 11 per cent). Nominal broad money (M2) increased by 60 per cent over 2005, largely reflecting the growth in official foreign reserves. Despite this relatively rapid rise in the money supply, inflation was held in check by higher money demand on the back of strong growth and greater confidence in the domestic currency. Exchange rate stability further underpinned disinflation.

## External sector

The current account recorded an estimated surplus of around 2 per cent in 2005. The trade deficit narrowed significantly to an estimated 1.5 per cent of GDP during the year (from 9.1 per cent in 2004), reflecting high prices for commodity exports and continued subsidies on gas imports from Russia. Apart from official financing from Russia (which provided a loan of US$146 million in 2005), other sources of external finance are limited and external debt remains low.

## Outlook and risks

The continued policy of enterprise support and directed wage increases, combined with the favourable external environment, should ensure positive growth in the short term. However, without significant progress in structural reforms, growth is unlikely to be sustainable at current levels. In the absence of deep enterprise restructuring, Belarussian exports may lose their competitiveness on the Russian market, even if preferential access is preserved (which is not guaranteed). Additional vulnerability stems from dependence on Russia as a cheap energy supplier and the major official creditor.

### Exports and industrial production growth year-on-year

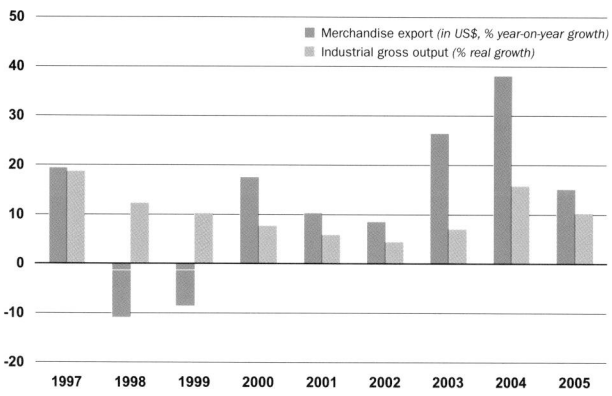

### Inflation, exchange rate developments and interest rates

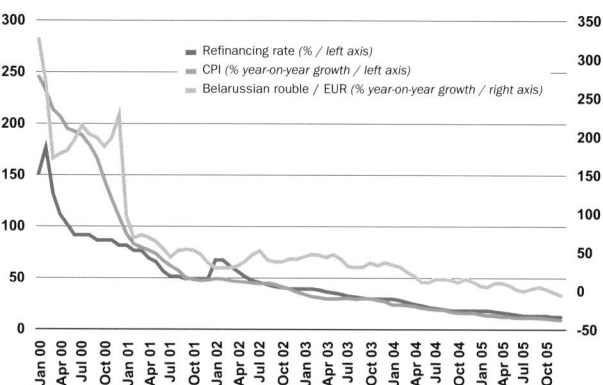

### Debt and fiscal balance

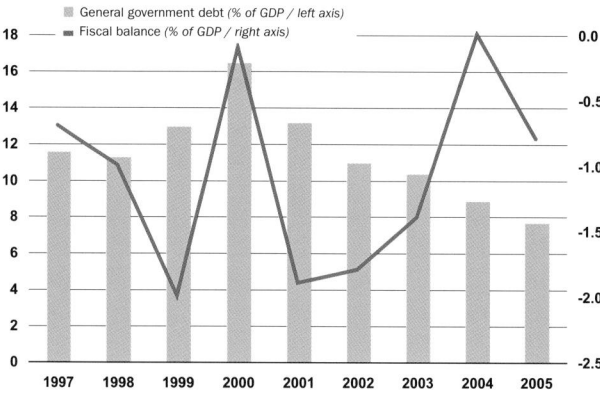

### Current account deficit and net FDI

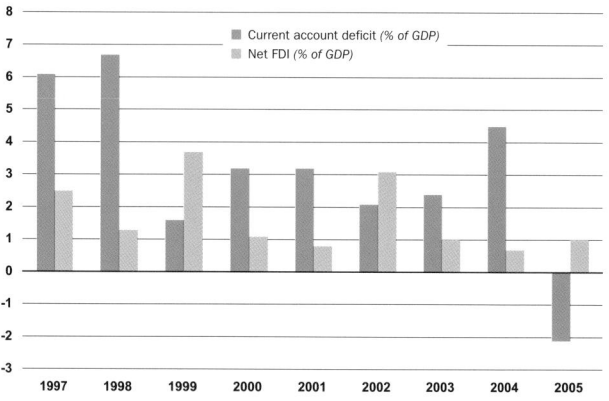

| | 2000 | 2001 | 2002 | 2003 | 2004 | 2005 Estimate | 2006 Projection |
|---|---|---|---|---|---|---|---|
| **Output and expenditure** | | | | *(Percentage change in real terms)* | | | |
| GDP | 5.8 | 4.7 | 5.0 | 7.0 | 11.4 | 9.2 | 7.0 |
| Private consumption | 8.0 | 17.9 | 11.4 | 7.4 | 9.6 | na | na |
| Public consumption | 5.8 | 3.3 | -1.1 | 0.2 | -0.2 | na | na |
| Gross fixed capital formation | 2.3 | -2.3 | 6.7 | 22.0 | 19.7 | 23.2 | na |
| Exports | na | na | na | na | na | na | na |
| Imports | na | na | na | na | na | na | na |
| Industrial gross output | 7.8 | 5.9 | 4.5 | 7.1 | 15.9 | 10.4 | na |
| Agricultural gross output | 9.3 | 1.8 | 0.7 | 6.6 | 12.6 | 2.1 | na |
| **Employment** | | | | *(Percentage change)* | | | |
| Labour force (end-year) | -0.1 | -0.4 | -0.4 | -0.5 | -1.2 | na | na |
| Employment (end-year) | -0.1 | -0.6 | -1.1 | -0.6 | 0.0 | na | na |
| | | | | *(In per cent of labour force)* | | | |
| Unemployment (end-year) | 2.1 | 2.3 | 3.0 | 3.1 | 1.9 | na | na |
| **Prices and wages** | | | | *(Percentage change)* | | | |
| Consumer prices (annual average) | 168.6 | 61.1 | 42.5 | 28.4 | 18.1 | 10.3 | 8.5 |
| Consumer prices (end-year) | 107.5 | 46.1 | 34.8 | 25.4 | 14.4 | 8.0 | 8.5 |
| Producer prices (annual average) | 185.6 | 71.8 | 40.4 | 37.5 | 24.1 | 12.1 | na |
| Producer prices (end-year) | 168.0 | 39.1 | 42.6 | 28.1 | 18.8 | 10.2 | na |
| Gross average monthly earnings in economy (annual average) | 200.9 | 108.8 | 53.8 | 32.5 | 38.6 | 35.1 | na |
| **Government sector** | | | | *(In per cent of GDP)* | | | |
| General government balance | -0.1 | -1.9 | -1.8 | -1.4 | 0.0 | -0.8 | -1.5 |
| General government expenditure | 45.9 | 46.8 | 46.4 | 47.2 | 45.6 | 47.0 | na |
| General government debt | 16.5 | 13.2 | 11.0 | 10.4 | 8.9 | 7.7 | na |
| **Monetary sector** | | | | *(Percentage change)* | | | |
| Broad money (M3, end-year) | 216.3 | 66.1 | 50.3 | 56.3 | 44.1 | 42.2 | na |
| Domestic credit (end-year) | 190.8 | 65.0 | 54.6 | 70.7 | 31.0 | 33.1 | na |
| | | | | *(In per cent of GDP)* | | | |
| Broad money (M3, end-year) | 17.2 | 15.2 | 15.0 | 16.8 | 17.7 | 19.7 | na |
| **Interest and exchange rates** | | | | *(In per cent per annum, end-year)* | | | |
| Refinancing rate | 80.0 | 48.0 | 38.0 | 28.0 | 17.0 | 11.0 | na |
| Treasury bill rate (3-month maturity) | na | na | na | na | na | na | na |
| Deposit rate (1 year) [1] | 37.6 | 34.2 | 26.9 | 17.4 | 12.7 | 9.2 | na |
| Lending rate (1 year) [2] | 67.7 | 47.0 | 36.9 | 24.0 | 16.9 | 11.4 | na |
| | | | | *(Belarussian roubles per US dollar)* | | | |
| Official exchange rate (end-year) | 1,180.0 | 1,580.0 | 1,920.0 | 2,156.0 | 2,170.0 | 2,152.0 | na |
| Official exchange rate (annual average) | 876.8 | 1,390.0 | 1,790.9 | 2,051.3 | 2,160.3 | 2,153.8 | na |
| **External sector** | | | | *(In millions of US dollars)* | | | |
| Current account | -338 | -394 | -311 | -424 | -1,043 | 624 | 840 |
| Trade balance | -884 | -807 | -914 | -1,256 | -2,066 | -452 | -500 |
| Merchandise exports | 6,641 | 7,334 | 7,965 | 10,073 | 13,917 | 16,031 | 17,500 |
| Merchandise imports | 7,525 | 8,141 | 8,879 | 11,329 | 15,983 | 16,483 | 18,000 |
| Foreign direct investment, net | 119 | 96 | 453 | 170 | 163 | 303 | 200 |
| Gross reserves, excluding gold (end-year) | 350 | 391 | 417 | 462 | 691 | 1,107 | na |
| External debt stock [3] | 1,265 | 1,381 | 1,655 | 1,615 | 1,351 | 1,366 | na |
| | | | | *(In months of imports of goods and services)* | | | |
| Gross reserves, excluding gold (end-year) | 0.5 | 0.5 | 0.5 | 0.5 | 0.5 | 0.7 | na |
| | | | | *(In per cent of exports of goods and services)* | | | |
| Debt service | 4.2 | 3.4 | 4.1 | 4.6 | 4.0 | 4.0 | na |
| **Memorandum items** | | | | *(Denominations as indicated)* | | | |
| Population (end-year, million) | 10.0 | 10.0 | 9.9 | 9.8 | 9.8 | 9.8 | na |
| GDP (in billions of Belarussian roubles) | 9,134 | 17,173 | 26,138 | 36,565 | 49,992 | 63,679 | 76,653 |
| GDP per capita (in US dollars) | 1,043 | 1,242 | 1,474 | 1,810 | 2,361 | 3,032 | na |
| Share of industry in GDP (in per cent) | 31.0 | 29.9 | 29.6 | 30.1 | 30.0 | na | na |
| Share of agriculture in GDP (in per cent) | 14.2 | 11.9 | 11.8 | 9.8 | 10.3 | na | na |
| Current account/GDP (in per cent) | -3.2 | -3.2 | -2.1 | -2.4 | -4.5 | 2.1 | 2.4 |
| External debt - reserves (in US$ million) | 914 | 991 | 1,238 | 1,154 | 660 | 259 | na |
| External debt/GDP (in per cent) | 12.1 | 11.2 | 11.3 | 9.1 | 5.8 | 4.6 | na |
| External debt/exports of goods and services (in per cent) | 16.6 | 16.4 | 17.8 | 14.0 | 8.6 | 7.5 | na |

[1] Data refer to weighted average interest rates on new one-year deposits in commercial banks.

[2] Data refer to weighted average interest rates for one-year loans by commercial banks.

[3] Includes medium and long-term public and publicly guaranteed debt and an estimate of private debt.

# Bosnia and Herzegovina[1]

## Economic performance and prospects

■ Growth remained steady and inflation low in 2005, but public spending continues to be high and the current account deficit remains one of the largest in the region.

■ Long-term sustainability depends on further administrative and governmental restructuring, an improved business environment and increased integration into the regional and world economy.

## Real economy

Economic growth continued at around 5 per cent in 2005 (based on preliminary figures for the first three quarters). Production in key industries revived and exports grew strongly. The private sector was boosted by wider access to credit and an overall improvement in the investment climate. However, corporate profitability remained weak, reflecting slow progress in privatisation.

## Economic policies

Monetary policy throughout the transition has been prudent, guided by the currency board of the central bank. Reserve requirements were raised twice in 2005 (to a rate of 15 per cent) in an effort to restrain consumer lending. The annual inflation rate rose in 2005 to around 3–4 per cent. Some significant price rises were recorded in January 2006 after the introduction of VAT, but the long-term effect of this measure is unlikely to raise inflation significantly. On the fiscal side, the budgets in both territorial Entities have been broadly in balance. The 2004 agreement among all parties (state and Entities) to restructure and substantially write down the level of domestic debt is on hold. This follows court rulings casting doubt on the legality of the original plan. It raises once again the potential for large liabilities facing governments at all levels in the country.

## External sector

The current account deficit remains one of the main macro-economic problems. It is estimated to be almost 20 per cent of GDP. However, the true figure may be much lower if GDP and remittances are, as many suspect, significantly under-recorded. The deficit continues to be covered fully by a combination of capital transfers, foreign direct investment (FDI) and other capital inflows. Foreign reserves rose steadily to more than €2 billion by September 2005. In addition, the level of public external debt remains moderate at about 30 per cent of GDP. Net FDI declined in 2005 but the overall trend is upwards, helping to offset the decline in war-related transfers.

## Outlook and risks

The outlook remains positive but clouded by uncertainty, much of it political. No IMF programme has been in place since the completion of the last Stand-By Arrangement in February 2004. A new agreement is on hold until fiscal issues are resolved. Further progress in state-building, reducing the public sector, and moving towards EU legal and regulatory standards will be necessary to convince outside investors that the country has a stable and prosperous future.

[1] The territorial constitutional entities distinguished in this assessment include the State of Bosnia and Herzegovina (BH), the Federation of Bosnia and Herzegovina (FBH), the Republika Srpska (RS) and the cantons of the Federation.

### Exports and industrial production growth year-on-year

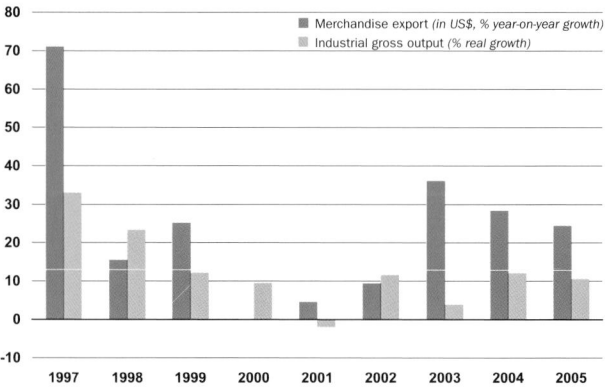

### Inflation, exchange rate developments and interest rates

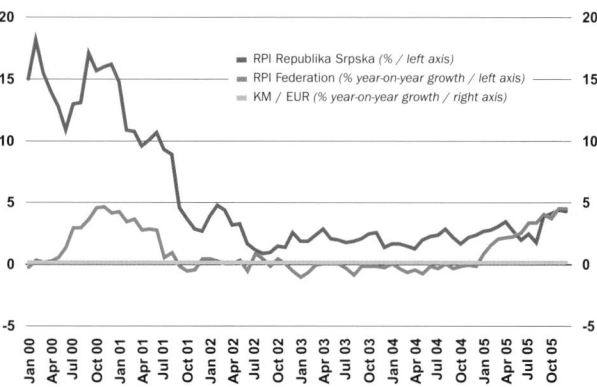

### Debt and fiscal balance

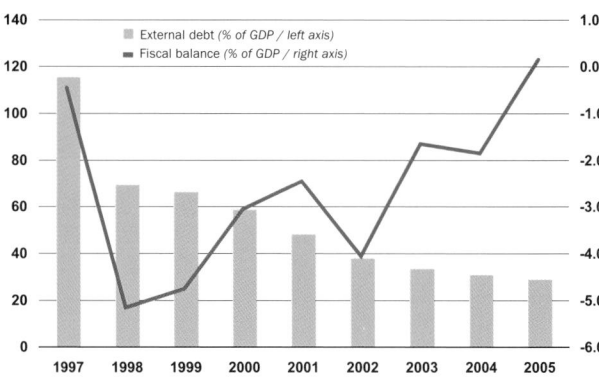

### Current account deficit and net FDI

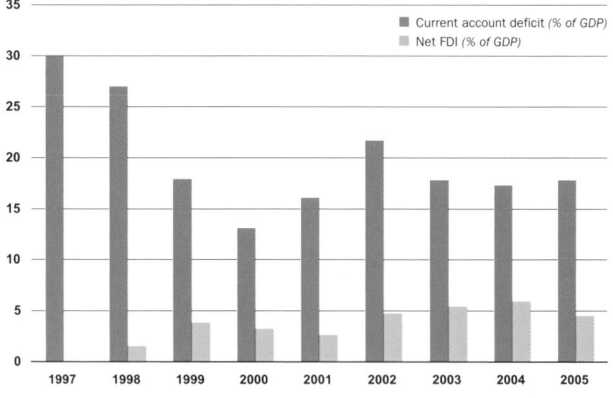

| | 2000 | 2001 | 2002 | 2003 | 2004 | 2005 Estimate | 2006 Projection |
|---|---|---|---|---|---|---|---|
| **Output and expenditure** | | | *(Percentage change in real terms)* | | | | |
| GDP | 5.5 | 4.3 | 5.3 | 3.0 | 6.0 | 5.0 | 5.0 |
| Total consumption | na | na | na | na | na | na | na |
| Gross fixed capital formation | na | na | na | na | na | na | na |
| Industrial gross output | 9.4 | -2.0 | 11.5 | 3.8 | 12.0 | 10.5 | na |
| Agricultural gross output | na | na | na | na | na | na | na |
| **Employment** | | | *(Percentage change)* | | | | |
| Labour force (end-year) | 2.1 | -1.3 | 3.1 | 1.3 | 0.5 | na | na |
| Employment (end-year) | 1.6 | -2.3 | 1.9 | -0.6 | 0.2 | na | na |
| | | | *(In per cent of labour force)* | | | | |
| Unemployment (end-year) | 39.6 | 40.3 | 40.9 | 42.0 | 0.0 | na | na |
| **Prices and wages** | | | *(Percentage change)* | | | | |
| Consumer prices (annual average) | | | | | | | |
| Federation (KM-based) | 1.9 | 1.9 | -0.2 | 0.2 | -0.3 | 2.1 | na |
| Republika Srpska (KM-based) | 14.0 | 7.0 | 1.7 | 1.8 | 2.2 | 2.7 | na |
| Consumer prices (end-year) | | | | | | | |
| Federation (KM-based) | 4.0 | 0.3 | -0.7 | 0.3 | -0.3 | 3.9 | na |
| Republika Srpska (KM-based) | 16.1 | 2.2 | 2.4 | 1.3 | 2.2 | 3.7 | na |
| Gross average monthly earnings in economy (annual average) | | | | | | | |
| Federation | 10.0 | 7.6 | 9.2 | 8.3 | 1.7 | na | na |
| Republika Srpska | 23.2 | 14.7 | 18.7 | 9.3 | 11.5 | na | na |
| **Government sector** | | | *(In per cent of GDP)* | | | | |
| General government balance | -3.1 | -2.5 | -4.1 | -1.7 | -1.9 | 0.1 | 0.3 |
| General government expenditure | 56.6 | 52.1 | 53.9 | 51.3 | 50.8 | 47.7 | na |
| **Monetary sector** | | | *(Percentage change)* | | | | |
| Broad money (M2, end-year) | 13.9 | 89.3 | 8.6 | 8.4 | 24.3 | 2.5 | na |
| Domestic credit (end-year) | 10.0 | 5.2 | 28.2 | 19.8 | 18.0 | 9.8 | na |
| | | | *(In per cent of GDP)* | | | | |
| Broad money (M2, end-year) | 24.5 | 42.5 | 43.6 | 44.8 | 52.6 | 50.6 | na |
| **Exchange rates** | | | *(KM per euro)* | | | | |
| Exchange rate (annual average) | 2.0 | 2.0 | 2.0 | 2.0 | 2.0 | 2.0 | na |
| **External sector** | | | *(In millions of US dollars)* | | | | |
| Current account | -621 | -811 | -1,218 | -1,259 | -1,431 | -1,592 | -1,552 |
| Trade balance | -1,715 | -1,831 | -2,259 | -2,520 | -2,832 | -3,123 | -3,107 |
| Merchandise exports | 832 | 870 | 952 | 1,296 | 1,664 | 2,072 | 2,434 |
| Merchandise imports | 2,547 | 2,701 | 3,211 | 3,816 | 4,496 | 5,195 | 5,541 |
| Foreign direct investment, net [1] | 150 | 130 | 266 | 382 | 490 | 400 | 570 |
| Gross reserves, excluding gold (end-year) | 497 | 1,221 | 1,295 | 1,765 | 2,389 | 2,600 | na |
| External debt stock | 2,814 | 2,382 | 2,113 | 2,356 | 2,570 | 2,700 | na |
| | | | *(In months of imports of goods and services)* | | | | |
| Gross reserves, excluding gold (end-year) | 2.2 | 5.1 | 4.5 | 5.3 | 6.1 | 5.8 | na |
| | | | *(In per cent of exports of goods and services)* | | | | |
| Debt service | 12.1 | 6.2 | 9.2 | 8.2 | 6.5 | 6.4 | na |
| **Memorandum items** | | | *(Denominations as indicated)* | | | | |
| Population (end-year, million) [2] | 3.8 | 3.8 | 3.8 | 3.8 | 3.8 | 3.8 | na |
| GDP (in millions of markas) | 10,086 | 10,986 | 11,636 | 12,261 | 12,997 | 13,829 | 14,882 |
| GDP per capita (in US dollars) | 1,251 | 1,323 | 1,475 | 1,862 | 2,172 | 2,353 | na |
| Share of industry in GDP (in per cent) | na | na | na | na | na | na | na |
| Share of agriculture in GDP (in per cent) | na | na | na | na | na | na | na |
| Current account/GDP (in per cent) | -13.1 | -16.1 | -21.7 | -17.8 | -17.3 | -17.8 | -16.4 |
| External debt - reserves (in US$ million) | 2,317 | 1,161 | 818 | 591 | 181 | 100 | na |
| External debt/GDP (in per cent) | 59.2 | 47.4 | 37.7 | 33.3 | 31.1 | 30.2 | na |
| External debt/exports of goods and services (in per cent) | 218.5 | 183.7 | 156.1 | 130.3 | 115.2 | 99.8 | na |

[1]  Excludes capital transfers for reconstruction.

[2]  Excludes refugees abroad.

# Bulgaria

## Economic performance and prospects

■ The economy continues to perform well, but remains vulnerable to any deterioration in external conditions.

■ A tight fiscal policy is essential to preserve macroeconomic stability and support the currency board regime.

### Real economy

The economy was estimated to have grown between 5.5 and 5.8 per cent in 2005, driven by sustained investment and private consumption. In 2005 agricultural production contracted by 8.6 per cent as a consequence of the 2004 flood, while industrial production increased by 7.3 per cent.

### Economic policies

The consolidated general government balance recorded a surplus of 2.4 per cent of GDP in 2005, maintaining the tight fiscal policy introduced in the previous year. The IMF precautionary stand-by programme was interrupted earlier in the year, but new fiscal measures were introduced and in May 2005 the programme was put back on track. In the context of the widening external imbalance, the IMF and the Bulgarian authorities managed to reach agreement on the 2006 parameters only after extensive negotiations. The IMF insisted on a fiscal surplus of 3 per cent of GDP for 2006, while parliament approved a balanced budget. The National Revenue Agency started operating in January 2006 with the aim of improving the tax collection rate (beyond 80 per cent). On the monetary side, annual inflation rose to 6.5 per cent in December 2005, the highest level in five years, due to higher fuel and food prices and the depreciation of the lev against the US dollar. The currency board arrangement remains in place and the central bank has announced the intention of adopting the euro between 2009 and 2010, three years after the target EU entry date of 2007.

### External sector

The current account deficit widened to 14.9 per cent of GDP in 2005, from 8.5 per cent in 2004. This mainly reflected the large deficit on the trade account (20.6 per cent of GDP in 2005). The financing of the current account deficit is being supported in the short term by strong net foreign direct investment (covering 73 per cent of the deficit in 2005) and other inflows, including bank lending. In December 2005 and January 2006 Bulgaria retired part of the debt (€339.1 million) owed to the IMF and World Bank. This left the Fiscal Reserve Account at almost twice the legal floor of €1.3 billion.

### Outlook and risks

The economy remains strong and growth prospects for the medium term are good. However, the external position is vulnerable to a further acceleration in import growth and to continuing high oil prices. The currency board regime will continue to constrain monetary policy. Therefore, further fiscal tightening may eventually be necessary to accommodate possible external shocks.

### Exports and industrial production growth year-on-year

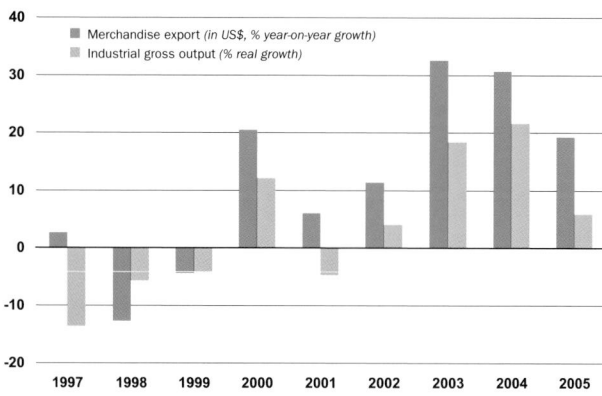

### Inflation, exchange rate developments and interest rates

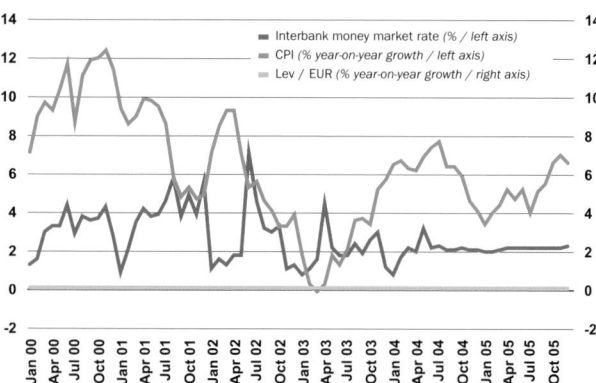

### Debt and fiscal balance

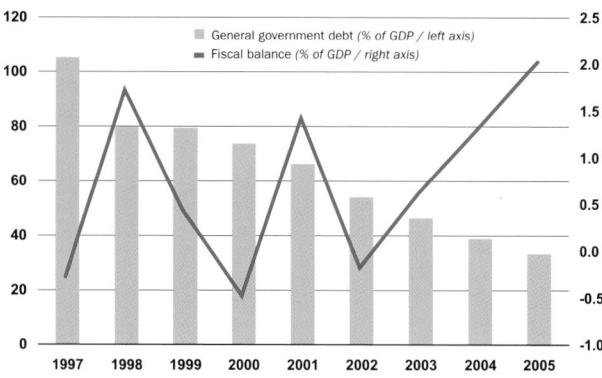

### Current account deficit and net FDI

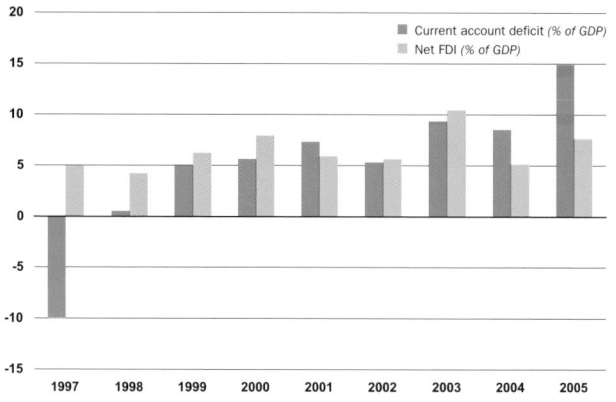

| | 2000 | 2001 | 2002 | 2003 | 2004 | 2005 Estimate | 2006 Projection |
|---|---|---|---|---|---|---|---|
| **Output and expenditure** | *(Percentage change in real terms)* | | | | | | |
| GDP | 5.4 | 4.0 | 4.8 | 4.5 | 5.6 | 5.8 | 5.5 |
| Private consumption | 4.9 | 4.5 | 3.9 | 7.1 | 4.8 | 7.4 | na |
| Public consumption | 13.3 | 4.7 | 6.2 | 3.0 | 5.8 | 2.2 | na |
| Gross fixed capital formation | 15.4 | 19.9 | 9.3 | 13.9 | 12.0 | 19.0 | na |
| Exports of goods and services | 16.6 | 8.5 | 6.2 | 8.0 | 13.1 | 7.2 | na |
| Imports of goods and services | 18.6 | 13.0 | 4.7 | 15.3 | 14.1 | 14.6 | na |
| Industrial gross output | 12.0 | -4.8 | 4.0 | 18.3 | 21.5 | 7.3 | na |
| Agricultural gross output | -9.1 | -0.1 | 4.2 | -1.4 | 5.6 | -8.6 | na |
| **Employment** | *(Percentage change)* | | | | | | |
| Labour force (end-year) | -3.4 | -0.2 | -0.5 | 1.1 | 1.2 | -0.3 | na |
| Employment (end-year) | -2.7 | -3.9 | 2.9 | 4.5 | 3.4 | 2.1 | na |
| | *(In per cent of labour force)* | | | | | | |
| Unemployment (end-year) | 16.4 | 19.5 | 16.8 | 13.7 | 12.0 | 9.9 | na |
| **Prices and wages** | *(Percentage change)* | | | | | | |
| Consumer prices (annual average) | 9.9 | 7.4 | 5.9 | 2.3 | 6.1 | 5.0 | 3.5 |
| Consumer prices (end-year) | 11.4 | 4.8 | 3.9 | 5.6 | 4.0 | 6.5 | 3.5 |
| Producer prices (annual average) | 17.3 | 3.6 | 1.3 | 4.9 | 6.0 | 6.5 | na |
| Producer prices (end-year) | 14.7 | -1.8 | 6.3 | 4.3 | 5.2 | 7.5 | na |
| Gross average monthly earnings in economy (annual average) | 25.8 | 6.5 | 3.4 | 9.2 | 9.1 | 4.3 | na |
| **Government sector** | *(In per cent of GDP)* | | | | | | |
| General government balance [1] | -0.5 | 1.4 | -0.2 | 0.6 | 1.3 | 2.4 | 3.0 |
| General government expenditure [1] | 39.7 | 40.6 | 39.4 | 40.9 | 40.0 | 37.8 | na |
| General government debt [2] | 73.6 | 66.2 | 54.0 | 46.3 | 38.8 | 33.3 | na |
| **Monetary sector** | *(Percentage change)* | | | | | | |
| Broad money (M2, end-year) | 7.5 | 53.0 | 11.7 | 18.8 | 23.3 | 24.3 | na |
| Domestic credit (end-year) | 31.0 | 26.0 | 27.4 | 33.9 | 34.3 | 32.9 | na |
| | *(In per cent of GDP)* | | | | | | |
| Broad money (M2, end-year) | 30.3 | 41.9 | 42.9 | 47.8 | 53.4 | 61.1 | na |
| **Interest and exchange rates** | *(In per cent per annum, end-year)* | | | | | | |
| Base interest rate [3] | 4.6 | 4.7 | 3.3 | 2.8 | 2.4 | 2.1 | na |
| Interbank interest rate (up to 1 month) | 3.0 | 3.7 | 2.5 | 1.1 | 2.0 | 2.2 | na |
| Deposit rate (1 month) | 3.1 | 2.9 | 2.8 | 2.8 | 3.3 | na | na |
| Lending rate (less than 1 year) | 11.5 | 11.1 | 9.4 | 9.1 | 8.4 | na | na |
| | *(Leva per US dollar)* | | | | | | |
| Exchange rate (end-year) | 2.1 | 2.2 | 1.9 | 1.5 | 1.4 | 1.7 | na |
| Exchange rate (annual average) | 2.1 | 2.2 | 2.1 | 1.7 | 1.6 | 1.6 | na |
| **External sector** | *(In millions of US dollars)* | | | | | | |
| Current account | -704 | -984 | -827 | -1,856 | -2,053 | -3,919 | -2,120 |
| Trade balance | -1,176 | -1,581 | -1,595 | -2,518 | -3,366 | -5,044 | -4,127 |
| Merchandise exports | 4,825 | 5,113 | 5,692 | 7,541 | 9,848 | 11,740 | 12,541 |
| Merchandise imports | 6,000 | 6,693 | 7,287 | 10,059 | 13,214 | 16,783 | 16,668 |
| Foreign direct investment, net | 998 | 803 | 876 | 2,070 | 1,232 | 1,991 | 2,106 |
| Gross reserves, excluding gold (end-year) | 3,460 | 3,591 | 4,407 | 6,291 | 8,776 | 9,213 | na |
| External debt stock | 11,165 | 10,626 | 11,312 | 13,437 | 16,713 | 17,906 | na |
| | *(In months of imports of goods and services)* | | | | | | |
| Gross reserves, excluding gold (end-year) | 5.4 | 5.1 | 5.8 | 6.0 | 6.3 | 5.4 | na |
| | *(In per cent of exports of goods and services)* | | | | | | |
| Debt service | 16.7 | 20.9 | 16.3 | 14.0 | 25.7 | 44.6 | na |
| **Memorandum items** | *(Denominations as indicated)* | | | | | | |
| Population (end-year, million) | 8.1 | 7.9 | 7.8 | 7.8 | 7.8 | 7.8 | na |
| GDP (in millions of leva) | 26,753 | 29,618 | 32,324 | 34,410 | 38,008 | 41,302 | 44,968 |
| GDP per capita (in US dollars) | 1,546 | 1,718 | 1,984 | 2,546 | 3,109 | 3,381 | na |
| Share of industry in GDP (in per cent) | 25.8 | 25.2 | 24.5 | 20.6 | 26.0 | 26.1 | na |
| Share of agriculture in GDP (in per cent) | 12.3 | 12.1 | 11.0 | 10.1 | 9.4 | 8.0 | na |
| Current account/GDP (in per cent) | -5.6 | -7.3 | -5.3 | -9.3 | -8.5 | -14.9 | -7.4 |
| External debt - reserves (in US$ million) | 7,705 | 7,035 | 6,905 | 7,146 | 7,937 | 8,693 | na |
| External debt/GDP (in per cent) | 88.6 | 78.4 | 72.7 | 67.7 | 69.3 | 68.2 | na |
| External debt/exports of goods and services (in per cent) | 159.5 | 146.8 | 140.4 | 125.5 | 119.6 | 110.7 | na |

[1]  In 2003 and 2004 general government expenditure includes capital transfers of about 0.4 per cent of GDP, which were classified below the line in the Budget Law.

[2]  From April 2001 direct debt to the Bulgarian National Bank (BNB) is excluded from domestic debt to avoid double reporting of IMF credit extended through the BNB.

[3]  Effective interest rate at end-month, based on the average annual yield attained at three-month government securities primary actions.

# Croatia

## Economic performance and prospects

■ The economy continues to grow steadily, aided by a positive contribution from net exports.

■ The economic outlook remains positive, although the large fiscal deficit and high level of external debt pose continuing risks.

## Real economy

Real GDP growth reached an estimated 4 per cent in 2005, compared with 3.8 per cent in 2004. After a slowdown in economic growth to 1.8 per cent in the first quarter, the second and third quarter figures of 5.1 per cent and 5.2 per cent were the highest since 2002. This improvement was driven primarily by a strong increase in investment activity and exports.

## Economic policies

There was some upward pressure on prices in 2005, mainly due to rising energy and food costs as well as higher excise taxes. This led to an increase in annual average inflation from 2.1 per cent in 2004 to 3.3 per cent in 2005. The Croatian National Bank (CNB) remains committed to tight monetary policies, mainly aimed at exchange rate stability. The general government deficit in 2005 was estimated to be in line with the target of 4.2 per cent of GDP. Achieving the 2006 target (3.3 per cent) will depend crucially on reforms in the pension and healthcare systems, state subsidies and privatisation.

## External sector

The current account deficit fell to around 6 per cent of GDP in 2005 (down from 7.2 per cent in 2003), reflecting significantly higher exports. Gross external debt exceeded €25 billion, or 83 per cent of GDP, as of November 2005. This was virtually the same (in ratio-to-GDP terms) as the level at the end of 2004. Domestic banks and other domestic sectors increased their share of total external debt, while the government's share fell substantially. To curb external indebtedness among commercial banks, a number of measures were undertaken by the CNB. These included three increases in 2005 in the reserve requirement on net foreign liabilities (the latest in December, from 40 to 55 per cent). Also, a 55 per cent mandatory reserve to be paid by commercial banks as a share of issued securities was introduced in February 2006.

## Outlook and risks

Sustained growth of between 3–5 per cent is forecast for the medium term, assuming some improvement in the external environment. The fiscal consolidation programme agreed with the IMF is expected to help the government to strengthen fiscal discipline, further reduce the current account deficit and cut the level of external indebtedness. The main risk to growth stems from the strong expansion in domestic credit and the growing commercial bank external indebtedness. These may have a negative effect on the already high foreign debt levels and may create appreciation pressures.

**Exports and industrial production growth year-on-year**

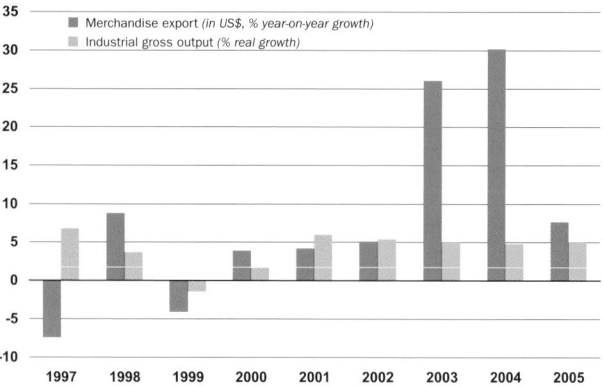

**Inflation, exchange rate developments and interest rates**

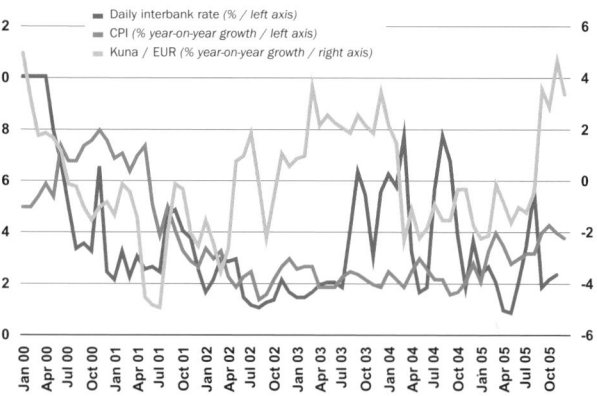

**Debt and fiscal balance**

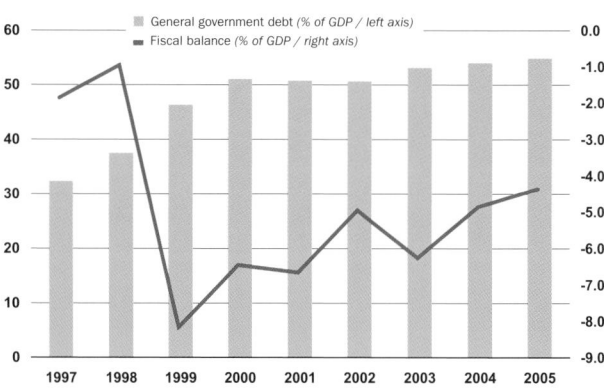

**Current account deficit and net FDI**

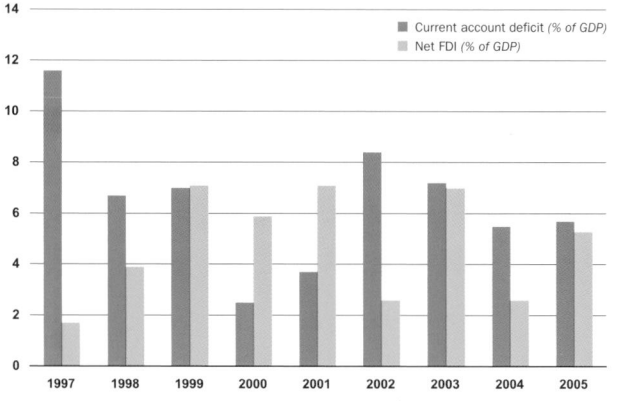

| | 2000 | 2001 | 2002 | 2003 | 2004 | 2005 Estimate | 2006 Projection |
|---|---|---|---|---|---|---|---|
| **Output and expenditure** | | | | | *(Percentage change in real terms)* | | |
| GDP | 2.9 | 4.4 | 5.2 | 4.3 | 3.8 | 4.0 | 3.8 |
|   Private consumption | 4.2 | 4.6 | 7.5 | 4.1 | 3.9 | na | na |
|   Public consumption | -8.9 | -4.3 | -1.8 | -1.8 | -0.3 | na | na |
|   Gross fixed capital formation | -3.8 | 9.7 | 10.1 | na | na | na | na |
|   Exports of goods and services | 12.0 | 8.1 | 1.3 | 10.1 | 5.4 | na | na |
|   Imports of goods and services | 3.7 | 9.3 | 8.8 | 10.9 | 3.5 | na | na |
| Industrial gross output | 1.7 | 6.0 | 5.4 | 5.0 | 4.8 | 5.0 | na |
| Agricultural gross output | 2.8 | 8.7 | 4.5 | 1.7 | 3.2 | na | na |
| **Employment** [1] | | | | | *(Percentage change)* | | |
| Labour force (end-year) | 7.2 | -5.6 | 2.7 | -0.1 | 1.1 | na | na |
| Employment (end-year) | 4.1 | -5.4 | 4.0 | 0.6 | 3.0 | na | na |
| | | | | | *(In per cent of labour force)* | | |
| Unemployment (end-year) | 16.1 | 15.8 | 14.8 | 14.3 | 13.8 | na | na |
| **Prices and wages** | | | | | *(Percentage change)* | | |
| Retail prices (annual average) | 6.2 | 4.9 | 2.2 | 1.8 | 2.1 | 3.3 | 3.0 |
| Retail prices (end-year) | 7.4 | 2.6 | 2.9 | 2.2 | 2.7 | 3.7 | 2.3 |
| Producer prices (annual average) | 9.7 | 3.7 | -0.5 | 1.9 | 3.5 | 4.0 | na |
| Producer prices (end-year) | 11.2 | -3.1 | 2.3 | 1.0 | 4.8 | 5.0 | na |
| Gross average monthly earnings in economy (annual average) | 7.0 | 3.9 | 6.0 | 4.8 | 3.1 | 3.5 | na |
| **Government sector** [2] | | | | | *(In per cent of GDP)* | | |
| General government balance | -6.5 | -6.7 | -5.0 | -6.3 | -4.9 | -4.4 | -4.2 |
| General government expenditure | 52.7 | 50.7 | 51.4 | 52.7 | 51.5 | 50.5 | na |
| General government debt | 51.1 | 50.8 | 50.7 | 53.2 | 54.1 | 54.9 | na |
| **Monetary sector** | | | | | *(Percentage change)* | | |
| Broad money (M4, end-year) | 28.9 | 45.2 | 9.5 | 11.0 | 9.4 | 9.9 | na |
| Domestic credit (end-year) | 9.3 | 21.6 | 28.4 | 12.3 | 10.0 | 9.4 | na |
| | | | | | *(In per cent of GDP)* | | |
| Broad money (M4, end-year) | 47.9 | 64.0 | 64.7 | 66.8 | 68.1 | 69.6 | na |
| **Interest and exchange rates** | | | | | *(In per cent per annum, end-year)* | | |
| Refinancing rate (3 months) | 7.0 | 4.3 | 2.7 | 2.5 | 3.9 | na | na |
| Interbank interest rate (daily) | 4.5 | 2.2 | 1.9 | 6.8 | 7.0 | 5.5 | na |
| Deposit rate [3] | 3.4 | 2.8 | 1.6 | 1.7 | 1.7 | 1.6 | na |
| Lending rate [3] | 10.5 | 9.5 | 10.9 | 12.0 | 11.8 | 11.7 | na |
| | | | | | *(Kuna per US dollar)* | | |
| Exchange rate (end-year) | 8.2 | 8.4 | 7.1 | 6.1 | 5.6 | 6.2 | na |
| Exchange rate (annual average) | 8.3 | 8.3 | 7.9 | 6.7 | 6.0 | 5.9 | na |
| **External sector** | | | | | *(In millions of US dollars)* | | |
| Current account | -469 | -726 | -1,920 | -2,072 | -1,896 | -2,136 | -2,386 |
| Trade balance | -3,204 | -4,101 | -5,649 | -7,908 | -8,350 | -8,546 | -8,974 |
|   Merchandise exports | 4,567 | 4,759 | 5,004 | 6,308 | 8,210 | 8,842 | 9,284 |
|   Merchandise imports | 7,771 | 8,860 | 10,652 | 14,216 | 16,560 | 17,388 | 18,258 |
| Foreign direct investment, net | 1,085 | 1,407 | 591 | 2,025 | 899 | 2,000 | 1,200 |
| Gross reserves, excluding gold (end-year) | 3,525 | 4,704 | 5,886 | 8,191 | 8,700 | 9,300 | na |
| External debt stock | 11,282 | 11,870 | 15,680 | 24,759 | 30,200 | 32,000 | na |
| | | | | | *(In months of imports of goods and services)* | | |
| Gross reserves, excluding gold (end-year) | 4.4 | 5.2 | 5.4 | 5.7 | 5.2 | 5.3 | na |
| | | | | | *(In per cent of exports of goods and services)* | | |
| Debt service | 22.9 | 19.6 | 23.2 | 19.5 | 22.6 | 23.9 | |
| **Memorandum items** | | | | | *(Denominations as indicated)* | | |
| Population (end-year, million) | 4.4 | 4.4 | 4.4 | 4.4 | 4.4 | 4.4 | na |
| GDP (in billions of kuna) | 153 | 166 | 179 | 193 | 207 | 223 | 245 |
| GDP per capita (in US dollars) | 4,206 | 4,476 | 5,131 | 6,484 | 7,721 | 8,426 | na |
| Share of industry in GDP (in per cent) | 20.7 | 20.4 | 19.6 | 19.2 | 19.1 | na | na |
| Share of agriculture in GDP (in per cent) [4] | 7.4 | 7.5 | 7.3 | 6.9 | 6.8 | na | na |
| Current account/GDP (in per cent) | -2.5 | -3.7 | -8.4 | -7.2 | -5.5 | -5.7 | -5.8 |
| External debt - reserves (in US$ million) | 7,757 | 7,166 | 9,794 | 16,568 | 21,500 | 22,700 | na |
| External debt/GDP (in per cent) [5] | 61.2 | 59.8 | 68.8 | 86.0 | 88.1 | 85.5 | na |
| External debt/exports of goods and services (in per cent) | 130.2 | 123.2 | 148.3 | 165.7 | 171.8 | 173.0 | na |

[1] Data from labour force surveys.

[2] Consolidated central government. Government expenditures include net lending. From 2002 data based on government finance statistics 2001.

[3] Weighted average over all maturities.

[4] Including hunting, forestry and fishing.

[5] Ratio calculated in euros.

# Czech Republic

## Economic performance and prospects

■ GDP growth remains strong, boosted by substantial foreign direct investment, but unemployment continues to be high.

■ Low labour market mobility and slow progress with urgently needed fiscal reforms pose significant risks to the economic outlook.

## Real economy

The economy grew by an estimated 6 per cent in 2005 (its highest level since the start of transition and compared with 4.7 per cent in 2004). Growth was driven particularly by exports and gross capital formation. Unemployment (estimated at 7.8 per cent) and non-wage labour costs remained high.

## Economic policies

The general government deficit, according to the ESA95 methodology, declined sharply from 12.4 per cent of GDP in 2003 to 3 per cent in 2004. In 2005 the deficit was an estimated 3.2 per cent, against a target of 4.8 per cent, primarily due to higher than expected tax revenues. However, given the lax expenditure controls, and the under-spending by government ministries of around 1.5 per cent of GDP, there is a risk of a significant loosening in fiscal policy in the run-up to parliamentary elections in June 2006. Nonetheless, the strength of revenues means that the 2006 deficit target of 3.8 per cent of GDP should be attainable. Public debt has increased sharply since 2000, reaching an estimated 26 per cent of GDP at the end of 2005. Meanwhile, annual average inflation remained very low at less than 2 per cent.

## External sector

The current account deficit decreased significantly to 2.1 per cent of GDP in 2005, down from 6 per cent in 2004. The economy recorded its first trade surplus since transition began due to sharply rising exports. Net foreign direct investment (FDI) inflows more than doubled in 2005, compared with the previous year, to US$10.1 billion mainly as a result of recent privatisations. External debt decreased slightly as a share of GDP to just under 40 per cent by the end of 2005. International reserves still exceeded four months of imports in 2005.

## Outlook and risks

Medium-term prospects for the economy are favourable. Record FDI inflows from previous years should sustain robust GDP growth, while consumer prices and the exchange rate are expected to remain stable. However, more determined action to enhance labour mobility, improve the business environment and reform the pensions, health and social security systems is necessary to lessen vulnerability to external shocks.

### Exports and industrial production growth year-on-year

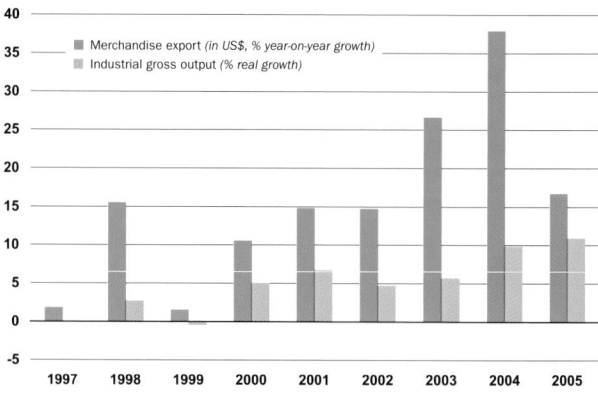

### Inflation, exchange rate developments and interest rates

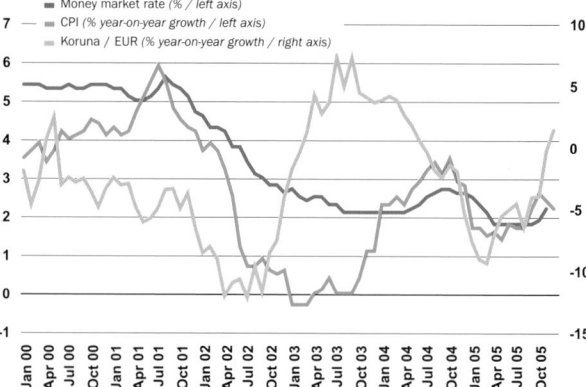

### Debt and fiscal balance

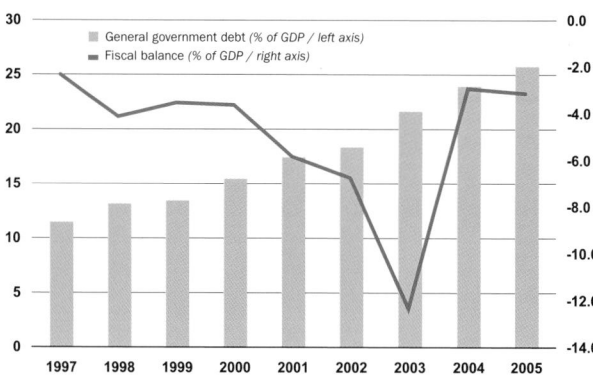

### Current account deficit and net FDI

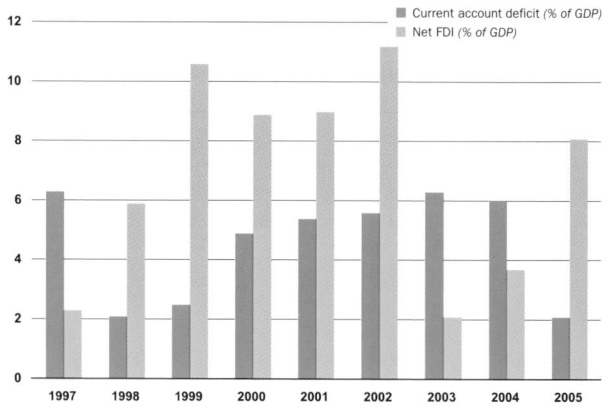

| | 2000 | 2001 | 2002 | 2003 | 2004 | 2005 Estimate | 2006 Projection |
|---|---|---|---|---|---|---|---|
| **Output and expenditure** | | | *(Percentage change in real terms)* | | | | |
| GDP | 3.9 | 2.6 | 1.5 | 3.2 | 4.7 | 6.0 | 5.5 |
| Private consumption | 2.9 | 2.8 | 2.7 | 4.6 | 3.3 | 2.6 | na |
| Public consumption | -1.0 | 5.3 | 4.5 | 3.8 | -2.7 | 0.1 | na |
| Gross fixed capital formation | 4.9 | 5.4 | 3.4 | 4.7 | 5.3 | 3.7 | na |
| Exports of goods and services | 16.5 | 11.5 | 2.1 | 7.5 | 21.4 | 11.1 | na |
| Imports of goods and services | 16.3 | 13.0 | 4.9 | 7.9 | 18.4 | 4.8 | na |
| Industrial gross output | 5.1 | 6.8 | 4.8 | 5.8 | 9.9 | 11.0 | na |
| Agricultural gross output | 5.5 | -7.1 | 2.4 | 4.9 | 22.3 | 5.4 | na |
| **Employment** | | | *(Percentage change)* | | | | |
| Labour force (end-year) | 0.2 | 0.0 | 1.0 | 0.4 | -0.1 | 1.6 | na |
| Employment (end-year) | -0.7 | -0.1 | 0.8 | -0.7 | -0.6 | 2.1 | na |
| | | | *(In per cent of labour force)* | | | | |
| Unemployment (end-year) | 8.8 | 8.1 | 7.3 | 7.8 | 8.2 | 7.8 | na |
| **Prices and wages** | | | *(Percentage change)* | | | | |
| Consumer prices (annual average) | 4.0 | 4.7 | 1.8 | 0.2 | 2.8 | 1.9 | 1.9 |
| Consumer prices (end-year) | 4.1 | 4.2 | 0.6 | 1.1 | 2.8 | 2.2 | 2.4 |
| Producer prices (annual average) | 4.9 | 2.9 | -0.5 | -0.3 | 5.7 | 3.0 | na |
| Producer prices (end-year) | 5.0 | 0.8 | -0.7 | 0.9 | 7.7 | -0.3 | na |
| Gross average monthly earnings in economy (annual average) | 7.0 | 8.6 | 7.5 | 7.0 | 6.6 | 5.5 | na |
| **Government sector** [1] | | | *(In per cent of GDP)* | | | | |
| General government balance | -3.7 | -5.9 | -6.8 | -12.4 | -3.0 | -3.2 | -3.9 |
| General government expenditure | 42.1 | 45.0 | 46.9 | 53.5 | 44.3 | 43.0 | na |
| General government debt | 15.5 | 17.5 | 18.4 | 21.7 | 24.0 | 25.8 | na |
| **Monetary sector** | | | *(Percentage change)* | | | | |
| Broad money (M2, end-year) | 6.8 | 7.9 | 3.2 | 7.2 | 4.4 | 5.7 | na |
| Domestic credit (end-year) | 1.0 | -5.3 | -7.1 | 21.9 | 0.1 | 4.6 | na |
| | | | *(In per cent of GDP)* | | | | |
| Broad money (M2, end-year) | 68.8 | 68.9 | 68.2 | 69.1 | 66.6 | 65.2 | na |
| **Interest and exchange rates** | | | *(In per cent per annum, end-year)* | | | | |
| 2-week repo rate | 5.3 | 4.8 | 2.8 | 2.0 | 2.5 | 2.0 | na |
| 3-month PRIBOR | 5.4 | 4.7 | 2.6 | 2.1 | 2.6 | na | na |
| Deposit rate | 3.4 | 2.6 | 1.7 | 1.3 | 1.4 | na | na |
| Lending rate | 7.2 | 8.7 | 8.8 | 8.2 | 8.0 | na | na |
| | | | *(Korunas per US dollar)* | | | | |
| Exchange rate (end-year) | 38.8 | 36.5 | 30.7 | 26.3 | 22.9 | 24.8 | na |
| Exchange rate (annual average) | 38.6 | 38.0 | 32.7 | 28.2 | 25.7 | 23.9 | na |
| **External sector** | | | *(In millions of US dollars)* | | | | |
| Current account | -2,718 | -3,273 | -4,166 | -5,690 | -6,511 | -2,575 | -3,500 |
| Trade balance | -3,131 | -3,068 | -2,179 | -2,473 | -1,029 | 1,685 | 2,000 |
| Merchandise exports | 29,052 | 33,378 | 38,319 | 48,568 | 67,027 | 78,307 | 96,000 |
| Merchandise imports | 32,183 | 36,446 | 40,497 | 51,041 | 68,056 | 76,622 | 94,000 |
| Foreign direct investment, net | 4,943 | 5,476 | 8,276 | 1,895 | 3,960 | 10,135 | 4,500 |
| Gross reserves, excluding gold (end-year) | 13,139 | 14,464 | 23,709 | 26,955 | 28,448 | 32,325 | na |
| External debt stock | 21,608 | 22,374 | 26,983 | 34,861 | 45,303 | 49,000 | na |
| | | | *(In months of imports of goods and services)* | | | | |
| Gross reserves, excluding gold (end-year) | 4.2 | 4.1 | 6.1 | 5.5 | 4.4 | 4.5 | na |
| | | | *(In per cent of exports of goods and services)* | | | | |
| Debt service | 12.3 | 8.6 | 9.1 | 6.4 | 4.7 | 4.5 | na |
| **Memorandum items** | | | *(Denominations as indicated)* | | | | |
| Population (end-year, million) | 10.3 | 10.2 | 10.2 | 10.2 | 10.2 | 10.2 | na |
| GDP (in billions of korunas) | 2,150 | 2,315 | 2,415 | 2,556 | 2,768 | 2,989 | 3,215 |
| GDP per capita (in US dollars) | 5,422 | 5,964 | 7,229 | 8,873 | 10,537 | 12,231 | na |
| Share of industry in GDP (in per cent) | 36.0 | 37.5 | 38.7 | 39.7 | 41.7 | 43.6 | na |
| Share of agriculture in GDP (in per cent) | 3.9 | 3.5 | 3.6 | 3.6 | 4.2 | 4.2 | na |
| Current account/GDP (in per cent) | -4.9 | -5.4 | -5.6 | -6.3 | -6.0 | -2.1 | -2.6 |
| External debt - reserves (in US$ million) | 8,469 | 7,910 | 3,274 | 7,906 | 16,855 | 16,675 | na |
| External debt/GDP (in per cent) | 38.8 | 36.8 | 36.6 | 38.5 | 42.1 | 39.2 | na |
| External debt/current account revenues, excluding transfers (in per cent) | 60.2 | 55.3 | 59.5 | 61.9 | 59.1 | 55.0 | na |

[1] Calculated according to Eurostat methodology (ESA95).

# Estonia

## Economic performance and prospects

■ Strong internal demand, supported by a sharp rise in domestic credit, is sustaining economic growth.

■ Under Estonia's monetary arrangement, fiscal discipline is essential to correct persistently high external imbalances and contain accelerating inflation.

### Real economy

Real growth in 2005 exceeded expectations, driven particularly by strong internal demand and technology sector exports. The economy grew by 9.6 per cent during 2005, with a peak of 10.6 per cent in the third quarter. Higher employment, real wage increases in line with productivity and rapid credit growth all fuelled the increase in investment and private consumption, while exports continued to expand rapidly.

### Economic policies

Despite an expansionary fiscal policy, the general government balance was in surplus by 1.5 per cent of GDP in 2005. Sustained fiscal discipline has led to record low public debt ratios, estimated at 5.1 per cent of GDP in 2005. Annual average inflation increased to 4.1 per cent, due mainly to supply side factors such as oil and EU accession-related price increases. Core inflation also accelerated, mostly through the indirect effects of oil prices on transport costs. Estonia entered the Exchange Rate Mechanism II (ERM II) in 2004, and the government remains committed to joining the European Monetary Union (EMU) by January 2007. Markets have not been perturbed by a possible delay in euro adoption and confidence in the currency board remains strong, as indicated by decreasing short-term interest rates differentials with the euro.

### External sector

Reflecting stronger export growth, the current account deficit declined to about 11 per cent of GDP in 2005, down from 13 per cent in 2004. The deficit has been financed through traditional foreign direct investment (FDI) inflows, borrowing by banks from foreign parents and increasing EU funding. Net FDI flows resumed in 2005 at an unprecedented pace. This was mainly due to portfolio investments being converted into direct investments following the buyout of Hansabank's shares. Gross external debt remains high at about 90 per cent of GDP, a large part of which is owed to the foreign parents of Estonian subsidiaries.

### Outlook and risks

Real GDP growth in 2006 is expected to be about 7 per cent. Growth will continue to be driven by internal demand as interest rates remain low and credit continues to expand. Domestic credit exceeded 70 per cent of GDP in 2005 and is expected to grow further in 2006. While such rapid credit growth is in line with Estonia's current phase of development, the country may be vulnerable to a sudden downturn in asset markets or a disruption to finance available from parent banks. It is unlikely that Estonia will meet the EU's Maastricht inflation criterion by the first possible test date in mid-2006.

**Exports and industrial production growth year-on-year**

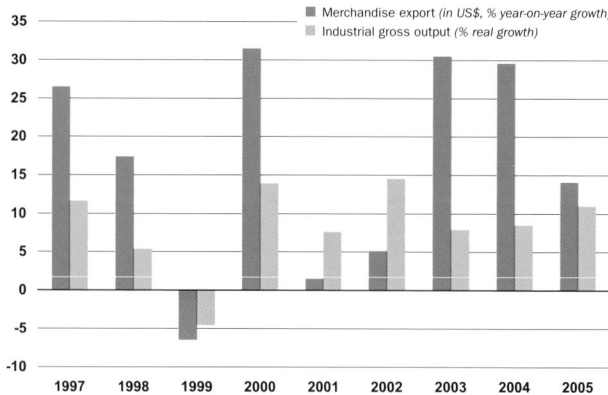

**Inflation, exchange rate developments and interest rates**

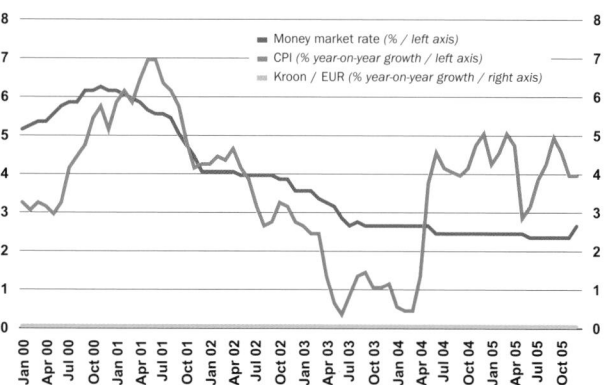

**Debt and fiscal balance**

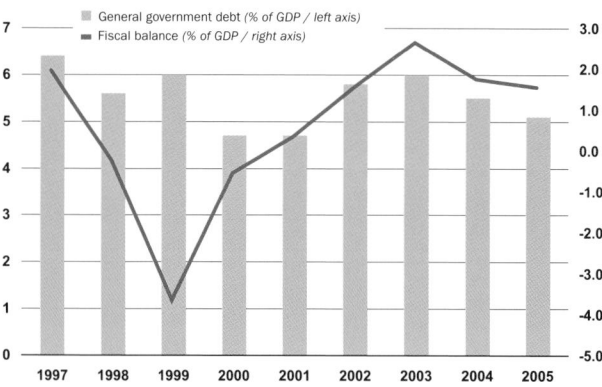

**Current account deficit and net FDI**

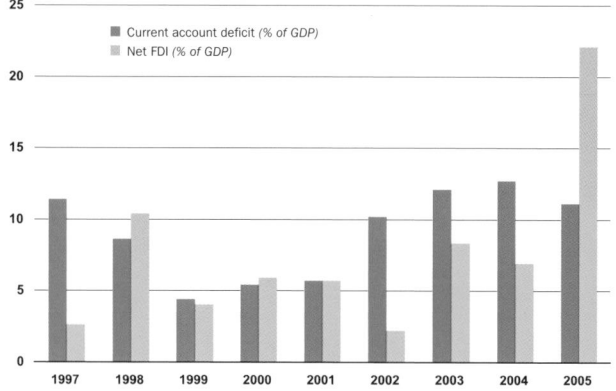

| | 2000 | 2001 | 2002 | 2003 | 2004 | 2005 Estimate | 2006 Projection |
|---|---|---|---|---|---|---|---|
| **Output and expenditure** | *(Percentage change in real terms)* | | | | | | |
| GDP | 7.9 | 6.5 | 7.2 | 6.7 | 7.8 | 9.6 | 6.8 |
| Private consumption | 8.6 | 6.2 | 10.3 | 5.7 | 4.4 | na | na |
| Public consumption | 1.1 | 1.8 | 5.9 | 5.8 | 9.1 | na | na |
| Gross fixed capital formation | 14.3 | 13.0 | 17.2 | 5.4 | 9.1 | na | na |
| Exports of goods and services | 28.3 | -0.2 | 0.6 | 6.0 | 16.5 | na | na |
| Imports of goods and services | 28.3 | 2.1 | 5.4 | 9.0 | 14.7 | na | na |
| Industrial gross output | 13.9 | 7.6 | 14.5 | 7.9 | 8.5 | 11.0 | na |
| Agricultural gross output | -0.8 | -5.4 | 0.1 | -1.5 | -8.0 | na | na |
| **Employment** | *(Percentage change)* | | | | | | |
| Labour force (annual average) | 0.4 | -0.2 | -1.2 | 1.2 | -0.2 | 0.3 | na |
| Employment (annual average) | -1.2 | 0.9 | 1.4 | 1.5 | 0.2 | 3.2 | na |
| | *(In per cent of labour force)* | | | | | | |
| Unemployment (annual average) | 13.6 | 12.6 | 10.3 | 10.0 | 9.6 | 7.0 | na |
| **Prices and wages** | *(Percentage change)* | | | | | | |
| Consumer prices (annual average) | 4.0 | 5.8 | 3.6 | 1.3 | 3.0 | 4.1 | 3.5 |
| Consumer prices (end-year) | 5.0 | 4.2 | 2.6 | 1.2 | 5.0 | 3.9 | 3.0 |
| Producer prices (annual average) | 4.9 | 4.4 | 0.4 | 0.2 | 2.9 | 2.1 | na |
| Producer prices (end-year) | 6.0 | 1.7 | 1.4 | 0.3 | 3.9 | na | na |
| Gross average monthly earnings in economy (annual average) | 10.6 | 12.1 | 11.6 | 9.4 | 8.4 | 6.8 | na |
| **Government sector** | *(In per cent of GDP)* | | | | | | |
| General government balance | -0.6 | 0.3 | 1.5 | 2.6 | 1.7 | 1.5 | 0.0 |
| General government expenditure | 36.2 | 34.9 | 35.5 | 35.6 | 37.1 | 32.6 | na |
| General government debt | 4.7 | 4.7 | 5.8 | 6.0 | 5.5 | 5.1 | na |
| **Monetary sector** | *(Percentage change)* | | | | | | |
| Broad money (M2, end-year) | 25.1 | 23.8 | 11.1 | 10.9 | 15.8 | 42.0 | na |
| Domestic credit (end-year) | 27.2 | 24.4 | 27.6 | 28.7 | 29.2 | 32.1 | na |
| | *(In per cent of GDP)* | | | | | | |
| Broad money (M2, end-year) | 35.5 | 39.0 | 38.8 | 39.5 | 41.1 | 51.2 | na |
| **Interest and exchange rates** | *(In per cent per annum, end-year)* | | | | | | |
| Interbank interest rate (up to 30-day maturity) | na | na | na | na | na | na | na |
| Deposit rate (over 12 months) | 6.8 | 4.5 | 3.7 | 2.4 | 2.1 | 3.0 | na |
| Lending rate (over 12 months) | 8.9 | 10.1 | 6.6 | 5.1 | 6.2 | 6.3 | na |
| | *(Kroons per US dollar)* | | | | | | |
| Exchange rate (end-year) | 16.7 | 17.6 | 14.9 | 12.4 | 11.5 | 12.5 | na |
| Exchange rate (annual average) | 17.0 | 17.5 | 16.6 | 13.9 | 12.6 | 12.4 | na |
| **External sector** | *(In millions of US dollars)* | | | | | | |
| Current account | -294 | -339 | -716 | -1,116 | -1,432 | -1,450 | -1,635 |
| Trade balance | -767 | -788 | -1,089 | -1,553 | -1,966 | -1,942 | -2,027 |
| Merchandise exports | 3,309 | 3,359 | 3,530 | 4,607 | 5,971 | 6,813 | 7,798 |
| Merchandise imports | 4,076 | 4,148 | 4,619 | 6,161 | 7,937 | 8,754 | 9,825 |
| Foreign direct investment, net | 324 | 343 | 153 | 763 | 781 | 2,882 | 1,200 |
| Gross reserves, excluding gold (end-year) | 921 | 820 | 1,000 | 1,373 | 1,640 | 4,483 | na |
| External debt stock [1] | 3,007 | 3,279 | 4,704 | 7,054 | 10,012 | 11,615 | na |
| | *(In months of imports of goods and services)* | | | | | | |
| Gross reserves, excluding gold (end-year) | 2.2 | 1.9 | 2.1 | 2.2 | 2.0 | 5.1 | na |
| | *(In per cent of exports of goods and services)* | | | | | | |
| Debt service | 8.9 | 10.7 | 12.5 | 11.7 | 11.1 | 10.5 | na |
| **Memorandum items** | *(Denominations as indicated)* | | | | | | |
| Population (end-year, million) | 1.4 | 1.4 | 1.4 | 1.4 | 1.4 | 1.3 | na |
| GDP (in billions of kroons) | 93 | 104 | 117 | 127 | 141 | 161 | 178 |
| GDP per capita (in US dollars) | 3,989 | 4,371 | 5,172 | 6,775 | 8,314 | 9,688 | na |
| Share of industry in gross value-added (in per cent) | 24.0 | 24.1 | 24.8 | 24.9 | 24.3 | na | na |
| Share of agriculture in gross value-added (in per cent) | 5.1 | 4.7 | 4.4 | 3.9 | 3.5 | na | na |
| Current account/GDP (in per cent) | -5.4 | -5.7 | -10.2 | -12.1 | -12.7 | -11.1 | -11.5 |
| External debt - reserves (in US$ million) | 2,086 | 2,458 | 3,703 | 5,680 | 8,371 | 7,132 | na |
| External debt/GDP (in per cent) | 54.9 | 54.9 | 66.8 | 76.8 | 89.1 | 89.0 | na |
| External debt/exports of goods and services (in per cent) | 62.6 | 65.5 | 89.7 | 103.1 | 113.8 | 118.4 | na |

[1] Data from the Bank of Estonia and include non-resident
currency and deposits, liabilities to affiliated enterprises and liabilities
to direct investors.

# FYR Macedonia

## Economic performance and prospects

■ Macroeconomic stability has been maintained, but economic performance is below potential and unemployment remains high.

■ Long-term prosperity depends on the acceleration of restructuring and privatisation, as well as job creation by new private enterprises.

## Real economy

Real GDP grew by 3.6 per cent in 2005, down from 4.1 per cent in 2004. Private consumption remained subdued by high unemployment, as large enterprises continued to lay off staff. However, industrial production recovered from a contraction in 2004 and grew by an estimated 6.7 per cent in 2005. Unemployment remains high, at 37 per cent of the labour force at the end of 2005.

## Economic policies

Following deflation in 2004, consumer prices started rising again in 2005, reaching 1.3 per cent year-on-year in December. Interest rates on central bank bills peaked mid-year at 10 per cent, and then declined by 150 basis points by the end of the year. The exchange rate remained stable at around 61 denar/€1, in line with a de facto near-peg to the euro.

The general government balance recorded a small surplus in 2005 of around 0.3 per cent of GDP. Public expenditure increased by more than 2 per cent of GDP to reach almost 38 per cent. Public debt remained below 50 per cent of GDP and interest payments were at about 1.3 per cent of GDP. Fiscal decentralisation was introduced in July 2005 as part of the overall plan included in the Ohrid Agreement.

## External sector

The current account deficit declined from 7.8 per cent of GDP in 2004 to 1.3 per cent in 2005, reflecting a fall in the trade deficit and a significant increase in net current transfers. In 2005 exports grew by more than 20 per cent as industry recovered, and the trade deficit declined from 21 per cent of GDP to less than 19 per cent. Inflows of foreign direct investment were US$97 million in 2005.

In December 2005 the authorities issued the first eurobond. Worth €150 million with a 10-year maturity (and a 4.7 per cent yield in December 2005), it has been rated BB+ by the international ratings agencies Fitch and Standard and Poor's. The government has used the proceeds to repay its US$221 million debt to the London Club of creditors. At the end of 2005, the level of external debt was 40 per cent of GDP (75 per cent of which was public long-term debt).

## Outlook and risks

The stable macroeconomic environment should be sustained in the medium term. High unemployment may eventually decline as a result of a new labour regulation and an easier enterprise registration process. Political instability, either internally or in neighbouring Kosovo, would pose the greatest risk to the economy.

### Exports and industrial production growth year-on-year

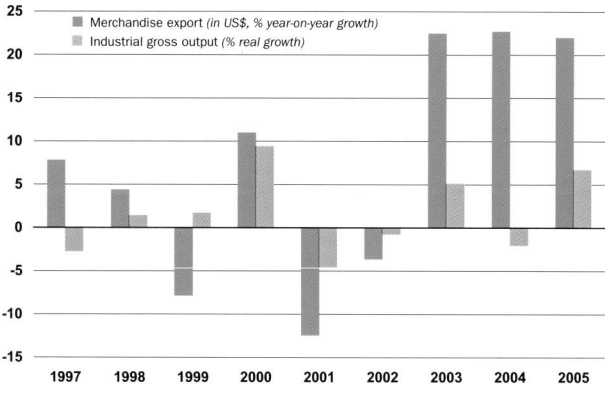

### Inflation, exchange rate developments and interest rates

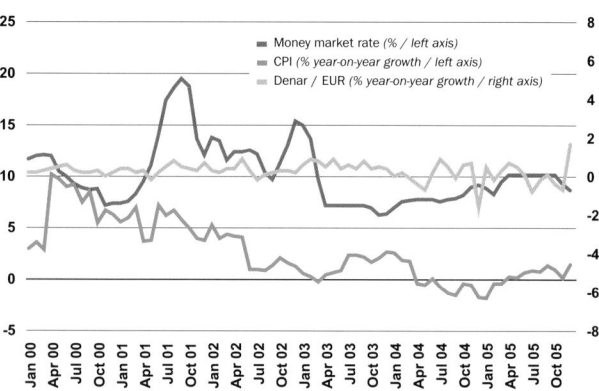

### Debt and fiscal balance

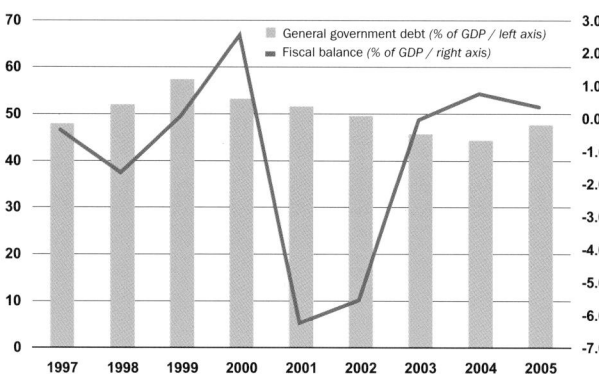

### Current account deficit and net FDI

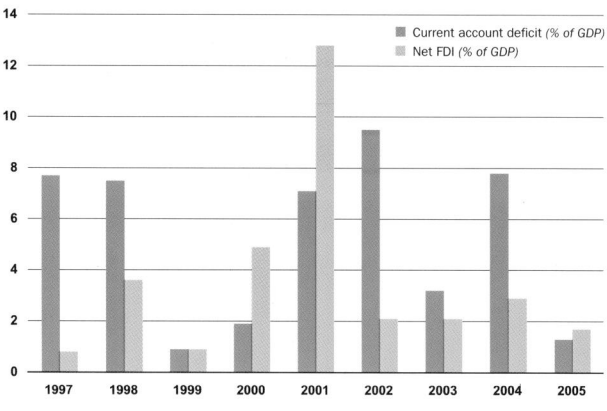

| | 2000 | 2001 | 2002 | 2003 | 2004 | 2005 Estimate | 2006 Projection |
|---|---|---|---|---|---|---|---|
| **Output and expenditure** | | | *(Percentage change in real terms)* | | | | |
| GDP | 4.5 | -4.5 | 0.9 | 2.8 | 4.1 | 3.6 | 4.0 |
| Industrial gross output | 9.4 | -4.6 | -0.8 | 5.1 | -2.1 | 6.7 | na |
| Agricultural gross output | 1.0 | -10.8 | -2.0 | 4.8 | 4.9 | 3.0 | na |
| **Employment** | | | *(Percentage change)* | | | | |
| Labour force (end-year) | 0.6 | 6.3 | -4.4 | 4.4 | -3.3 | 6.9 | na |
| Employment (end-year) | 0.8 | 9.0 | -6.3 | -2.9 | 3.0 | 8.0 | na |
| | | | *(In per cent of labour force)* | | | | |
| Unemployment (end-year) | 32.1 | 30.5 | 31.9 | 36.7 | 37.2 | 36.5 | na |
| **Prices and wages** | | | *(Percentage change)* | | | | |
| Consumer prices (annual average) | 5.8 | 5.3 | 2.4 | 1.1 | -0.3 | 0.1 | 2.0 |
| Consumer prices (end-year) | 6.1 | 3.7 | 1.0 | 2.5 | -1.9 | 1.3 | 2.0 |
| Producer prices (annual average) | 8.9 | 2.0 | -0.9 | -0.3 | 0.9 | 3.0 | na |
| Producer prices (end-year) | 7.9 | -2.5 | 1.1 | -0.2 | 1.3 | 2.9 | na |
| Gross average monthly earnings in economy (annual average) | 5.5 | 3.6 | 6.9 | 4.8 | 3.5 | 3.8 | na |
| **Government sector** | | | *(In per cent of GDP)* | | | | |
| General government balance | 2.5 | -6.3 | -5.6 | -0.1 | 0.7 | 0.3 | -0.6 |
| General government expenditure | 33.7 | 40.3 | 40.5 | 38.5 | 35.8 | 38.0 | na |
| General government debt | 53.2 | 51.6 | 49.6 | 45.7 | 44.3 | 47.6 | na |
| **Monetary sector** | | | *(Percentage change)* | | | | |
| Broad money (M2, end-year) | 24.4 | 66.3 | -8.0 | 18.4 | 16.1 | 17.7 | na |
| Domestic credit (end-year) | -10.7 | -11.5 | 28.8 | 14.1 | 20.0 | 16.7 | na |
| | | | *(In per cent of GDP)* | | | | |
| Broad money (M2, end-year) | 17.7 | 29.8 | 26.3 | 30.2 | 33.3 | 37.8 | na |
| **Interest and exchange rates** | | | *(In per cent per annum, end-year)* | | | | |
| Basic rate of the National Bank | 8.9 | 10.7 | 10.7 | 7.0 | 6.5 | 6.5 | na |
| Interbank interest rate | 7.2 | 11.9 | 14.4 | 5.8 | 7.9 | 8.5 | na |
| Deposit rate | 10.7 | 10.0 | 9.2 | 6.7 | 6.5 | 5.2 | na |
| Lending rate | 19.0 | 19.2 | 17.7 | 14.5 | 12.0 | 12.1 | na |
| | | | *(Denars per US dollar)* | | | | |
| Exchange rate (end-year) | 65.3 | 69.2 | 58.6 | 49.9 | 49.4 | 48.9 | na |
| Exchange rate (annual average) | 65.9 | 68.1 | 64.7 | 54.3 | 50.0 | 48.5 | na |
| **External sector** | | | *(In millions of US dollars)* | | | | |
| Current account | -69 | -244 | -358 | -149 | -415 | -76 | -300 |
| Trade balance | -690 | -526 | -804 | -848 | -1,112 | -1,052 | -1,100 |
| Merchandise exports | 1,321 | 1,155 | 1,112 | 1,363 | 1,672 | 2,040 | 2,300 |
| Merchandise imports | 2,011 | 1,682 | 1,916 | 2,211 | 2,785 | 3,092 | 3,400 |
| Foreign direct investment, net | 175 | 441 | 78 | 96 | 156 | 97 | 300 |
| Gross reserves, excluding gold (end-year) | 700 | 760 | 730 | 890 | 980 | 1,401 | na |
| External debt stock | 1,548 | 1,494 | 1,641 | 1,831 | 2,034 | 2,253 | na |
| | | | *(In months of imports of goods and services)* | | | | |
| Gross reserves, excluding gold (end-year) | 3.5 | 4.8 | 4.1 | 4.2 | 3.8 | 4.9 | na |
| | | | *(In per cent of exports of goods and services)* | | | | |
| Debt service | 11.5 | 14.7 | 17.2 | 14.8 | 12.2 | 8.9 | na |
| **Memorandum items** | | | *(Denominations as indicated)* | | | | |
| Population (end-year, million) | 2.0 | 2.0 | 2.0 | 2.0 | 2.0 | 2.0 | na |
| GDP (in billions of denars) | 236 | 234 | 244 | 251 | 265 | 275 | 292 |
| GDP per capita (in US dollars) | 1,793 | 1,717 | 1,885 | 2,316 | 2,653 | 2,839 | na |
| Share of industry in GDP (in per cent) | 18.1 | 17.5 | 17.2 | 17.6 | 16.5 | 17.0 | na |
| Share of agriculture in GDP (in per cent) | 10.0 | 9.8 | 9.5 | 9.7 | 9.8 | 9.7 | na |
| Current account/GDP (in per cent) | -1.9 | -7.1 | -9.5 | -3.2 | -7.8 | -1.3 | -5.0 |
| External debt - reserves (in US$ million) | 848 | 734 | 911 | 941 | 1,054 | 852 | na |
| External debt/GDP (in per cent) | 43.2 | 43.5 | 43.5 | 39.5 | 38.3 | 39.7 | na |
| External debt/exports of goods and services (in per cent) | 94.6 | 106.9 | 120.0 | 108.8 | 100.6 | 93.1 | na |

# Georgia

## Economic performance and prospects

■ Strong economic growth in 2005 was supported by major projects in the natural resources sector and by a prudent policy framework.

■ Maintaining macroeconomic stability while implementing structural reforms is crucial to sustaining growth and managing external indebtedness.

## Real economy

Economic growth is estimated to have reached more than 8 per cent in 2005, compared with 6.2 per cent in 2004. The industrial sector grew by 18 per cent during January–September, due in part to the privatisation of key enterprises, and to structural reforms aimed at reducing the informal economy. The services sector maintained its robust performance, with domestic credit growing by 36 per cent overall (and by 78 per cent in the private sector). Growth in agricultural production continued to recover despite spring flooding.

## Economic policies

Fiscal performance remained strong during 2005, reflecting improved tax and customs administration and anti-corruption measures. These contributed to an increase in budget revenues by 55 per cent year-on-year as of end-November 2005. However, due to an increase in government expenditure (mainly capital spending on infrastructure), the general government budget recorded a deficit of 1.5 per cent of GDP (on a commitments basis). This compared with an overall surplus of 2.3 per cent in 2004. The money supply grew significantly due to strong capital inflows and increased fiscal spending. Combined with the increase in energy costs, this led to average annual inflation of 8.4 per cent during 2005 (although end-year inflation was 6.4 per cent).

## External sector

The current account deficit fell to 7.4 per cent of GDP in 2005 from 8.3 per cent in 2004. The rise in imports related to oil and gas infrastructure investment slowed from May 2005. This followed the completion of the Baku-Tbilisi-Ceyhan (BTC) oil pipeline. The external deficit has been mainly financed by privatisations and other private capital inflows. Since the Paris Club debt rescheduling in July 2004, bilateral agreements for debt relief have been reached with a number of creditors. The ratio of public external debt to GDP fell to 27 per cent in 2005 from 36 per cent in 2004.

## Outlook and risks

Real GDP growth in the medium term is expected to moderate with the completion of the BTC and South Caucasus gas pipelines. The current account deficit should decline, reflecting the expected increase in transit fees as well as the reduction in imports related to pipeline construction. The main economic risks to sustained long-term growth are the country's persistent significant external indebtedness, decaying physical infrastructure and the poor financial and technical conditions of the energy sector. Internal and regional political instability could similarly undermine future prospects.

## Exports and industrial production growth year-on-year

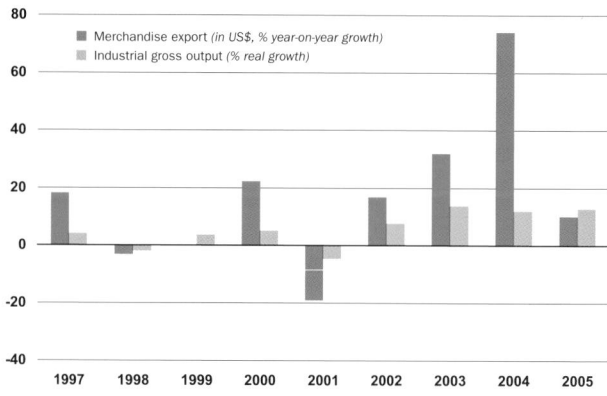

## Inflation, exchange rate developments and interest rates

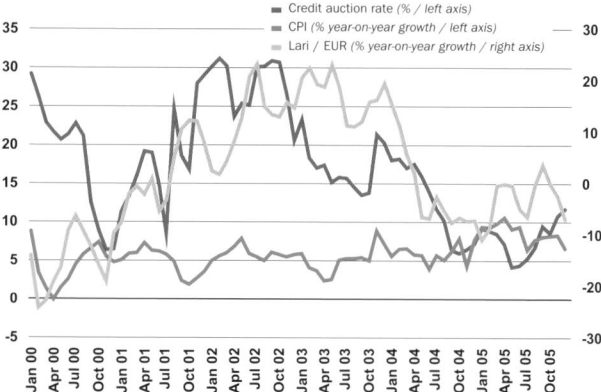

## Debt and fiscal balance

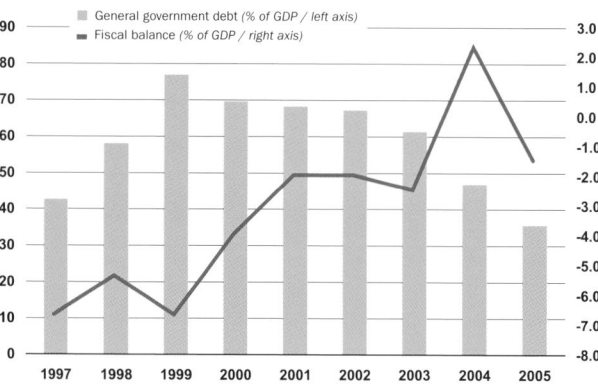

## Current account deficit and net FDI

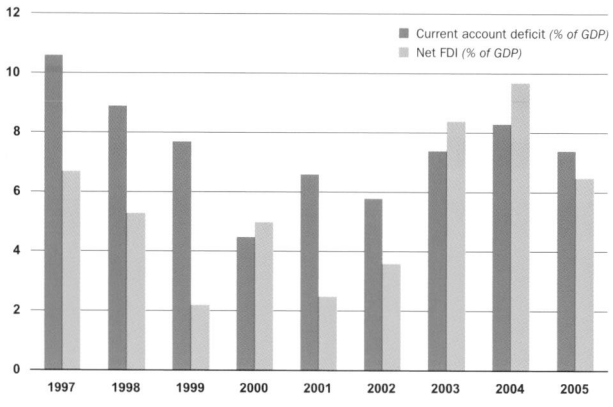

| | 2000 | 2001 | 2002 | 2003 | 2004 | 2005 Estimate | 2006 Projection |
|---|---|---|---|---|---|---|---|
| **Output and expenditure** | | | | *(Percentage change in real terms)* | | | |
| GDP | 1.9 | 4.7 | 5.5 | 11.1 | 6.2 | 8.5 | 6.5 |
| Private consumption | na | na | na | na | na | na | na |
| Public consumption | na | na | na | na | na | na | na |
| Gross fixed capital formation | na | na | na | na | na | na | na |
| Exports of goods and services | na | na | na | na | na | na | na |
| Imports of goods and services | na | na | na | na | na | na | na |
| Industrial gross output | 5.3 | -4.5 | 7.8 | 14.0 | 12.2 | 13.0 | na |
| Agricultural gross output | -12.0 | 8.2 | -1.4 | 7.0 | -6.7 | na | na |
| **Employment** [1] | | | | *(Percentage change)* | | | |
| Labour force (end-year) | 9.3 | -2.2 | -5.0 | 8.1 | -4.4 | na | na |
| Employment (end-year) | 15.0 | -2.1 | -6.8 | 9.6 | -6.3 | na | na |
| | | | | *(In per cent of labour force)* | | | |
| Unemployment (end-year) | 10.4 | 10.3 | 11.9 | 10.7 | 12.5 | na | na |
| **Prices and wages** | | | | *(Percentage change)* | | | |
| Consumer prices (annual average) | 4.1 | 4.6 | 5.7 | 4.9 | 5.7 | 8.4 | 5.5 |
| Consumer prices (end-year) | 4.6 | 3.4 | 5.6 | 7.0 | 7.5 | 6.4 | 4.8 |
| Producer prices (annual average) | 5.8 | 3.6 | 6.0 | 2.3 | 3.8 | na | na |
| Producer prices (end-year) | 2.4 | 8.9 | 1.5 | 5.4 | 0.7 | na | na |
| Gross average monthly earnings in economy (annual average) | 7.1 | 30.8 | 20.5 | 10.4 | 19.9 | 22.5 | na |
| **Government sector** [2] | | | | *(In per cent of GDP)* | | | |
| General government balance | -4.0 | -2.0 | -2.0 | -2.5 | 2.3 | -1.5 | -1.1 |
| General government expenditure | 19.2 | 18.3 | 17.8 | 18.7 | 19.5 | 24.9 | na |
| General government debt | 69.8 | 68.4 | 67.4 | 61.5 | 47.0 | 35.8 | na |
| **Monetary sector** | | | | *(Percentage change)* | | | |
| Broad money (M3, end-year) | 39.4 | 18.5 | 17.1 | 22.7 | 43.6 | 26.4 | na |
| Domestic credit (end-year) | 17.5 | 2.3 | 9.5 | 14.7 | 7.4 | 39.8 | na |
| | | | | *(In per cent of GDP)* | | | |
| Broad money (M3, end-year) | 10.4 | 11.1 | 11.6 | 12.4 | 15.3 | 16.6 | na |
| **Interest and exchange rates** | | | | *(In per cent per annum, end-year)* | | | |
| Money market rate | 18.2 | 17.5 | 27.7 | 16.9 | 11.9 | 7.7 | na |
| Treasury bill rate (3-month maturity) [3] | 26.0 | 29.9 | 43.4 | 44.3 | 19.2 | na | na |
| Deposit rate (3 months) [4] | 12.0 | 7.8 | 9.8 | 9.3 | 7.2 | 7.6 | na |
| Lending rate (3 months) | 32.8 | 27.0 | 31.8 | 32.3 | 31.2 | 21.6 | na |
| | | | | *(Laris per US dollar)* | | | |
| Exchange rate (end-year) | 2.0 | 2.1 | 2.1 | 2.1 | 1.8 | 1.8 | na |
| Exchange rate (annual average) | 2.0 | 2.1 | 2.2 | 2.1 | 1.9 | 1.8 | na |
| **External sector** | | | | *(In millions of US dollars)* | | | |
| Current account | -136 | -210 | -196 | -294 | -430 | -473 | -537 |
| Trade balance | -398 | -486 | -439 | -598 | -719 | -907 | -1,048 |
| Merchandise exports | 584 | 473 | 553 | 730 | 1,272 | 1,403 | 1,522 |
| Merchandise imports | 982 | 959 | 992 | 1,328 | 1,991 | 2,310 | 2,570 |
| Foreign direct investment, net | 153 | 80 | 122 | 335 | 503 | 415 | 390 |
| Gross reserves, excluding gold (end-year) | 109 | 161 | 198 | 191 | 383 | 493 | na |
| External debt stock | 1,582 | 1,712 | 1,858 | 1,954 | 2,039 | 2,137 | na |
| | | | | *(In months of imports of goods and services)* | | | |
| Gross reserves, excluding gold (end-year) | 0.9 | 1.4 | 1.6 | 1.3 | 1.8 | 2.1 | na |
| | | | | *(In per cent of current account revenues, excluding transfers)* | | | |
| Debt service | 16.7 | 19.3 | 7.4 | 10.0 | 10.2 | 9.8 | na |
| **Memorandum items** | | | | *(Denominations as indicated)* | | | |
| Population (end-year, million) | 4.6 | 4.6 | 4.6 | 4.6 | 4.6 | 4.6 | na |
| GDP (in millions of laris) | 6,013 | 6,638 | 7,448 | 8,565 | 9,951 | 11,600 | 13,080 |
| GDP per capita (in US dollars) | 659 | 693 | 734 | 864 | 1,124 | 1,385 | na |
| Share of industry in GDP (in per cent) | 13.7 | 12.2 | 12.4 | 13.3 | 13.2 | na | na |
| Share of agriculture in GDP (in per cent) | 20.2 | 20.7 | 19.3 | 20.3 | 16.2 | na | na |
| Current account/GDP (in per cent) | -4.5 | -6.6 | -5.8 | -7.4 | -8.3 | -7.4 | -7.3 |
| External debt - reserves (in US$ million) | 1,473 | 1,551 | 1,660 | 1,763 | 1,656 | 1,644 | na |
| External debt/GDP (in per cent) | 52.0 | 53.5 | 54.8 | 49.0 | 39.3 | 33.4 | na |
| External debt/exports of goods and services (in per cent) | 143.8 | 175.6 | 167.2 | 151.7 | 111.4 | 110.7 | na |

[1] Figures consistent with ILO methodology.
[2] General government includes the state, municipalities and extra-budgetary funds.

[3] Data from 2000 relate to average auction rates during that year.
[4] Data refer to average rates for local currency from International Financial Statistics.

# Hungary

## Economic performance and prospects

■ The economy continues to expand, but inconsistent policy making has resulted in large deficits.

■ Fiscal discipline and coherent economic policies will be essential for sustained growth and stability in the run-up to the adoption of the euro.

## Real economy

Real GDP grew by 4.1 per cent in 2005, compared with 4.6 per cent in 2004. Growth in 2005 was driven primarily by net exports and investments, while private consumption remained subdued. The unemployment rate edged up to 7.3 per cent at the end of 2005, compared with 6.3 per cent a year earlier. The employment rate was just above 50 per cent of the population.

## Economic policies

The general government deficit in 2005 was an estimated 6.1 per cent of GDP (according to the ESA95 methodology which treats part of the contributions to the pension system as budgetary revenues). This was substantially above the original target and followed Eurostat's ruling that the government account transparently for costs of infrastructure investments. Annual inflation fell to about 2.5 per cent by February 2006. The decline over the year allowed the central bank to lower the reference rate, in a series of cuts, to 6 per cent by September 2005, down from 9.5 per cent in January 2005. The government has also officially postponed the target date for accession to the eurozone from 2008 to 2010 to allow more time to meet the EU's Maastricht criteria.

## External sector

The current account deficit was 7.6 per cent of GDP in 2005, compared with 8.8 per cent in 2004. During the year exports increased by 9.6 per cent, imports rose by 6.1 per cent, and the trade deficit shrank to around €2.8 billion. The deficit was financed by government and corporate borrowing, significant (but volatile) portfolio investments and foreign direct investment (FDI). Net FDI benefited from substantial reinvested profits by foreign companies, and is estimated to have reached between 3.2 and 4.4 per cent of GDP in 2005.

## Outlook and risks

The strong economy has benefited from a sound banking sector, sustained market-oriented reforms and large-scale foreign investment since the beginning of transition. However, there are substantial fiscal challenges over the medium term. Large infrastructure projects will weigh heavily on the budget in the future. With elections in April 2006, necessary fiscal adjustments may be delayed and possible tax reforms may have uncertain overall consequences for the central budget. Any further fiscal slippage may lead to volatility of the exchange rate, with possible negative consequences for overall economic performance.

**Exports and industrial production growth year-on-year**

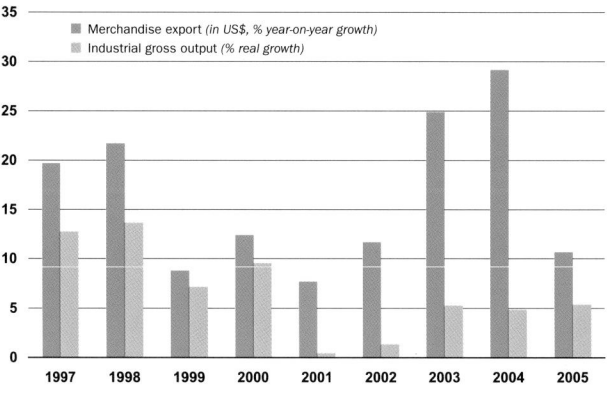

**Inflation, exchange rate developments and interest rates**

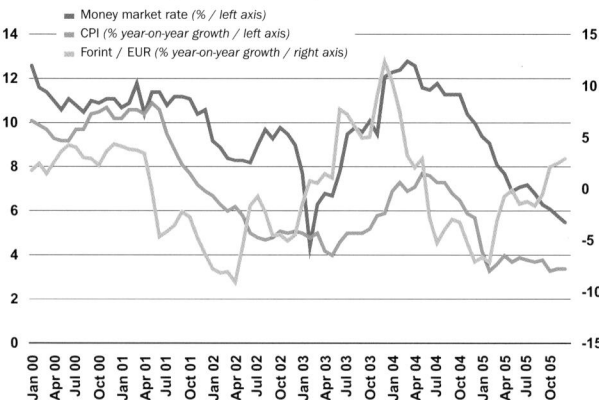

**Debt and fiscal balance**

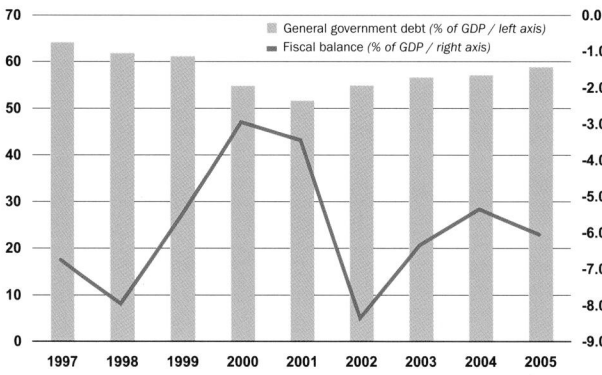

**Current account deficit and net FDI**

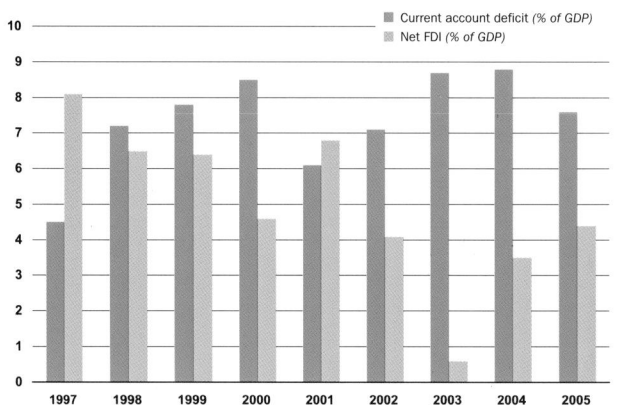

| | 2000 | 2001 | 2002 | 2003 | 2004 | 2005 Estimate | 2006 Projection |
|---|---|---|---|---|---|---|---|
| **Output and expenditure** | | | | *(Percentage change in real terms)* | | | |
| GDP | 5.2 | 4.3 | 3.8 | 3.4 | 4.6 | 4.1 | 4.2 |
| Private consumption | 5.0 | 5.8 | 9.7 | 7.8 | 3.1 | 2.1 | na |
| Public consumption | 1.2 | 1.2 | 6.6 | 7.9 | 0.9 | -1.4 | na |
| Gross fixed capital formation | 7.7 | 5.9 | 9.3 | 2.5 | 8.4 | 6.6 | na |
| Exports of goods and services | 21.0 | 8.0 | 3.9 | 7.8 | 16.4 | 10.6 | na |
| Imports of goods and services | 19.4 | 5.2 | 6.6 | 11.1 | 13.2 | 5.8 | na |
| Industrial gross output | 9.6 | 0.5 | 1.4 | 5.3 | 4.9 | 5.4 | na |
| Agricultural gross output | -7.9 | 24.6 | -12.9 | -4.2 | 37.9 | -11.8 | na |
| **Employment** | | | | *(Percentage change)* | | | |
| Labour force (annual average) | 0.6 | -0.4 | 0.2 | 1.4 | 0.1 | 1.3 | na |
| Employment (annual average) [1] | 1.2 | 0.3 | 0.1 | 1.3 | -0.3 | 0.2 | na |
| | | | | *(In per cent of labour force)* | | | |
| Unemployment (end-year) | 6.4 | 5.7 | 5.8 | 5.9 | 6.3 | 7.3 | na |
| **Prices and wages** | | | | *(Percentage change)* | | | |
| Consumer prices (annual average) | 9.8 | 9.2 | 5.3 | 4.7 | 6.8 | 3.6 | 1.9 |
| Consumer prices (end-year) | 10.1 | 6.8 | 4.8 | 5.7 | 5.5 | 3.3 | 2.2 |
| Producer prices (annual average) | 11.7 | 5.2 | -1.8 | 2.4 | 3.5 | 4.3 | na |
| Producer prices (end-year) | 12.4 | -0.4 | -1.3 | 6.2 | 1.6 | 4.7 | na |
| Gross average monthly earnings in economy (annual average) | 13.5 | 18.2 | 18.3 | 12.0 | 6.2 | 7.3 | na |
| **Government sector** | | | | *(In per cent of GDP)* | | | |
| General government balance [2] | -3.0 | -3.5 | -8.4 | -6.4 | -5.4 | -6.1 | -6.2 |
| General government expenditure | 47.4 | 48.0 | 52.1 | 49.8 | 49.7 | 49.4 | na |
| General government debt | 54.9 | 51.7 | 55.0 | 56.7 | 57.2 | 58.9 | na |
| **Monetary sector** | | | | *(Percentage change)* | | | |
| Broad money (M2, end-year) | 12.1 | 16.8 | 13.8 | 13.6 | 9.9 | 13.0 | na |
| Domestic credit (end-year) | 11.8 | 4.7 | 15.3 | 19.8 | 11.9 | 23.3 | na |
| | | | | *(In per cent of GDP)* | | | |
| Broad money (M2, end-year) | 42.8 | 44.3 | 44.6 | 46.0 | 46.2 | 48.5 | na |
| **Interest and exchange rates** | | | | *(In per cent per annum, end-year)* | | | |
| Refinance rate | 11.0 | 9.8 | 8.5 | 12.5 | 9.5 | 6.0 | na |
| Interbank interest rate (up to 30-day maturity) | 11.9 | 10.0 | 8.9 | 12.2 | 9.7 | 6.1 | na |
| Deposit rate weighted average (fixed for less than 1 year) | 9.9 | 9.4 | 7.4 | 8.7 | 9.1 | 5.2 | na |
| Lending rate weighted average (maturing within 1 year) | 12.8 | 12.0 | 9.7 | 11.2 | 11.0 | 7.4 | na |
| | | | | *(Forints per US dollar)* | | | |
| Exchange rate (end-year) | 284.7 | 279.0 | 225.2 | 207.9 | 180.3 | 213.6 | na |
| Exchange rate (annual average) | 282.2 | 286.5 | 257.9 | 224.3 | 202.7 | 199.6 | na |
| **External sector** | | | | *(In millions of US dollars)* | | | |
| Current account [3] | -4,011 | -3,201 | -4,643 | -7,204 | -8,863 | -8,400 | -8,600 |
| Trade balance [3] | -2,930 | -2,234 | -2,076 | -3,271 | -3,038 | -3,500 | -4,500 |
| Merchandise exports [3] | 28,822 | 31,054 | 34,684 | 43,325 | 55,984 | 62,000 | 68,300 |
| Merchandise imports [3] | 31,752 | 33,288 | 36,760 | 46,596 | 59,023 | 65,500 | 72,800 |
| Foreign direct investment, net [3] | 2,151 | 3,573 | 2,722 | 479 | 3,542 | 3,500 | 3,500 |
| Gross reserves, excluding gold (end-year) | 11,229 | 10,766 | 10,394 | 12,791 | 15,963 | 14,280 | na |
| External debt stock | 30,287 | 33,951 | 36,883 | 53,761 | 70,574 | 74,800 | na |
| | | | | *(In months of imports of goods and services)* | | | |
| Gross reserves, excluding gold (end-year) | 3.7 | 3.3 | 2.9 | 2.8 | 2.8 | 2.2 | na |
| | | | | *(In per cent of exports of goods and services)* | | | |
| Debt service [4] | 15.3 | 14.5 | 13.7 | 14.2 | 15.2 | na | na |
| **Memorandum items** | | | | *(Denominations as indicated)* | | | |
| Population (end-year, million) | 10.0 | 10.2 | 10.1 | 10.1 | 10.1 | 10.1 | na |
| GDP (in billions of forints) | 13,272 | 14,990 | 16,915 | 18,651 | 20,413 | 21,952 | 23,412 |
| GDP per capita (in US dollars) | 4,683 | 5,140 | 6,467 | 8,219 | 9,971 | 10,911 | na |
| Share of industry in GDP (in per cent) | 27.9 | 27.2 | 26.8 | 27.5 | 28.3 | na | na |
| Share of agriculture in GDP (in per cent) | 4.6 | 5.5 | 4.7 | 4.4 | 4.6 | na | na |
| Current account/GDP (in per cent) | -8.5 | -6.1 | -7.1 | -8.7 | -8.8 | -7.6 | -7.8 |
| External debt - reserves (in US$ million) | 19,058 | 23,185 | 26,490 | 40,970 | 54,611 | 60,520 | na |
| External debt/GDP (in per cent) | 64.4 | 64.9 | 56.2 | 64.7 | 70.1 | 68.0 | na |
| External debt/exports of goods and services (in per cent) | 87.2 | 89.1 | 87.7 | 103.4 | 106.5 | 101.6 | na |

[1] Data from labour force survey.

[2] Calculated according to Eurostat methodology (ESA95), excluding part of the cost of pension reform. Figures from 2003 onwards are subject to methodological revisions as accounting is brought into compliance with the Eurostat standards.

[3] Data from balance of payments.

[4] Excluding inter-company loans.

# Kazakhstan

## Economic performance and prospects

- Strong external and domestic demand, underpinned by buoyant oil prices and increased fiscal expenditures on civil service wages and social outlays, has sustained growth.

- Medium-term fiscal management must improve and banking regulations must be further tightened to mitigate risks arising from external shocks.

## Real economy

The economy continued to grow strongly by 9.4 per cent in 2005. Fiscal loosening and the easing of credit stimulated domestic consumption and investment. However, the growth of industrial output slowed, mainly due to the sluggish hydrocarbon sector (hindered by export capacity constraints) and a decline in production of metals and iron ores.

## Economic policies

The general government surplus narrowed from 2.7 per cent in 2004 to 0.7 per cent in 2005. Expenditure on social outlays and civil service salaries increased, and the government made a one-off payment of around 1.6 per cent of GDP to purchase a stake in the Kashagan oil field from a foreign owner. During 2005 the National Bank of Kazakhstan (NBK) scaled back interventions in the foreign exchange market. This followed increased demand for foreign currency, primarily due to the amortisation of inter-company loans linked to oil prices. The National Fund also absorbed around US$ 3 billion (5.8 per cent of GDP). Money supply (M2) growth eased from 69 per cent in 2004 to 26 per cent in 2005, but domestic credit remained buoyant at 55 per cent. The annual inflation rate edged upwards from 6.9 per cent in 2004 to 7.6 per cent in 2005.

## External sector

The current account recorded a surplus of 2.1 per cent of GDP in 2005. Exports of mineral products, including hydrocarbons and metal products, increased sharply in US dollar terms. This more than offset the strong surge in oil-related imports and interest and income payments. Net foreign direct investment declined to around US$ 1 billion in 2005, compared with US$ 5.5 billion in 2004. The fall reflected the government's purchase of a stake in the Kashagan oil field and the accelerated amortisation of inter-company loans. Total external debt declined from 79 per cent of GDP to 76 per cent during 2005 due to the faster debt amortisation of hydrocarbon-related investments. However, total external debt of Kazakh banks increased to around 23 per cent of GDP at the end of 2005 from 17 per cent a year earlier.

## Outlook and risks

The short-term economic outlook remains favourable. However, a further deceleration of growth to 8.5 per cent is expected in 2006, reflecting constraints on hydrocarbon production. Fiscal tightening should ease inflationary pressures. The main medium-term risk stems from the rapid credit expansion. Further regulatory improvements may be required in the banking sector to minimise the impact from a possible tightening of credit. The planned integration of the National Fund into the budgetary framework (in 2007) should improve fiscal management.

## Exports and industrial production growth year-on-year

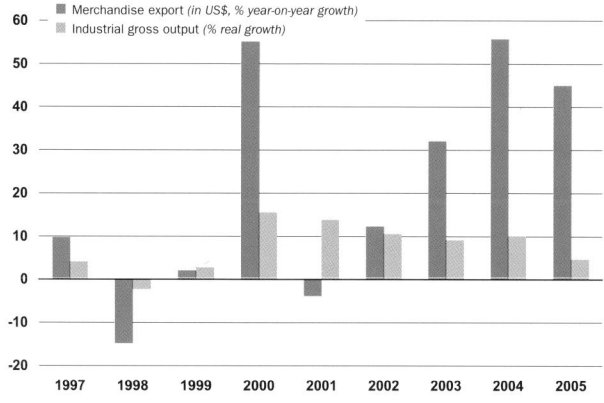

## Inflation, exchange rate developments and interest rates

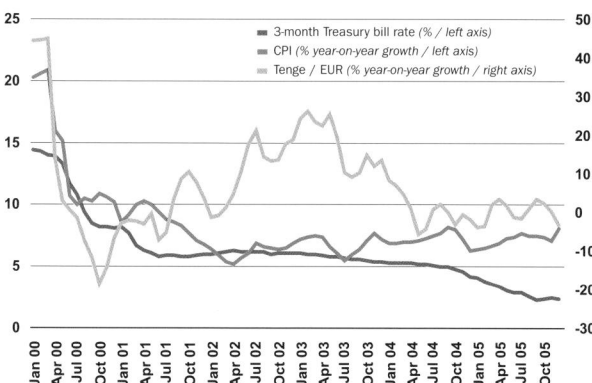

## Debt and fiscal balance

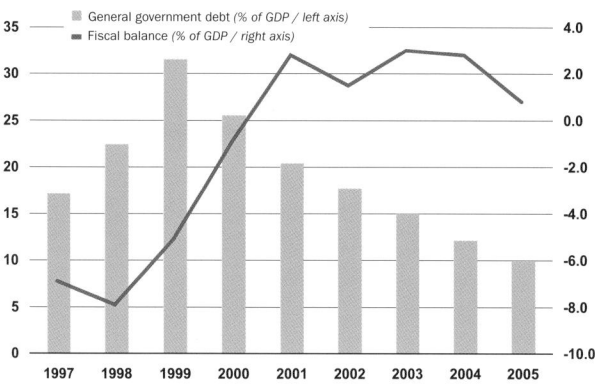

## Current account deficit and net FDI

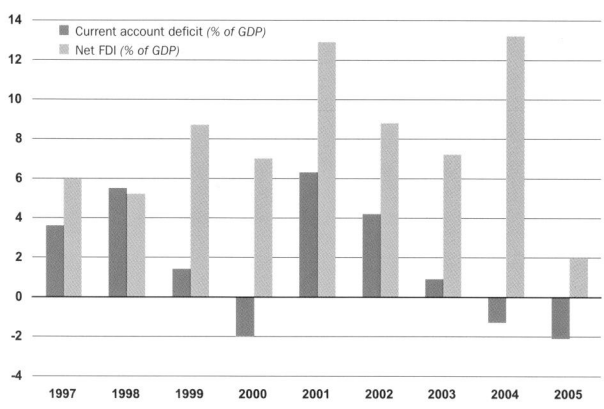

| | 2000 | 2001 | 2002 | 2003 | 2004 | 2005 Estimate | 2006 Projection |
|---|---|---|---|---|---|---|---|
| **Output and expenditure** | | | *(Percentage change in real terms)* | | | | |
| GDP | 9.8 | 13.5 | 9.8 | 9.3 | 9.4 | 9.4 | 8.5 |
| Private consumption | 1.2 | 7.8 | 12.2 | 3.5 | 9.5 | na | na |
| Public consumption | 15.0 | 19.2 | -4.3 | 7.5 | 18.4 | na | na |
| Gross fixed capital formation | 16.1 | 25.3 | 10.2 | 8.9 | 12.4 | na | na |
| Exports of goods and services | 28.7 | -1.8 | 22.6 | 5.5 | 10.5 | na | na |
| Imports of goods and services | 26.1 | 0.3 | 4.3 | -4.1 | 14.5 | na | na |
| Industrial gross output | 15.5 | 13.8 | 10.5 | 9.1 | 10.1 | 4.6 | na |
| Agricultural gross output | -4.2 | 17.3 | 3.4 | 1.6 | 1.0 | 6.7 | na |
| **Employment** [1] | | | *(Percentage change)* | | | | |
| Labour force (end-year) | 0.7 | 5.2 | -1.1 | 3.5 | 2.4 | 0.5 | na |
| Employment (end-year) | 1.6 | 8.0 | 0.2 | 4.1 | 2.8 | 0.8 | na |
| | | | *(In per cent of labour force)* | | | | |
| Unemployment (end-year) | 12.8 | 10.4 | 9.3 | 8.8 | 8.4 | 8.1 | na |
| **Prices and wages** | | | *(Percentage change)* | | | | |
| Consumer prices (annual average) | 13.2 | 8.4 | 5.9 | 6.4 | 6.9 | 7.6 | 7.7 |
| Consumer prices (end-year) | 9.8 | 6.4 | 6.6 | 6.8 | 6.7 | 7.5 | 7.5 |
| Producer prices (annual average) | 38.0 | 0.3 | 0.3 | 9.3 | 16.7 | 23.7 | na |
| Producer prices (end-year) | 19.4 | -14.1 | 11.9 | 5.9 | 23.8 | 20.3 | na |
| Gross average monthly earnings in economy (annual average) | 21.2 | 20.4 | 17.5 | 13.8 | 22.2 | 16.6 | na |
| **Government sector** [2] | | | *(In per cent of GDP)* | | | | |
| General government balance [3] | -1.0 | 2.7 | 1.4 | 2.9 | 2.7 | 0.7 | 3.1 |
| General government expenditure [4] | 23.2 | 23.0 | 21.0 | 22.5 | 23.3 | 31.4 | na |
| General government debt | 25.5 | 20.4 | 17.7 | 15.0 | 12.1 | 10.0 | na |
| **Monetary sector** | | | *(Percentage change)* | | | | |
| Broad money (M2, end-year) | 45.0 | 40.2 | 30.1 | 29.5 | 69.3 | 24.8 | na |
| Domestic credit (end-year) [5] | 57.3 | 17.1 | 30.2 | 24.1 | 69.6 | 82.5 | na |
| | | | *(In per cent of GDP)* | | | | |
| Broad money (M2, end-year) | 15.3 | 17.1 | 19.2 | 20.3 | 28.7 | 30.4 | na |
| **Interest and exchange rates** | | | *(In per cent per annum, end-year)* | | | | |
| Refinancing rate | 14.0 | 9.0 | 7.5 | 7.0 | 7.0 | 8.0 | na |
| Treasury bill rate (3-month maturity) [6] | 6.6 | 5.3 | 5.2 | 5.9 | 3.3 | 3.3 | na |
| Deposit rate [7] | 15.6 | 12.8 | 11.0 | 10.9 | 9.3 | 9.1 | na |
| Lending rate [8] | 18.8 | 15.3 | 14.1 | 14.9 | 13.7 | 13.0 | na |
| | | | *(Tenges per US dollar)* | | | | |
| Exchange rate (end-year) | 144.5 | 150.2 | 155.6 | 144.2 | 130.0 | 134.0 | na |
| Exchange rate (annual average) | 142.1 | 146.7 | 153.3 | 149.6 | 136.0 | 132.9 | na |
| **External sector** | | | *(In millions of US dollars)* | | | | |
| Current account | 366 | -1,390 | -1,024 | -273 | 530 | 1,031 | -1,784 |
| Trade balance [9] | 2,168 | 983 | 1,987 | 3,679 | 6,786 | 11,912 | 12,205 |
| Merchandise exports | 9,288 | 8,928 | 10,027 | 13,233 | 20,603 | 29,875 | 32,862 |
| Merchandise imports | 7,120 | 7,944 | 8,040 | 9,554 | 13,818 | 17,963 | 20,657 |
| Foreign direct investment, net | 1,278 | 2,861 | 2,164 | 2,213 | 5,383 | 1,000 | 2,500 |
| Gross reserves, excluding gold (end-year) | 1,594 | 1,997 | 2,555 | 4,236 | 8,473 | 6,084 | na |
| External debt stock [10] | 12,685 | 15,158 | 18,252 | 22,920 | 32,095 | 36,095 | na |
| | | | *(In months of imports of goods and services)* | | | | |
| Gross reserves, excluding gold (end-year) [11] | 2.1 | 2.3 | 2.6 | 3.8 | 5.4 | 2.9 | na |
| | | | *(In per cent of exports of goods and services)* | | | | |
| Debt service | 31.7 | 37.6 | 35.4 | 35.2 | 38.3 | 33.9 | na |
| **Memorandum items** | | | *(Denominations as indicated)* | | | | |
| Population (end-year, million) | 14.9 | 14.9 | 14.9 | 15.0 | 15.1 | 15.1 | na |
| GDP (in billions of tenges) | 2,600 | 3,251 | 3,776 | 4,612 | 5,542 | 6,524 | 7,624 |
| GDP per capita (in US dollars) | 1,231 | 1,492 | 1,657 | 2,062 | 2,703 | 3,250 | na |
| Share of industry in GDP (in per cent) | 25.2 | 25.2 | 25.3 | 25.3 | 25.4 | na | na |
| Share of agriculture in GDP (in per cent) | 9.8 | 10.1 | 9.5 | 8.9 | 8.1 | na | na |
| Current account/GDP (in per cent) | 2.0 | -6.3 | -4.2 | -0.9 | 1.3 | 2.1 | -2.9 |
| External debt - reserves (in US$ million) | 11,090 | 13,160 | 15,696 | 18,684 | 23,621 | 30,010 | na |
| External debt/GDP (in per cent) | 69.3 | 68.4 | 74.1 | 74.3 | 78.8 | 73.5 | na |
| External debt/exports of goods and services (in per cent) | 122.7 | 148.8 | 157.8 | 153.4 | 142.0 | 113.2 | na |

[1] Data from labour force surveys.

[2] General government includes the state, municipalities and extra-budgetary funds and is on a cash basis.

[3] Government balance includes quasi-fiscal operations and transfers to the National Fund. Balance excludes privatisation revenues.

[4] Expenditures include extra-budgetary funds.

[5] Domestic credit from International Financial Statistics. Break in series in 2001. From 2001, data include National Fund.

[6] Average effective yield of short-term NBK notes.

[7] Deposit rate refers to the weighted average of interest rates on time deposits of individuals, in tenge by maturity.

[8] Lending rate refers to weighted average of interest rates on credits extended to legal entities, excluding banks, in tenge by maturity.

[9] Exports at declared customs prices and are not corrected for under-invoicing of oil and gas exports.

[10] Includes inter-company debt by branches of non-resident foreign enterprises and short-term debt.

[11] Excludes National Fund.

# Kyrgyz Republic

## Economic performance and prospects

- Political upheaval severely affected the economy in 2005, as did the downturn in production at the Kumtor gold mine.

- Confidence in public institutions needs to be restored and the business environment further improved to achieve high growth over the medium term.

## Real economy

The economy suffered from the political events of March 2005 and a decline in output from the Kumtor gold mine (which accounts for about 9 per cent of GDP). Real GDP growth fell by 0.6 per cent in 2005, according to preliminary estimates. Agricultural output, accounting for around 33 per cent of GDP, decreased markedly by 4.2 per cent, as the instability disrupted the spring planting season. The tourism sector was also affected as visitors from neighbouring countries stayed away due to security concerns.

## Economic policies

Fiscal policy has been tightened in recent years under the IMF's Poverty Reduction and Growth Facility (PRGF). However, following the March events, revisions to the programme allowed for a fiscal expansion in 2005. The 2005 deficit was an estimated 4.8 per cent, compared with 4.1 per cent in 2004. Meanwhile, the political situation delayed the adoption of a new tax code and the planned overhaul in the tax structure. The employers' contribution to the social security tax was reduced by 1 per cent and the VAT exemption threshold was raised. These changes, however, had little downward impact on tax revenues as tax collection continued to improve. The March events also led temporarily to reduced money demand and pushed consumer prices up as commodity distribution channels were disrupted. However, prices subsequently stabilised, resulting in an annual average inflation rate of 4.9 per cent year-on-year.

## External sector

Despite a record level of remittances, the current account deficit widened in 2005 to 5.2 per cent of GDP from 3.4 per cent in 2004. This was due to the decline in the volume of gold exports, which more than offset the increase in gold prices. Net foreign direct investment was similar to previous years at around US$60 million. Total external debt continued to decline from 95 per cent of GDP in 2004 to 89 per cent in 2005, following further debt relief by the Paris Club in March 2005.

## Outlook and risks

Growth is projected to accelerate to more than 5 per cent in 2006, provided agriculture and other sectors affected adversely by the 2005 events recover and the decline in output at the Kumtor mine decelerates. With IMF and World Bank approval, the country could initiate a highly indebted poor countries (HIPC) public external debt relief process in 2006. This, combined with relief from the IMF and World Bank under a new G8 initiative, should substantially reduce the debt servicing burden and relieve pressure on budgets. However, medium and long-term growth depends on private investment, which will require improvements to the business environment.

### Exports and industrial production growth year-on-year

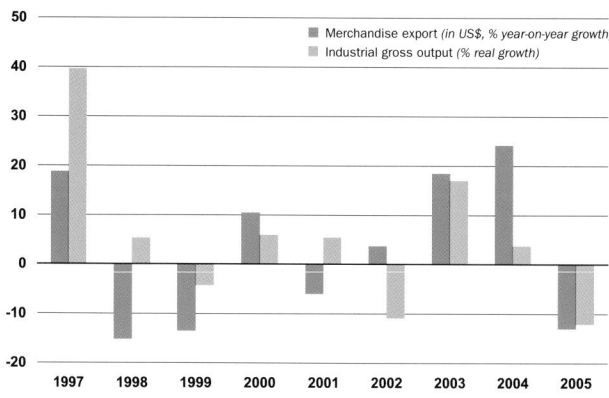

### Inflation, exchange rate developments and interest rates

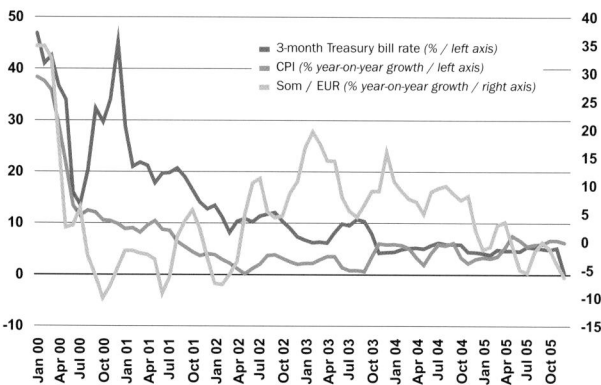

### Debt and fiscal balance

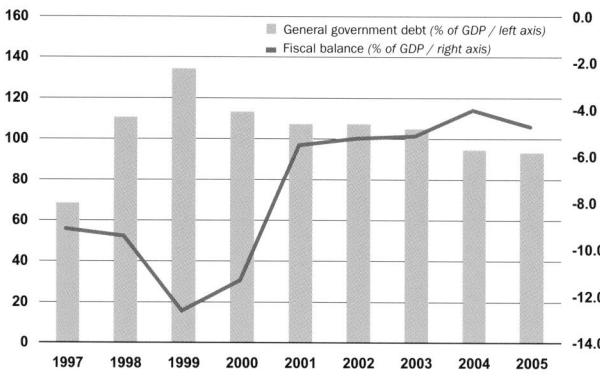

### Current account deficit and net FDI

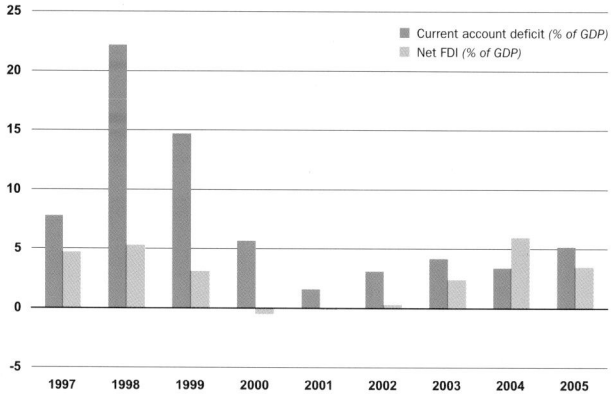

| | 2000 | 2001 | 2002 | 2003 | 2004 | 2005 Estimate | 2006 Projection |
|---|---|---|---|---|---|---|---|
| **Output and expenditure** | | | | *(Percentage change in real terms)* | | | |
| GDP | 5.4 | 5.3 | 0.0 | 6.7 | 7.1 | -0.6 | 5.2 |
| Private consumption | -4.2 | 1.6 | 4.2 | 22.1 | 9.9 | na | na |
| Public consumption | 7.5 | 0.0 | -0.2 | -2.0 | 6.7 | na | na |
| Gross fixed capital formation | 26.4 | -1.9 | -7.3 | -6.3 | -2.9 | na | na |
| Exports of goods and services | 10.5 | -3.2 | 8.1 | 5.3 | 14.8 | na | na |
| Imports of goods and services | 0.4 | -13.8 | 13.1 | 16.0 | 18.5 | na | na |
| Industrial gross output | 6.0 | 5.4 | -10.9 | 17.0 | 3.7 | -12.1 | na |
| Agricultural gross output | 2.6 | 7.3 | 3.1 | 3.2 | 4.1 | -4.2 | na |
| **Employment** | | | | *(Percentage change)* | | | |
| Labour force (end-year) [1] | 1.7 | 1.8 | 2.0 | 4.7 | na | na | na |
| Employment (end-year) [2] | 0.2 | 1.1 | 1.1 | 1.7 | na | na | na |
| | | | | *(In per cent of labour force)* | | | |
| Unemployment (end-year) | 7.5 | 7.8 | 8.6 | 8.9 | 9.0 | na | na |
| **Prices and wages** | | | | *(Percentage change)* | | | |
| Consumer prices (annual average) | 18.7 | 6.9 | 2.0 | 3.1 | 4.1 | 4.3 | 5.0 |
| Consumer prices (end-year) | 9.5 | 3.7 | 2.3 | 5.6 | 2.8 | 4.9 | 4.4 |
| Producer prices (annual average) | 30.7 | 12.0 | 4.8 | 4.6 | 5.9 | na | na |
| Producer prices (end-year) | 22.9 | 5.2 | 6.0 | 7.8 | 4.5 | na | na |
| Gross average monthly earnings in economy (annual average) | 16.9 | 18.6 | 15.8 | 13.7 | 14.9 | 16.6 | na |
| **Government sector [3]** | | | | *(In per cent of GDP)* | | | |
| General government balance | -11.4 | -5.6 | -5.3 | -5.2 | -4.1 | -4.8 | -3.7 |
| General government expenditure | 29.9 | 26.0 | 28.1 | 27.4 | 27.1 | 28.6 | na |
| General government debt | 113.3 | 107.3 | 107.3 | 104.9 | 94.6 | 93.4 | na |
| **Monetary sector** | | | | *(Percentage change)* | | | |
| Broad money (M2, end-year) | 11.7 | 11.3 | 33.9 | 33.4 | 32.1 | 18.0 | na |
| Domestic credit (end-year) | 10.0 | -8.1 | 21.6 | 11.3 | -18.8 | 22.0 | na |
| | | | | *(In per cent of GDP)* | | | |
| Broad money (M2, end-year) | 11.3 | 11.1 | 14.6 | 17.5 | 20.6 | 23.5 | na |
| **Interest and exchange rates** | | | | *(In per cent per annum, end-year)* | | | |
| Official rate | 32.8 | 10.7 | 4.4 | 4.0 | 4.0 | 4.3 | na |
| Money market rate [4] | 32.3 | 19.1 | 7.0 | 4.0 | 4.0 | 4.4 | na |
| Deposit rate [5] | 18.4 | 12.5 | 5.9 | 5.0 | 6.7 | 5.8 | na |
| Lending rate [5] | 51.9 | 37.3 | 24.8 | 21.7 | 29.3 | 26.6 | na |
| | | | | *(Soms per US dollar)* | | | |
| Exchange rate (end-year) | 48.3 | 47.7 | 46.1 | 44.2 | 41.6 | 41.3 | na |
| Exchange rate (annual average) | 47.7 | 48.3 | 46.9 | 43.7 | 42.6 | 41.0 | na |
| **External sector** | | | | *(In millions of US dollars)* | | | |
| Current account | -78 | -24 | -49 | -81 | -75 | -124 | -56 |
| Trade balance | 4 | 31 | -74 | -133 | -171 | -285 | -281 |
| Merchandise exports | 511 | 480 | 498 | 590 | 733 | 638 | 734 |
| Merchandise imports | 507 | 450 | 572 | 724 | 904 | 922 | 1,015 |
| Foreign direct investment, net | -7 | -1 | 5 | 46 | 131 | 83 | 65 |
| Gross reserves, excluding gold (end-year) | 205 | 230 | 289 | 365 | 549 | 562 | na |
| External debt stock | 1,704 | 1,678 | 1,785 | 1,978 | 2,104 | 2,154 | na |
| | | | | *(In months of imports of goods and services)* | | | |
| Gross reserves, excluding gold (end-year) | 3.8 | 4.8 | 4.8 | 5.0 | 5.8 | 5.7 | na |
| | | | | *(In per cent of exports of goods and services)* | | | |
| Debt service [6] | 28.1 | 30.8 | 21.0 | 22.3 | 19.1 | 16.3 | na |
| **Memorandum items** | | | | *(Denominations as indicated)* | | | |
| Population (end-year, million) | 4.9 | 4.9 | 5.0 | 5.0 | 5.1 | 5.1 | na |
| GDP (in millions of soms) | 65,358 | 73,883 | 75,367 | 83,872 | 94,078 | 97,535 | 107,669 |
| GDP per capita (in US dollars) | 279 | 309 | 322 | 381 | 433 | 464 | na |
| Share of industry in GDP (in per cent) | 27.2 | 26.8 | 21.3 | 20.2 | 19.0 | na | na |
| Share of agriculture in GDP (in per cent) | 34.2 | 34.5 | 34.4 | 33.6 | 32.9 | na | na |
| Current account/GDP (in per cent) | -5.7 | -1.6 | -3.1 | -4.2 | -3.4 | -5.2 | -2.1 |
| External debt - reserves (in US$ million) | 1,499 | 1,448 | 1,496 | 1,614 | 1,555 | 1,592 | na |
| External debt/GDP (in per cent) | 124.4 | 109.6 | 111.1 | 103.0 | 95.3 | 90.6 | na |
| External debt/exports of goods and services (in per cent) | 297.5 | 299.3 | 278.8 | 265.5 | 223.3 | 248.2 | na |

[1] Based on labour force data from World Bank *World Development Indicators*.

[2] Based on data from the National Statistical Committee (NSC). Includes people employed in legal entities and excludes employment in agriculture and forestry.

[3] General government includes the state, municipalities and extra-budgetary funds. It also includes expenditure under the foreign-financed public investment programme and net lending.

[4] Weighted average rate on interbank loans in soms with 1-90 days maturity. Data from International Financial Statistics.

[5] Weighted average over all maturities. Data from International Financial Statistics.

[6] Debt service scheduled and excludes debt rescheduling granted by the Paris Club of official creditors for 2002-05.

# Latvia

## Economic performance and prospects

- Strong domestic demand continues to boost growth, but there has been a resurgence of inflation and the current account deficit remains large.

- In the absence of a tighter fiscal policy, continuing credit expansion could exacerbate inflationary pressures and delay membership to the European Monetary Union.

## Real economy

Real GDP grew by 10.2 per cent in 2005, driven mainly by the trade, transport, communications and construction sectors. Manufacturing also improved during the year after a slow first quarter. On the demand side, low interest rates and longer available maturities for local bank loans continued to stimulate rapid credit growth for businesses and households.

## Economic policies

The general government deficit for 2005 was an estimated 1 per cent of GDP. This was lower than planned due to increased tax revenue collection and lower expenditure. The deficit is expected to remain below 2 per cent in 2006 and 2007. As a result of a prudent fiscal policy in recent years, public debt remained modest at less than 15 per cent of GDP by the end of 2005. Following the re-pegging of the currency to the euro in January 2005, Latvia was admitted to the Exchange Rate Mechanism II (ERM II) in May. However, global increases in oil prices, EU-related administrative changes and increases in food prices resulted in annual average inflation of 6.7 per cent in 2005. The authorities are aware of the risk that higher inflation poses to EU convergence, and are addressing the issue through a working group of ministers and Bank of Latvia officials.

## External sector

The current account deficit was at least 11 per cent of GDP in 2005. This was below the level in 2004 and reflected a significant growth in exports. Latvian exports are becoming more diversified, with food products and metals adding to the traditional staples of timber and wood products. The current account deficit continues to be financed by foreign direct investment (FDI) and other investments. FDI coverage of the deficit remained below 50 per cent in 2005 as a result of decreasing reinvested earnings and repayment of FDI loans. Other investments make up the largest proportion of the financial account, with increased borrowing from parent banks financing domestic lending. Gross external debt is high at over 90 per cent of GDP, but assets owned by foreigners in the country account for some 60 per cent of GDP.

## Outlook and risks

A slight decline in annual real GDP growth to around 8 per cent is expected in 2006. Rapid credit growth is contributing to financial deepening, but is also fuelling the high current account deficit. Fiscal policy needs to be tightened, or a continuing credit expansion could exacerbate inflationary pressures and delay membership to the European Monetary Union.

### Exports and industrial production growth year-on-year

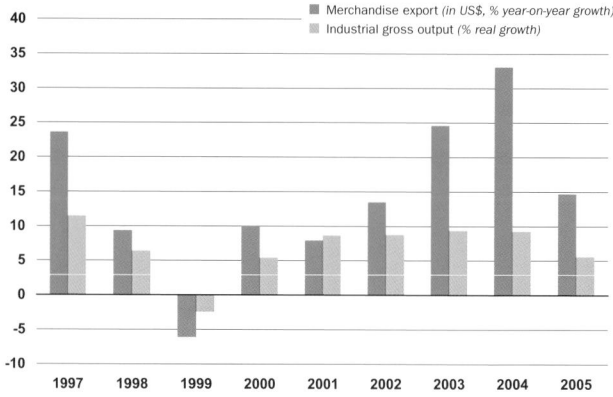

### Inflation, exchange rate developments and interest rates

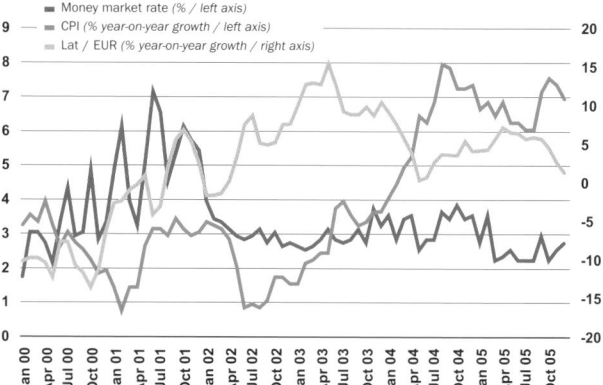

### Debt and fiscal balance

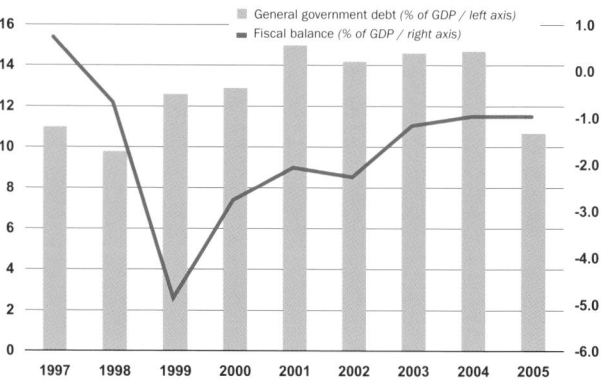

### Current account deficit and net FDI

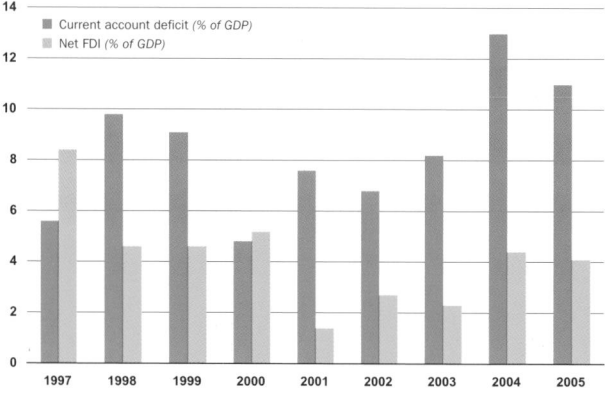

| | 2000 | 2001 | 2002 | 2003 | 2004 | 2005 Estimate | 2006 Projection |
|---|---|---|---|---|---|---|---|
| **Output and expenditure** | | | | *(Percentage change in real terms)* | | | |
| GDP | 6.9 | 8.0 | 6.4 | 7.2 | 8.3 | 10.2 | 7.7 |
| Private consumption | 6.3 | 7.3 | 7.4 | 8.6 | 8.9 | 7.8 | na |
| Public consumption | -1.9 | 0.3 | 2.4 | 2.5 | 1.4 | 2.0 | na |
| Gross fixed capital formation | 10.2 | 11.4 | 13.0 | 7.4 | 21.1 | 15.0 | na |
| Exports of goods and services | 12.0 | 6.9 | 6.3 | 4.3 | 8.9 | 18.6 | na |
| Imports of goods and services | 4.9 | 12.6 | 4.5 | 13.3 | 15.5 | 11.4 | na |
| Industrial gross output | 5.4 | 8.7 | 8.8 | 9.4 | 9.3 | 5.6 | na |
| Agricultural gross output | 11.5 | 6.4 | 4.4 | 1.0 | 4.0 | na | na |
| **Employment** | | | | *(Percentage change)* | | | |
| Labour force (end-year) | -2.9 | 0.9 | 1.5 | 0.3 | -1.6 | 1.5 | na |
| Employment (end-year) | -2.8 | 2.2 | 2.8 | 1.8 | 1.1 | 2.5 | na |
| | | | | *(In per cent of labour force)* | | | |
| Unemployment (end-year) | 14.4 | 13.1 | 12.4 | 10.6 | 10.4 | 9.9 | na |
| **Prices and wages** | | | | *(Percentage change)* | | | |
| Consumer prices (annual average) | 2.6 | 2.5 | 1.9 | 2.9 | 6.2 | 6.7 | 6.0 |
| Consumer prices (end-year) | 1.9 | 3.0 | 1.5 | 3.6 | 7.3 | 7.0 | 6.0 |
| Producer prices (annual average) | 0.6 | 1.7 | 1.0 | 3.2 | 8.6 | 7.8 | na |
| Producer prices (end-year) | 1.0 | 1.8 | 0.8 | 4.1 | 11.3 | 6.8 | na |
| Gross average monthly earnings in economy (annual average) | 6.2 | 6.5 | 8.7 | 11.2 | 9.6 | 17.5 | na |
| **Government sector** | | | | *(In per cent of GDP)* | | | |
| General government balance | -2.8 | -2.1 | -2.3 | -1.2 | -1.0 | -1.0 | -1.5 |
| General government expenditure [1] | 37.2 | 34.9 | 35.7 | 35.0 | 36.0 | 10.7 | na |
| General government debt | 12.9 | 15.0 | 14.2 | 14.6 | 14.7 | 12.6 | na |
| **Monetary sector** | | | | *(Percentage change)* | | | |
| Broad money (M2, end-year) | 27.9 | 20.8 | 21.0 | 21.1 | 27.0 | 36.1 | na |
| Domestic credit (end-year) | 44.3 | 36.2 | 39.8 | 39.2 | 40.2 | 66.1 | na |
| | | | | *(In per cent of GDP)* | | | |
| Broad money (M2, end-year) | 27.2 | 29.8 | 32.8 | 35.8 | 39.1 | 45.3 | na |
| **Interest and exchange rates** | | | | *(In per cent per annum, end-year)* | | | |
| Refinancing rate | 3.5 | 3.5 | 3.0 | 3.0 | 4.0 | 4.0 | na |
| Interbank market rate [2] | 3.3 | 5.4 | 2.7 | 3.2 | 3.5 | na | na |
| Deposit rate (short-term, under 1 year) | 4.4 | 5.3 | 3.2 | 3.0 | 3.3 | 2.8 | na |
| Lending rate (short-term, under 1 year) | 12.1 | 10.8 | 7.5 | 5.4 | 7.5 | 5.9 | na |
| | | | | *(Lats per US dollar)* | | | |
| Exchange rate (end-year) | 0.6 | 0.6 | 0.6 | 0.5 | 0.5 | 0.6 | na |
| Exchange rate (annual average) | 0.6 | 0.6 | 0.6 | 0.6 | 0.5 | 0.6 | na |
| **External sector** | | | | *(In millions of US dollars)* | | | |
| Current account | -372 | -626 | -625 | -910 | -1,766 | -1,682 | -1,725 |
| Trade balance | -1,044 | -1,335 | -1,479 | -2,003 | -2,781 | -3,110 | -3,270 |
| Merchandise exports | 2,080 | 2,243 | 2,545 | 3,171 | 4,221 | 4,840 | 5,670 |
| Merchandise imports | 3,123 | 3,578 | 4,024 | 5,174 | 7,002 | 7,950 | 8,940 |
| Foreign direct investment, net | 400 | 114 | 250 | 256 | 596 | 622 | 740 |
| Gross reserves, excluding gold (end-year) | 851 | 1,149 | 1,241 | 1,432 | 1,909 | 2,579 | na |
| External debt stock [3] | 4,702 | 5,571 | 7,043 | 9,343 | 12,689 | 13,000 | na |
| | | | | *(In months of imports of goods and services)* | | | |
| Gross reserves, excluding gold (end-year) | 2.6 | 3.2 | 3.1 | 2.8 | 2.8 | 3.4 | na |
| | | | | *(In per cent of exports of goods and services)* | | | |
| Debt service | 14.8 | 20.5 | 15.8 | 19.8 | 19.9 | 18.7 | na |
| **Memorandum items** | | | | *(Denominations as indicated)* | | | |
| Population (end-year, million) | 2.4 | 2.4 | 2.3 | 2.3 | 2.3 | 2.3 | na |
| GDP (in millions of lats) | 4,686 | 5,168 | 5,689 | 6,318 | 7,333 | 8,622 | 9,844 |
| GDP per capita (in US dollars) | 3,250 | 3,484 | 3,924 | 4,743 | 5,854 | 6,618 | na |
| Share of industry in GDP (in per cent) | 20.7 | 20.4 | 20.3 | 20.4 | 20.6 | na | na |
| Share of agriculture in GDP (in per cent) | 4.9 | 4.7 | 4.5 | 4.3 | 5.3 | na | na |
| Current account/GDP (in per cent) | -4.8 | -7.6 | -6.8 | -8.2 | -13.0 | -11.0 | -10.4 |
| External debt - reserves (in US$ million) | 3,851 | 4,422 | 5,802 | 7,911 | 10,780 | 10,421 | na |
| External debt/GDP (in per cent) | 60.9 | 67.6 | 76.5 | 84.5 | 93.5 | 85.2 | na |
| External debt/exports of goods and services (in per cent) | 142.8 | 162.3 | 185.5 | 198.9 | 211.4 | 194.6 | na |

[1]  General government expenditure includes net lending.
[2]  Weighted average interest rates in the interbank market.

[3]  Includes non-resident currency and deposits, liabilities to affiliated enterprises and liabilities to direct investors.

# Lithuania

## Economic performance and prospects

■ The economy continues to perform well, supported by strong domestic consumption and export growth.

■ A prudent fiscal policy should be maintained to control inflation and adhere to the EU Maastricht criteria.

## Real economy

After a slow start the economy picked up during 2005, recording an estimated GDP growth rate of 7.5 per cent for the year as a whole. Domestic consumption provided much of the momentum, fuelled by low interest rates, declining unemployment and rising wages. Financial sector deepening also contributed to increased household spending.

## Economic policies

The fiscal stance loosened during 2005 due to public salary increases, higher pension benefits and rising investment. At the same time, however, revenues were better than expected because of high economic growth and improved tax collection. During the year, parliament approved rate cuts on personal income tax from 33 per cent to 27 per cent from July 2006 and to 24 per cent in 2008. To compensate for the loss in revenues, the government introduced a temporary increase in the corporate profits tax rate from 15 per cent to 19 per cent for 2006 and 2007. The currency board continues to enjoy broad support. Inflation accelerated in 2005 and reached 2.7 per cent year-on-year by December. There was upward pressure from rising excise taxes, administered prices and oil and gas costs. The authorities are aware of the risk of increasing inflation to EU convergence, but believe that it can be contained within the EU Maastricht limit.

## External sector

The current account deficit stabilised at around 7 per cent of GDP in 2005 as a result of an improved export performance. In the first half of the year, export growth picked up significantly, especially in mineral products and the re-export of food products and chemical goods. In the January–September period, foreign direct investment (FDI) flows decreased due to declining reinvestment and other capital flows. However, FDI increased in the last quarter due to a greenfield investment in a plastic bottle plant in Klaipeda. The levels of net FDI per capita remain among the lowest in the EU.

## Outlook and risks

With continued strong internal demand, real GDP is projected to grow by more than 6 per cent in 2006. Medium-term growth prospects depend on Lithuania's ability to shift the basis of its competitiveness from cheap labour to value added. Also, the country needs to maintain fiscal discipline, control inflation and address its weak external position. Failure to do so would risk missing the Maastricht criteria and delaying accession to the European Monetary Union.

### Exports and industrial production growth year-on-year

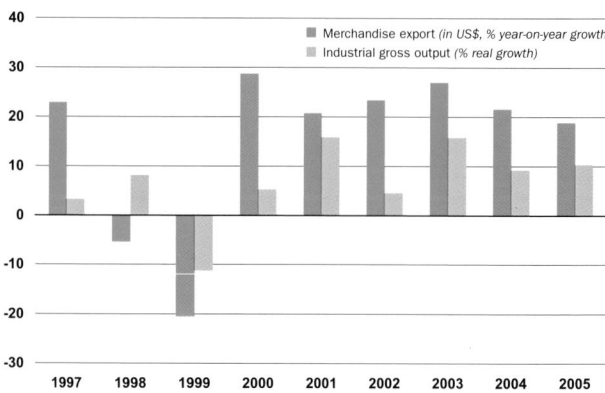

### Inflation, exchange rate developments and interest rates

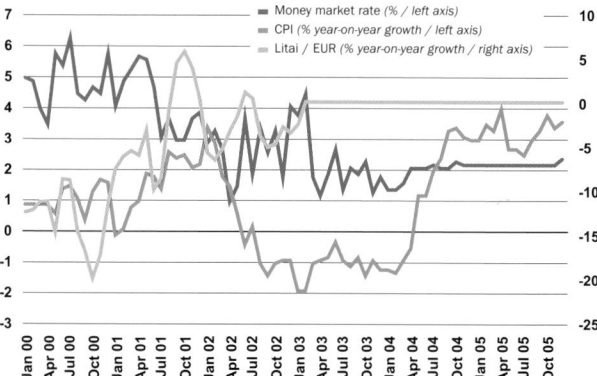

### Debt and fiscal balance

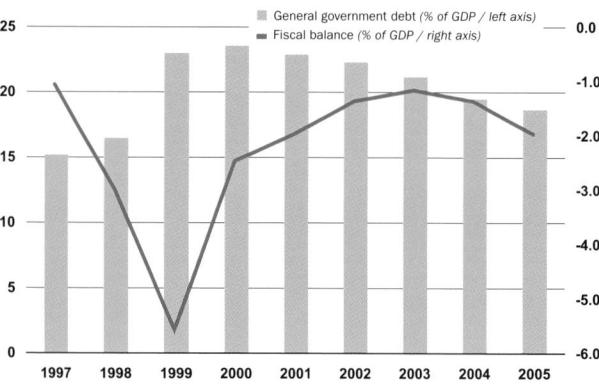

### Current account deficit and net FDI

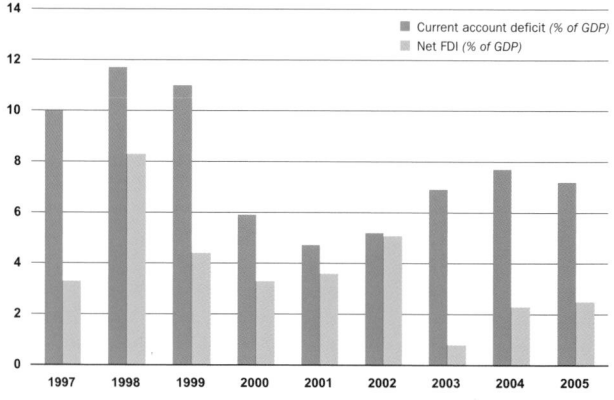

| | 2000 | 2001 | 2002 | 2003 | 2004 | 2005 Estimate | 2006 Projection |
|---|---|---|---|---|---|---|---|
| **Output and expenditure** | | | *(Percentage change in real terms)* | | | | |
| GDP | 4.7 | 6.4 | 6.8 | 10.5 | 7.0 | 7.5 | 6.2 |
| Private consumption | 5.9 | 3.7 | 5.8 | 11.1 | 9.7 | na | na |
| Public consumption | 4.5 | 0.7 | 1.4 | 3.8 | 7.5 | na | na |
| Gross fixed capital formation | -9.0 | 13.5 | 8.7 | 11.4 | 12.3 | 13.0 | na |
| Exports of goods and services | 9.9 | 21.2 | 19.5 | 6.9 | 4.2 | 13.0 | na |
| Imports of goods and services | 4.8 | 17.6 | 17.7 | 10.3 | 14.8 | 11.0 | na |
| Industrial gross output | 5.3 | 15.9 | 4.6 | 15.8 | 9.3 | 10.4 | na |
| Agricultural gross output | 0.9 | -5.0 | 7.9 | 7.7 | -0.8 | na | na |
| **Employment** [1] | | | *(Percentage change)* | | | | |
| Labour force (end-year) | -2.0 | -2.1 | -0.3 | 0.7 | -1.3 | na | na |
| Employment (end-year) | -4.0 | -3.3 | 4.0 | 2.3 | -0.1 | 3.9 | na |
| | | | *(In per cent of labour force)* | | | | |
| Unemployment (end-year) | 16.4 | 17.4 | 13.8 | 12.4 | 11.4 | 7.2 | na |
| **Prices and wages** | | | *(Percentage change)* | | | | |
| Consumer prices (annual average) | 1.0 | 1.5 | 0.3 | -1.2 | 1.2 | 2.7 | 2.8 |
| Consumer prices (end-year) | 1.5 | 2.1 | -1.0 | -1.3 | 2.9 | 3.5 | 2.5 |
| Producer prices (annual average) | 16.0 | -3.0 | -2.8 | -0.5 | 6.0 | na | na |
| Producer prices (end-year) | 2.6 | -7.8 | 1.9 | -0.2 | 6.8 | 13.5 | na |
| Gross average monthly earnings in economy (annual average) | -1.5 | 1.4 | 3.2 | 4.1 | 8.5 | 15.8 | na |
| **Government sector** | | | *(In per cent of GDP)* | | | | |
| General government balance | -2.5 | -2.0 | -1.4 | -1.2 | -1.4 | -2.0 | -1.8 |
| General government expenditure [2] | 32.7 | 31.0 | 30.6 | 31.1 | 31.9 | 30.5 | na |
| General government debt | 24.3 | 23.4 | 22.8 | 21.9 | 19.5 | 17.5 | na |
| **Monetary sector** | | | *(Percentage change)* | | | | |
| Broad money (M2, end-year) | 16.5 | 21.4 | 16.9 | 18.2 | 24.1 | 32.9 | na |
| Domestic credit (end-year) | 1.7 | 13.7 | 22.3 | 42.4 | 41.0 | 61.6 | na |
| | | | *(In per cent of GDP)* | | | | |
| Broad money (M2, end-year) | 22.8 | 26.1 | 28.6 | 30.9 | 34.9 | 40.9 | na |
| **Interest and exchange rates** | | | *(In per cent per annum, end-year)* | | | | |
| Interbank interest rate | 10.4 | 5.5 | 10.0 | 4.3 | 3.0 | 3.3 | na |
| Treasury bill rate (3-month maturity) | 5.9 | 4.8 | 3.3 | 2.5 | 2.1 | na | na |
| Deposit rate [3] | 1.0 | 0.8 | 0.3 | 0.2 | 0.2 | na | na |
| Lending rate [4] | 10.7 | 8.1 | 6.1 | 5.1 | 5.6 | 4.7 | na |
| | | | *(Litai per US dollar)* | | | | |
| Exchange rate (end-year) | 4.0 | 4.0 | 3.3 | 2.7 | 2.5 | 2.8 | na |
| Exchange rate (annual average) | 4.0 | 4.0 | 3.7 | 3.1 | 2.8 | 2.7 | na |
| **External sector** | | | *(In millions of US dollars)* | | | | |
| Current account | -675 | -574 | -734 | -1,278 | -1,724 | -1,875 | -1,957 |
| Trade balance | -1,104 | -1,108 | -1,337 | -1,704 | -2,382 | -2,421 | -2,758 |
| Merchandise exports | 4,050 | 4,889 | 6,031 | 7,658 | 9,305 | 11,056 | 11,015 |
| Merchandise imports | 5,154 | 5,997 | 7,368 | 9,363 | 11,688 | 13,477 | 13,773 |
| Foreign direct investment, net [5] | 375 | 439 | 714 | 142 | 510 | 655 | 667 |
| Gross reserves, excluding gold (end-year) | 1,359 | 1,669 | 2,413 | 3,450 | 3,594 | 3,816 | na |
| External debt stock [6] | 4,857 | 5,268 | 6,199 | 8,338 | 10,472 | 11,409 | na |
| | | | *(In months of imports of goods and services)* | | | | |
| Gross reserves, excluding gold (end-year) | 2.8 | 3.0 | 3.5 | 3.9 | 3.2 | 3.0 | na |
| | | | *(In per cent of exports of goods and services)* | | | | |
| Debt service | 20.5 | 15.5 | 39.1 | 19.6 | 16.6 | 16.5 | na |
| **Memorandum items** | | | *(Denominations as indicated)* | | | | |
| Population (end-year, million) | 3.5 | 3.5 | 3.5 | 3.5 | 3.4 | 3.4 | na |
| GDP (in millions of litai) | 45,848 | 48,563 | 51,948 | 56,772 | 62,440 | 70,763 | 77,255 |
| GDP per capita (in US dollars) | 3,260 | 3,478 | 4,068 | 5,360 | 6,518 | 7,568 | na |
| Share of industry in GDP (in per cent) | 26.3 | 27.3 | 26.4 | 28.3 | 29.4 | na | na |
| Share of agriculture in GDP (in per cent) | 7.0 | 6.3 | 6.3 | 5.8 | 5.3 | na | na |
| Current account/GDP (in per cent) | -5.9 | -4.7 | -5.2 | -6.9 | -7.7 | -7.2 | -7.0 |
| External debt - reserves (in US$ million) | 3,498 | 3,599 | 3,786 | 4,888 | 6,878 | 7,593 | na |
| External debt/GDP (in per cent) | 42.4 | 43.4 | 43.8 | 44.9 | 46.6 | 44.0 | na |
| External debt/exports of goods and services (in per cent) | 95.1 | 87.1 | 82.5 | 87.4 | 89.1 | 82.9 | na |

[1] Data from population census.
[2] General government expenditure includes net lending.
[3] Average interest rate on demand deposits in litai.

[4] Average interest rate on loans in litai.
[5] Covers equity capital and reinvested earnings.
[6] Includes non-resident currency and deposits and loans to foreign subsidiaries.

# Moldova

## Economic performance and prospects

The economy continues to perform well, supported by strong exports, but the country continues to depend on remittances from abroad.

Reforms aimed at improving the business environment and corporate governance are required to reduce external vulnerabilities and strengthen competitiveness.

### Real economy

The economy has maintained its momentum, growing by 7.1 per cent in 2005. The main impetus came from the booming retail trade and construction sectors, as well as growing external demand for Moldovan agricultural produce. Industrial production increased substantially in the second half of 2005, leading to full-year output growth of 6.3 per cent. On the demand side, investment was the main driver of growth, supported by strong private consumption fuelled by rising credit and remittances.

### Economic policies

The rise in energy costs and large inflows of foreign exchange have undermined the single-digit inflation objective of the National Bank of Moldova (NBM). The exchange rate depreciated by 3 per cent against the US dollar in 2005, reflecting high imports and large foreign currency reserve accumulation. The NBM was active on the foreign exchange market, purchasing substantial amounts of foreign exchange to prevent currency appreciation, maintain competitiveness and contain inflation. The consolidated budget recorded a modest 0.2 per cent surplus in 2005, due mainly to higher revenues from indirect taxes on products.

### External sector

Despite growing barriers to Moldovan products in the main export market of Russia, export growth continued in 2005, driven by exports of agricultural products and textiles to the EU and other transition countries. Nevertheless, import growth substantially outpaced the increases in exports and the trade deficit exceeded US$1 billion in 2005. The NBM estimated a significant increase in remittances in 2005, while reinvested earnings of foreign companies maintained net foreign direct investment levels above 5 per cent of GDP. The external debt stock at the end of 2005 remained at just below US$2 billion.

### Outlook and risks

The recent deterioration of economic relations with Russia, which has led to export barriers and higher energy prices, has highlighted the need for economic diversification in Moldova. In the absence of substantial productivity gains, economic growth in the short term could be hindered by rising energy costs and the inability to diversify export markets. Additionally, prudent macroeconomic policies and restructuring of the bilateral debt could contain the external debt burden. Long-term prospects, however, will depend on the effective implementation of the reform agenda outlined in the Economic Growth and Poverty Reduction Strategy and the EU-Moldova Action Plan. Durable growth depends on improvements in the competitiveness of Moldovan products and successful diversification of export markets.

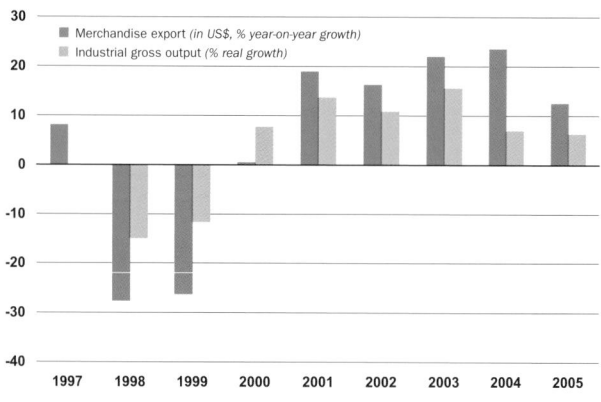

**Exports and industrial production growth year-on-year**

- Merchandise export *(in US$, % year-on-year growth)*
- Industrial gross output *(% real growth)*

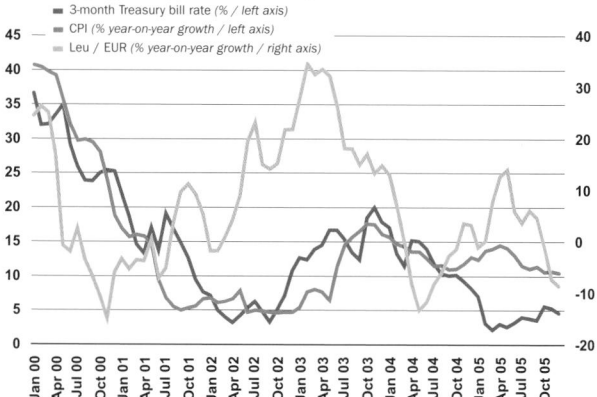

**Inflation, exchange rate developments and interest rates**

- 3-month Treasury bill rate *(% / left axis)*
- CPI *(% year-on-year growth / left axis)*
- Leu / EUR *(% year-on-year growth / right axis)*

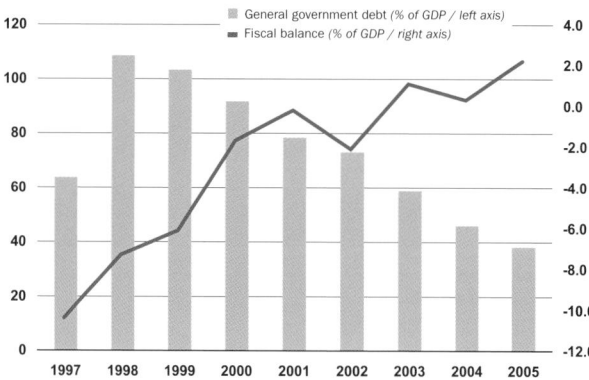

**Debt and fiscal balance**

- General government debt *(% of GDP / left axis)*
- Fiscal balance *(% of GDP / right axis)*

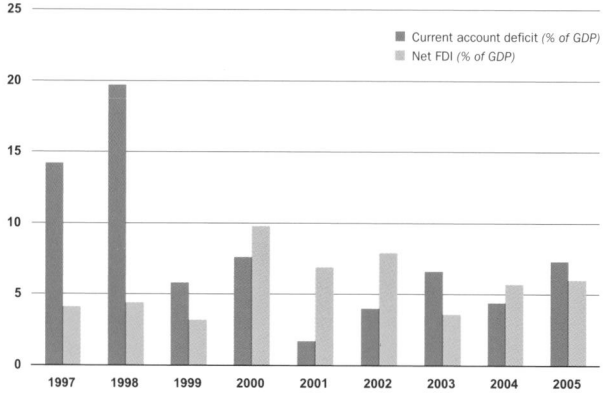

**Current account deficit and net FDI**

- Current account deficit *(% of GDP)*
- Net FDI *(% of GDP)*

|  | 2000 | 2001 | 2002 | 2003 | 2004 | 2005 Estimate | 2006 Projection |
|---|---|---|---|---|---|---|---|
| **Output and expenditure** | | | | *(Percentage change in real terms)* | | | |
| GDP | 2.1 | 6.1 | 7.8 | 6.6 | 7.3 | 7.1 | 5.5 |
| Private consumption | 27.6 | 6.1 | 5.9 | 18.5 | 6.9 | na | na |
| Public consumption | -17.9 | -5.8 | 31.4 | 3.2 | -17.5 | na | na |
| Gross fixed capital formation | -0.7 | 5.2 | 1.1 | 13.5 | 3.4 | na | na |
| Exports of goods and services | 6.8 | 15.7 | 18.9 | 19.2 | 4.7 | na | na |
| Imports of goods and services | 29.8 | 11.1 | 15.8 | 28.7 | -1.7 | na | na |
| Industrial gross output | 7.7 | 13.7 | 10.8 | 15.6 | 6.9 | 6.3 | na |
| Agricultural gross output | -3.3 | 6.4 | 3.4 | -13.6 | 20.4 | na | na |
| **Employment** | | | | *(Percentage change)* | | | |
| Labour force (end-year) | -1.7 | -2.3 | -0.1 | -8.8 | -3.3 | -2.2 | na |
| Employment (end-year) | 1.4 | -1.0 | 0.4 | -9.9 | -3.4 | -0.6 | na |
|  | | | | *(In per cent of labour force)* | | | |
| Unemployment (end-year) [1] | 8.5 | 7.3 | 6.8 | 7.9 | 8.0 | 6.4 | na |
| **Prices and wages** | | | | *(Percentage change)* | | | |
| Consumer prices (annual average) | 31.1 | 9.6 | 5.2 | 11.6 | 12.5 | 12.0 | 10.2 |
| Consumer prices (end-year) | 18.4 | 6.3 | 4.4 | 15.7 | 12.5 | 10.2 | 10.5 |
| Producer prices (annual average) | 28.5 | 12.3 | 4.7 | 7.8 | 5.6 | 5.9 | na |
| Producer prices (end-year) | 24.3 | 5.7 | 6.7 | 9.2 | 4.9 | 7.0 | na |
| Gross average monthly earnings in economy (annual average) | 33.9 | 33.3 | 27.2 | 28.8 | 23.8 | 19.7 | na |
| **Government sector** | | | | *(In per cent of GDP)* | | | |
| General government balance [2] | -1.8 | -0.3 | -2.2 | 1.0 | 0.2 | 2.1 | -0.9 |
| General government expenditure [2] | 34.5 | 29.4 | 31.5 | 33.1 | 35.2 | 37.9 | na |
| General government debt [3] | 91.7 | 78.4 | 73.1 | 58.9 | 46.0 | 38.2 | na |
| **Monetary sector** | | | | *(Percentage change)* | | | |
| Broad money (M2, end-year) | 39.0 | 37.8 | 30.4 | 24.4 | 44.7 | 36.7 | na |
| Domestic credit (end-year) | 14.4 | 29.6 | 25.2 | 24.3 | 25.8 | 20.4 | na |
|  | | | | *(In per cent of GDP)* | | | |
| Broad money (M2, end-year) | 15.7 | 18.2 | 20.0 | 20.4 | 25.4 | 30.3 | na |
| **Interest and exchange rates** | | | | *(In per cent per annum, end-year)* | | | |
| Refinancing rate | 27.0 | 13.0 | 9.5 | 14.0 | 14.5 | 12.5 | na |
| Interbank interest rate (up to 30-day maturity) | 20.3 | 10.8 | 7.5 | 13.0 | 13.3 | 5.8 | na |
| Deposit rate (1 year) | 24.6 | 20.6 | 14.4 | 12.7 | 15.2 | 13.2 | na |
| Lending rate (1 year) | 33.3 | 28.5 | 23.1 | 19.2 | 21.0 | 19.3 | na |
|  | | | | *(Lei per US dollar)* | | | |
| Exchange rate (end-year) | 12.4 | 13.1 | 13.8 | 13.2 | 12.5 | 12.8 | na |
| Exchange rate (annual average) | 12.4 | 12.9 | 13.6 | 13.9 | 12.3 | 12.6 | na |
| **External sector** | | | | *(In millions of US dollars)* | | | |
| Current account | -98 | -25 | -67 | -130 | -113 | -213 | -201 |
| Trade balance | -294 | -313 | -378 | -623 | -758 | -1,140 | -1,424 |
| Merchandise exports | 477 | 567 | 660 | 805 | 995 | 1,119 | 1,287 |
| Merchandise imports | 770 | 880 | 1,038 | 1,429 | 1,754 | 2,259 | 2,711 |
| Foreign direct investment, net | 127 | 102 | 132 | 71 | 148 | 175 | 150 |
| Gross reserves, excluding gold (end-year) | 222 | 229 | 269 | 302 | 470 | 597 | na |
| External debt stock | 1,721 | 1,675 | 1,815 | 1,925 | 1,924 | 1,950 | na |
|  | | | | *(In months of imports of goods and services)* | | | |
| Gross reserves, excluding gold (end-year) | 2.7 | 2.5 | 2.5 | 2.1 | 2.6 | 2.7 | na |
|  | | | | *(In per cent of exports of goods and services)* | | | |
| Debt service | 16.8 | 13.4 | 13.8 | 12.2 | 8.5 | 4.1 | na |
| **Memorandum items** | | | | *(Denominations as indicated)* | | | |
| Population (end-year, million) [4] | 3.6 | 3.6 | 3.6 | 3.6 | 3.4 | 3.4 | na |
| GDP (in millions of lei) | 16,020 | 19,052 | 22,556 | 27,619 | 31,992 | 36,755 | 42,732 |
| GDP per capita (in US dollars) | 353 | 407 | 458 | 547 | 766 | 862 | na |
| Share of industry in GDP (in per cent) | 19.0 | 21.8 | 20.2 | 20.9 | 20.5 | na | na |
| Share of agriculture in GDP (in per cent) | 25.4 | 22.4 | 21.0 | 19.1 | 18.2 | na | na |
| Current account/GDP (in per cent) | -7.6 | -1.7 | -4.0 | -6.6 | -4.4 | -7.3 | -6.0 |
| External debt - reserves (in US$ million) | 1,498 | 1,447 | 1,546 | 1,622 | 1,454 | 1,353 | na |
| External debt/GDP (in per cent) | 133.6 | 113.1 | 109.2 | 97.2 | 74.2 | 66.8 | na |
| External debt/exports of goods and services (in per cent) | 268.3 | 226.9 | 207.1 | 181.7 | 146.1 | 126.8 | na |

[1]  According to ILO methodology.
[2]  General government includes the state, local government, social security and healthcare.
[3]  Includes public and publicly guaranteed debt.
[4]  Excludes Transnistria

# Poland

## Economic performance and prospects

Despite strong economic growth in 2005, unemployment remains high and the fiscal deficit is large.

The medium-term outlook remains positive, provided that the government takes robust measures to curb the fiscal deficit and further improve the business environment.

## Real economy

Real GDP growth slowed to 3.2 per cent in 2005, down from 5.3 per cent in 2004. It did pick up in the last quarter of 2005, however, reaching 4 per cent year-on-year. Growth was driven mainly by a net increase in exports, although investment and consumption demand rose during the last three months of the year. Falling unemployment, improved retail sales and rising industrial production may herald GDP growth of around 4.5 per cent in 2006. Although the unemployment rate declined in 2005, it was 18 per cent of the labour force in February 2006, the highest level in the EU.

## Economic policies

Despite the economic slowdown, the general government deficit fell to an estimated 2.9 per cent of GDP in 2005 from 3.8 per cent in 2004 (according to ESA95 methodology which allows for the exclusion of some pension costs from the general budget). Public debt and guarantees reached around 47.5 per cent of GDP in 2005 (according to the same methodology). Annual consumer price inflation declined to 0.7 per cent in February 2006, well below the 2.5 per cent target rate of the National Bank of Poland. Between March 2005 and February 2006, the Monetary Policy Council reduced the policy rate in seven steps to 4 per cent, a historical low, down from 6.5 per cent.

## External sector

Strong export growth (particularly in services) and a stable inflow of transfers kept the current account deficit at around 1.6 per cent of GDP in 2005, compared with 4.1 per cent in 2004. On the capital account, portfolio inflows continued to dominate. Although below 2004 levels, foreign direct investment (FDI) reached around 2.8 per cent of GDP in 2005, supported by stronger economic growth and EU membership. External debt stabilised below 50 per cent of GDP, and international reserves remained above four months of imports of goods and services. The current account deficit was covered comfortably by inflows of FDI, complemented by sizeable portfolio inflows.

## Outlook and risks

Given further improvements in key infrastructure sectors and the business environment, the outlook remains positive. However, a number of risks remain. In the short term, the fiscal stance of the new minority government is unclear, particularly regarding the uncertain costs of planned social welfare measures promised in the election campaign. Also, foreign residents hold more than 40 per cent of government debt and portfolio inflows are substantial. Fiscal reforms will therefore be crucial to reduce the risk of volatility in the exchange rate and a destabilisation of the economy.

### Exports and industrial production growth year-on-year

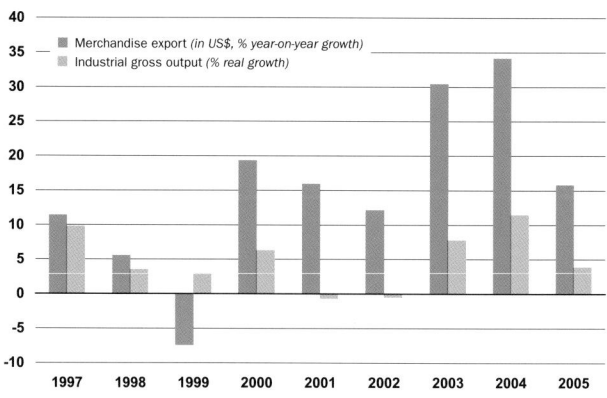

### Inflation, exchange rate developments and interest rates

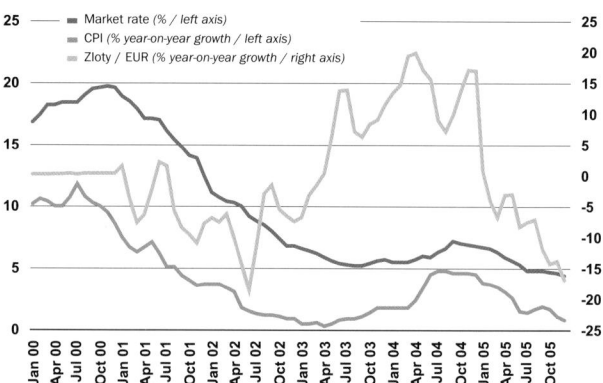

### Debt and fiscal balance

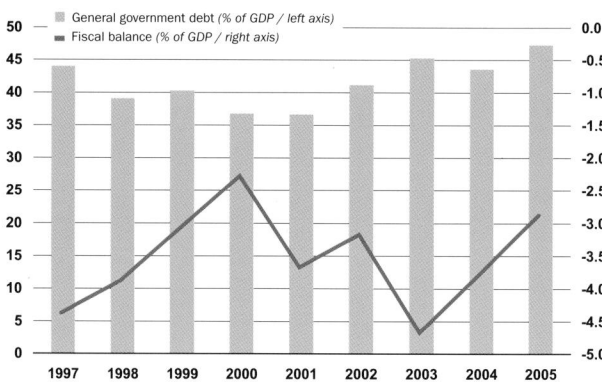

### Current account deficit and net FDI

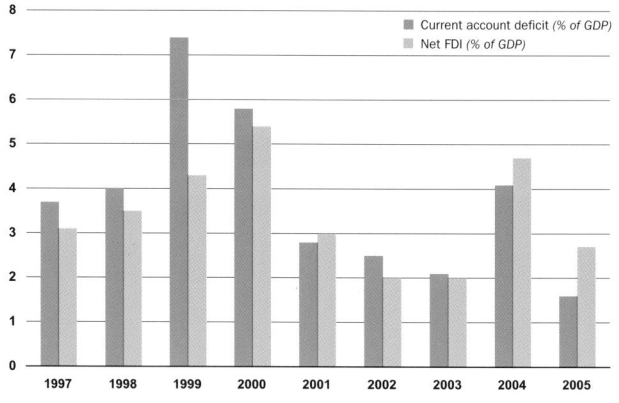

| | 2000 | 2001 | 2002 | 2003 | 2004 | 2005 Estimate | 2006 Projection |
|---|---|---|---|---|---|---|---|
| **Output and expenditure** | | | | *(Percentage change in real terms)* | | | |
| GDP | 4.2 | 1.1 | 1.4 | 3.8 | 5.3 | 3.2 | 4.5 |
| Private consumption | 3.0 | 2.2 | 3.3 | 1.9 | 4.0 | 2.3 | na |
| Public consumption | 2.4 | 2.5 | 1.5 | 4.7 | 3.9 | 2.2 | na |
| Gross fixed capital formation | 2.7 | -9.7 | -6.3 | -0.1 | 6.3 | 1.1 | na |
| Exports of goods and services | 23.2 | 3.1 | 4.8 | 14.2 | 14.0 | 10.0 | na |
| Imports of goods and services | 15.5 | -5.3 | 2.7 | 9.3 | 15.2 | 8.0 | na |
| Industrial gross output | 6.3 | -0.7 | -0.5 | 7.8 | 11.5 | 3.9 | na |
| Agricultural gross output | -4.1 | 6.6 | 1.0 | 2.7 | 6.0 | 0.0 | na |
| **Employment** | | | | *(Percentage change)* | | | |
| Labour force (end-year) | -6.1 | 1.8 | -2.9 | -3.4 | -2.0 | 0.3 | na |
| Employment (end-year) | -9.4 | -0.8 | -4.5 | -4.5 | -1.9 | 2.2 | na |
| | | | | *(In per cent of labour force)* | | | |
| Unemployment (end-year) | 16.4 | 18.5 | 19.8 | 19.2 | 19.1 | 17.6 | na |
| **Prices and wages** | | | | *(Percentage change)* | | | |
| Consumer prices (annual average) | 10.1 | 5.5 | 1.9 | 0.8 | 3.5 | 2.1 | 0.8 |
| Consumer prices (end-year) | 8.5 | 3.6 | 0.8 | 1.7 | 4.4 | 0.7 | 1.0 |
| Producer prices (annual average) | 7.9 | 1.9 | 1.1 | 2.6 | 7.3 | 0.8 | na |
| Producer prices (end-year) | 5.5 | -0.3 | 2.3 | 3.7 | 5.4 | 0.5 | na |
| Gross average monthly earnings in economy (annual average) | 12.7 | 7.2 | 3.5 | 3.2 | 4.0 | 4.0 | na |
| **Government sector** | | | | *(In per cent of GDP)* | | | |
| General government balance [1] | -2.3 | -3.7 | -3.2 | -4.7 | -3.8 | -2.9 | -3.2 |
| General government expenditure | 43.6 | 43.6 | 44.1 | 44.4 | 43.0 | 41.4 | na |
| General government debt [2] | 36.8 | 36.7 | 41.2 | 45.3 | 43.6 | 47.4 | na |
| **Monetary sector** | | | | *(Percentage change)* | | | |
| Broad money (M2, end-year) | 11.8 | 9.2 | -2.6 | 5.6 | 7.3 | 11.0 | na |
| Domestic credit (end-year) | 20.2 | 9.7 | 6.7 | 10.1 | 6.0 | 16.8 | na |
| | | | | *(In per cent of GDP)* | | | |
| Broad money (M2, end-year) | 40.3 | 42.1 | 39.6 | 40.1 | 39.3 | 41.8 | na |
| **Interest and exchange rates** | | | | *(In per cent per annum, end-year)* | | | |
| Rate on 28-day open market operations | 19.0 | 11.5 | 6.8 | 5.3 | 6.5 | 4.5 | na |
| 3-month WIBOR | 19.5 | 12.3 | 6.7 | 5.6 | 6.7 | 4.3 | na |
| Deposit rate | 14.3 | 7.9 | 4.2 | 2.9 | 3.8 | 2.8 | na |
| Lending rate | 21.5 | 16.2 | 11.6 | 9.6 | 10.4 | 8.6 | na |
| | | | | *(Zlotys per US dollar)* | | | |
| Exchange rate (end-year) | 4.3 | 4.0 | 3.9 | 3.8 | 3.0 | 3.3 | na |
| Exchange rate (annual average) | 4.3 | 4.1 | 4.1 | 3.9 | 3.7 | 3.2 | na |
| **External sector** | | | | *(In millions of US dollars)* | | | |
| Current account | -9,981 | -5,376 | -5,011 | -4,599 | -10,357 | -4,857 | -5,700 |
| Trade balance | -12,307 | -7,661 | -7,249 | -5,725 | -5,622 | -3,096 | -4,300 |
| Merchandise exports | 35,902 | 41,663 | 46,742 | 61,007 | 81,862 | 94,918 | 107,300 |
| Merchandise imports | 48,209 | 49,324 | 53,991 | 66,732 | 87,484 | 98,014 | 111,600 |
| Foreign direct investment, net | 9,327 | 5,804 | 3,901 | 4,284 | 11,826 | 8,177 | 8,400 |
| Gross reserves, excluding gold (end-year) | 27,466 | 26,564 | 29,794 | 34,168 | 36,783 | 44,408 | na |
| External debt stock | 69,463 | 71,971 | 84,875 | 106,961 | 128,266 | 140,000 | na |
| | | | | *(In months of imports of goods and services)* | | | |
| Gross reserves, excluding gold (end-year) | 5.8 | 5.5 | 5.7 | 5.3 | 4.4 | 4.8 | na |
| | | | | *(In per cent of exports of goods and services)* | | | |
| Debt service | 13.6 | 13.0 | 11.7 | 8.9 | 8.3 | 9.3 | na |
| **Memorandum items** | | | | *(Denominations as indicated)* | | | |
| Population (end-year, million) | 38.6 | 38.6 | 38.2 | 38.2 | 38.2 | 38.1 | na |
| GDP (in billions of zlotys) | 745 | 779 | 808 | 842 | 922 | 963 | 1,016 |
| GDP per capita (in US dollars) | 4,433 | 4,928 | 5,181 | 5,670 | 6,609 | 7,809 | na |
| Share of industry in GDP (in per cent) | 29.5 | 27.0 | 26.5 | 26.6 | 28.0 | 28.2 | na |
| Share of agriculture in GDP (in per cent) | 3.0 | 3.2 | 2.7 | 2.6 | 2.5 | 2.5 | na |
| Current account/GDP (in per cent) | -5.8 | -2.8 | -2.5 | -2.1 | -4.1 | -1.6 | -1.8 |
| External debt - reserves (in US$ million) | 41,997 | 45,407 | 55,081 | 72,793 | 91,483 | 95,592 | na |
| External debt/GDP (in per cent) | 40.5 | 37.8 | 42.9 | 49.4 | 50.8 | 47.0 | na |
| External debt/exports of goods and services (in per cent) | 150.0 | 140.0 | 149.5 | 148.2 | 134.5 | 125.8 | na |

[1] Calculated according to Eurostat methodology (ESA95), including private pension funds in the general government balance.

[2] Calculated according to Eurostat methodology (ESA95).

# Romania

## Economic performance and prospects

■ Although direct taxation has been reduced, the capital account liberalised and formal inflation targeting introduced, these measures have not been matched by appropriate economic policies.

■ Growth should continue, but widening domestic and external deficits and a lack of funds for major social sector reforms and investments in infrastructure pose risks.

## Real economy

Real growth slowed to 4.0 per cent in 2005, from a record rate of 8.3 per cent in 2004. Growth was driven by a 9.9 per cent year-on-year increase in private consumption and by a 8.1 per cent rise in investment. On the supply side, services grew by 8.1 per cent, agriculture contracted by 13.9 per cent and industrial production grew by 2.1 per cent.

## Economic policies

Disinflation was slower than expected, especially in view of the 15 per cent real appreciation of the currency in the first nine months of 2005. End-year inflation fell from 9.3 per cent in 2004 to 8.6 per cent in 2005. In August 2005 the monetary authorities moved from an exchange rate-based monetary framework to a formal inflation targeting regime. To prevent speculative short-term capital inflows and possible currency appreciation, the central bank cut the reference rate by a cumulative 1,375 basis points between June 2004 and December 2005. However, the currency continued to appreciate.

During the second and third reviews under the precautionary Stand-By Arrangement (SBA) with the IMF, an agreement was reached on a new 2005 budget deficit target of 0.7 per cent of GDP. The government subsequently increased the target to 1 per cent of GDP to deal with the costs of flood damage in 2005. The fiscal targets for 2005–06 were deemed unsuitable by the IMF, given the large and widening external deficit and the loss of competitiveness resulting from exchange rate appreciation and wage increases. These factors, among others, caused the IMF to declare that the SBA programme was off-track in October 2005. The consolidated general government deficit at the end of the year reached 0.8 per cent of GDP.

## External sector

The trade deficit contributed to a current account deficit of €6.9 billion in 2005, representing 9.3 per cent of GDP. Foreign direct investment covered 75 per cent of the current account deficit. International reserves reached record levels of €16.8 billion at the end of 2005, following significant central bank interventions in the foreign exchange market during the year.

## Outlook and risks

Economic growth is moderating in the run-up to EU membership, with private consumption fuelling an import boom. Reducing direct taxation, liberalising the capital account and introducing a formal inflation targeting regime pose new monetary and fiscal challenges.

### Exports and industrial production growth year-on-year

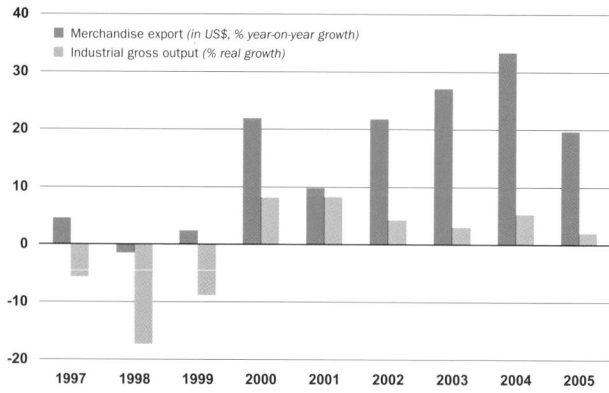

### Inflation, exchange rate developments and interest rates

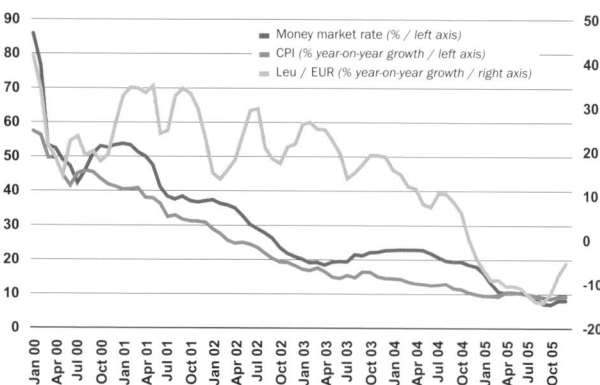

### Debt and fiscal balance

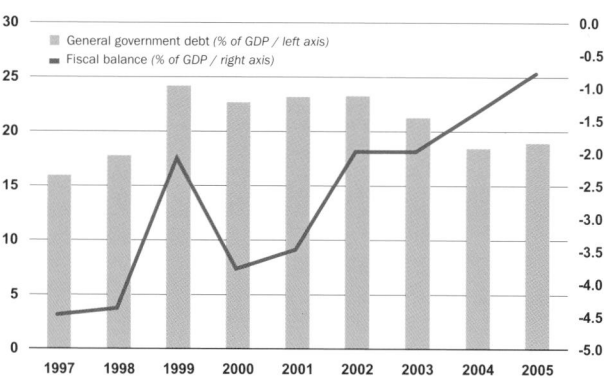

### Current account deficit and net FDI

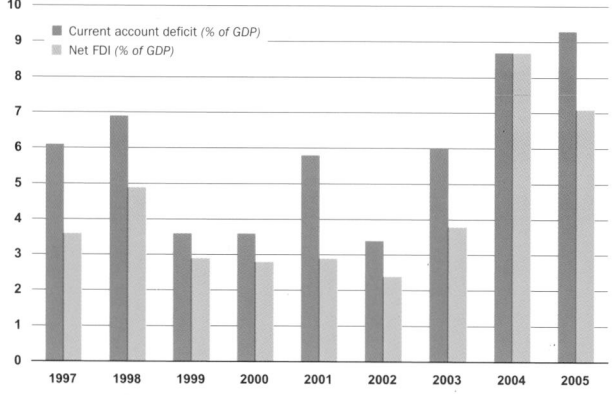

| | 2000 | 2001 | 2002 | 2003 | 2004 | 2005 Estimate | 2006 Projection |
|---|---|---|---|---|---|---|---|
| **Output and expenditure** | *(Percentage change in real terms)* | | | | | | |
| GDP [1] | 1.8 | 5.3 | 4.9 | 5.2 | 8.3 | 4.0 | 5.0 |
| Private consumption | 0.2 | 6.4 | 3.0 | 7.2 | 10.8 | 9.9 | na |
| Public consumption | 20.4 | -1.9 | 2.1 | 4.6 | 4.6 | 4.0 | na |
| Gross fixed capital formation | 4.6 | 6.6 | 8.3 | 9.1 | 10.1 | 8.1 | na |
| Exports of goods and services | 23.9 | 10.6 | 16.9 | 11.4 | 14.1 | 7.6 | na |
| Imports of goods and services | 29.1 | 17.5 | 12.1 | 16.4 | 17.8 | 17.2 | na |
| Industrial gross output, unadjusted series | 8.2 | 8.3 | 4.3 | 3.1 | 5.3 | 2.1 | na |
| Agricultural gross output | -14.1 | 22.7 | -3.5 | 3.0 | na | -13.9 | na |
| **Employment** | *(Percentage change)* | | | | | | |
| Labour force (end-year) | 0.2 | -1.2 | -12.0 | -1.6 | -10.7 | 0.1 | na |
| Employment (end-year) | -0.1 | -0.6 | -13.7 | -0.1 | -52.3 | 2.3 | na |
| | *(In per cent of labour force)* | | | | | | |
| Unemployment (end-year) [2] | 7.1 | 6.6 | 8.4 | 7.0 | 6.3 | 5.9 | na |
| **Prices and wages** | *(Percentage change)* | | | | | | |
| Consumer prices (annual average) | 45.7 | 34.5 | 22.5 | 15.3 | 11.9 | 9.5 | 7.5 |
| Consumer prices (end-year) | 40.7 | 30.3 | 17.8 | 14.1 | 9.3 | 8.6 | 6.5 |
| Producer prices (annual average) | 53.4 | 40.3 | 24.5 | 19.6 | 18.6 | 12.3 | na |
| Producer prices (end-year) | 50.3 | 32.6 | 20.1 | 20.0 | 16.3 | 10.4 | na |
| Gross average monthly earnings in economy (annual average) | 46.9 | 48.9 | 27.3 | 23.6 | 22.5 | 17.0 | na |
| **Government sector** | *(In per cent of GDP)* | | | | | | |
| General government balance [3] | -3.8 | -3.5 | -2.0 | -2.0 | -1.4 | -0.8 | -1.4 |
| General government expenditure | 34.8 | 33.4 | 32.3 | 32.1 | 30.5 | na | na |
| General government debt [3] | 22.7 | 23.2 | 23.3 | 21.3 | 18.5 | 19.0 | na |
| **Monetary sector** | *(Percentage change)* | | | | | | |
| Broad money (M2, end-year) | 38.0 | 46.2 | 38.1 | 23.3 | 39.9 | 33.9 | na |
| Domestic credit (end-year) | 11.4 | 26.9 | 39.8 | 50.4 | 21.2 | 49.7 | na |
| | *(In per cent of GDP)* | | | | | | |
| Broad money (M2, end-year) | 23.0 | 23.2 | 24.7 | 24.2 | 27.0 | 31.7 | na |
| **Interest and exchange rates** | *(In per cent per annum, end-year)* | | | | | | |
| Discount rate | 35.0 | 35.0 | 29.0 | 20.4 | 18.0 | 7.5 | na |
| 1-week BUBOR | 53.0 | 36.6 | 20.5 | 22.3 | 17.6 | 7.6 | na |
| Deposit rate (average) | 32.4 | 26.2 | 18.4 | 10.8 | 11.3 | 4.2 | na |
| Lending rate (average) | 53.2 | 45.7 | 36.7 | 26.2 | 25.8 | 15.7 | na |
| | *(Lei per US dollar)* | | | | | | |
| Exchange rate (end-year) [4] | 25.9 | 31.6 | 33.5 | 32.6 | 29.1 | 31.1 | na |
| Exchange rate (annual average) [4] | 21.7 | 29.1 | 33.1 | 33.2 | 32.6 | 29.1 | na |
| **External sector** | *(In millions of US dollars)* | | | | | | |
| Current account | -1,347 | -2,349 | -1,573 | -3,455 | -5,468 | -8,716 | -11,200 |
| Trade balance | -1,684 | -2,969 | -2,613 | -4,465 | -6,612 | -9,873 | -13,125 |
| Merchandise exports | 10,366 | 11,385 | 13,869 | 17,627 | 23,518 | 28,149 | 35,468 |
| Merchandise imports | 12,050 | 14,354 | 16,482 | 22,092 | 30,130 | 38,022 | 48,592 |
| Foreign direct investment, net | 1,051 | 1,154 | 1,080 | 2,156 | 5,020 | 5,230 | 4,480 |
| Gross reserves, excluding gold (end-year) | 2,497 | 3,960 | 6,145 | 8,050 | 14,806 | 20,994 | na |
| External debt stock | 10,673 | 12,399 | 16,021 | 20,621 | 26,500 | 32,510 | na |
| | *(In months of imports of goods and services)* | | | | | | |
| Gross reserves, excluding gold (end-year) | 2.1 | 2.9 | 3.9 | 3.9 | 5.2 | 5.8 | na |
| | *(In per cent of exports of goods and services)* | | | | | | |
| Debt service [5] | 25.9 | 21.1 | 18.9 | 16.3 | 18.6 | 18.2 | na |
| **Memorandum items** | *(Denominations as indicated)* | | | | | | |
| Population (end-year, million) | 22.4 | 22.4 | 21.8 | 21.7 | 21.7 | 21.7 | na |
| GDP (in billions of lei) [4] | 803,773 | 1,167,243 | 1,512,617 | 1,903,354 | 2,387,914 | 2,719,773 | 3,069,944 |
| GDP per capita (in US dollars) | 1,652 | 1,792 | 2,100 | 2,638 | 3,376 | 4,295 | na |
| Share of industry in GDP (in per cent) | 27.3 | 28.2 | 28.4 | 28.4 | na | na | na |
| Share of agriculture in GDP (in per cent) | 11.1 | 13.3 | 11.3 | 11.7 | na | na | na |
| Current account/GDP (in per cent) | -3.6 | -5.8 | -3.4 | -6.0 | -7.5 | -9.3 | -10.6 |
| External debt - reserves (in US$ million) | 8,176 | 8,439 | 9,877 | 12,571 | 11,694 | 11,516 | na |
| External debt/GDP (in per cent) | 28.8 | 30.9 | 35.0 | 36.0 | 36.2 | 34.8 | na |
| External debt/exports of goods and services (in per cent) | 88.1 | 93.0 | 98.9 | 99.9 | 97.7 | 98.2 | na |

[1] From 2001 growth rates are calculated by the National Statistical Institute using a new methodology that complies with European standards of national accounting.

[2] Officially registered unemployed. According to the ILO methodology, unemployment in Romania is lower than the official rate.

[3] Calculated according to Eurostat methodology (ESA95).

[4] The Romanian lei was redenominated in July 2005. Data are expressed in new lei.

[5] Debt service payments on private and public external debt.

# Russia

## Economic performance and prospects

- Economic growth is faltering despite strong household consumption and a recovery in investment.

- Long-term growth will need to be driven by productivity and innovation and will therefore depend on a revival of the liberal reform course.

## Real economy

Real GDP growth for 2005 was 6.4 per cent, below the levels registered in 2003 and 2004. There was, however, a slight recovery in the last quarter of the year. Growth has been driven by household consumption. This increased by about 11 per cent year-on-year, underpinned by the expansion of private incomes and credit to the private sector. Investment also continued to recover as uncertainty surrounding the Yukos renationalisation dissipated and as capacity constraints elsewhere became increasingly apparent. Industrial output was largely supported by manufacturing industries, despite the roughly 11 per cent appreciation in the real effective exchange rate.

## Economic policies

The federal budget recorded an estimated surplus of over 7 per cent of GDP in 2005, reflecting higher revenues from the natural resources sector. At the same time, the Stabilisation Fund recorded an increase in assets to over US$ 43 billion, following the repayment of IMF and Paris Club debt. By the end of 2005, inflation had eased. CPI inflation was at 10.9 per cent, the lowest level in seven years, but above the authorities' earlier target.

## External sector

High commodity prices raised the current account surplus to about 12 per cent of GDP in 2005. They also contributed to another record level of official foreign reserves (US$ 182 billion) by the end of the year. Despite lingering political uncertainties, gross foreign direct investment inflows to the non-financial sector reached a record US$ 16.7 billion in 2005. Private external transactions also recorded a net inflow over the year. With growth in exports (principally metals and hydrocarbons) expected to slow sharply in 2006 and imports continuing to increase, the rate of reserve accumulation and money growth will also decelerate. This will put further pressure on real interest rates.

## Outlook and risks

Despite continued high commodity prices, growth is expected to moderate in 2006. Medium-term prospects depend on whether the confidence of domestic and foreign investors can be revived, and whether capital formation, which is low compared with other emerging markets, can be stimulated. However, given the prospect of enduring high energy prices and the approaching presidential elections, incentives for further reforms to improve the investment climate are likely to be limited. The key risks to price stability are further fiscal loosening and the failure to adapt exchange rate policy to inflation objectives. The financial sector will need to play a key role in absorbing liquidity, and in allocating funds to the private sector.

### Exports and industrial production growth year-on-year

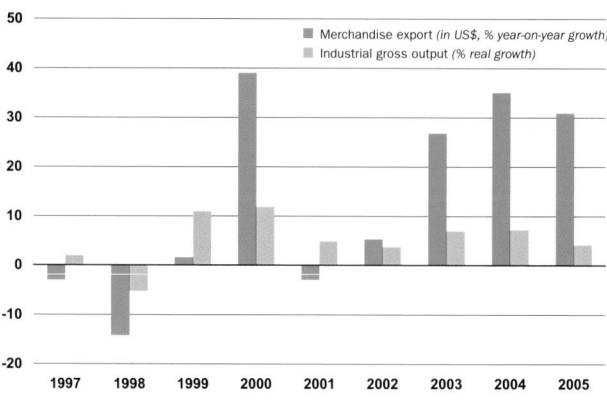

### Inflation, exchange rate developments and interest rates

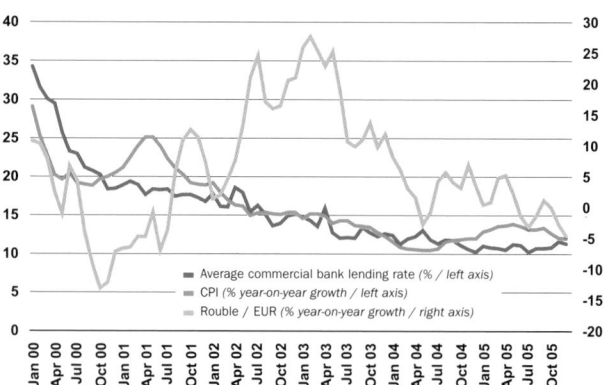

### Debt and fiscal balance

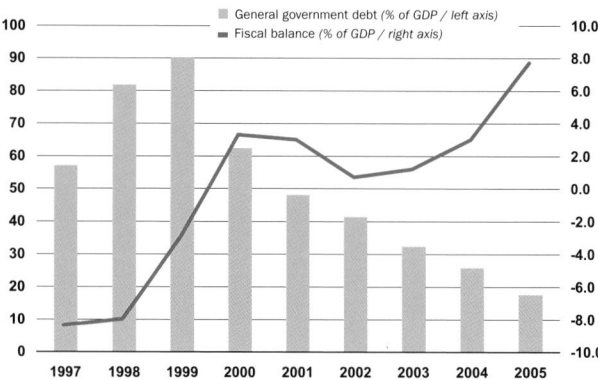

### Current account deficit and net FDI

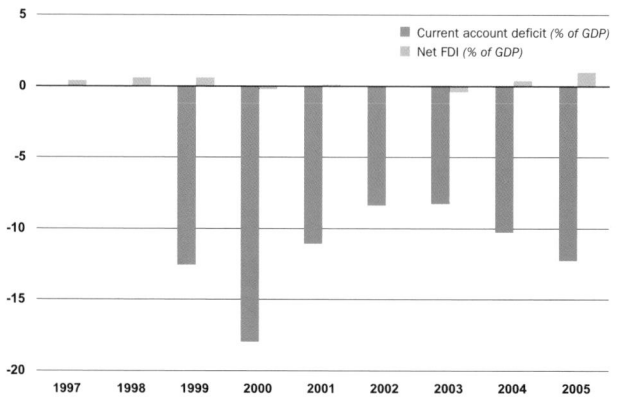

| | 2000 | 2001 | 2002 | 2003 | 2004 | 2005 Estimate | 2006 Projection |
|---|---|---|---|---|---|---|---|
| **Output and expenditure** | *(Percentage change in real terms)* | | | | | | |
| GDP | 10.0 | 5.1 | 4.7 | 7.3 | 7.1 | 6.4 | 5.5 |
| Private consumption | 7.3 | 10.1 | 8.5 | 7.5 | 11.6 | 11.1 | na |
| Public consumption | 1.9 | -0.8 | 2.6 | 2.2 | 2.1 | 1.8 | na |
| Gross fixed capital formation | 21.5 | 10.3 | 2.8 | 12.8 | 11.3 | 10.5 | na |
| Exports of goods and services | 9.4 | 4.2 | 10.3 | 12.5 | 11.9 | 5.6 | na |
| Imports of goods and services | 31.5 | 18.7 | 14.6 | 17.7 | 22.5 | 16.2 | na |
| Industrial gross output | 11.9 | 4.9 | 3.7 | 7.0 | 7.3 | 4.2 | na |
| Agricultural gross output | 7.7 | 7.5 | 1.5 | 1.5 | 2.9 | na | na |
| **Employment** | *(Percentage change)* | | | | | | |
| Labour force (end-year) | 0.4 | -1.9 | 1.1 | 0.8 | 1.5 | na | na |
| Employment (end-year) | 3.2 | -0.3 | 2.3 | 0.2 | 2.0 | na | na |
| | *(In per cent of labour force)* | | | | | | |
| Unemployment (end-year) | 10.2 | 8.7 | 8.8 | 8.6 | 8.5 | na | na |
| **Prices and wages** | *(Percentage change)* | | | | | | |
| Consumer prices (annual average) | 20.8 | 21.6 | 15.7 | 13.7 | 11.0 | 11.3 | 10.5 |
| Consumer prices (end-year) | 20.1 | 18.6 | 15.0 | 12.0 | 11.7 | 10.9 | 11.1 |
| Producer prices (annual average) | 46.6 | 19.2 | 14.0 | 15.6 | 24.0 | 21.9 | na |
| Producer prices (end-year) | 31.6 | 10.7 | 17.1 | 13.1 | 28.8 | 15.0 | na |
| Gross average monthly earnings in economy (annual average) | 42.5 | 45.7 | 34.5 | 24.8 | 24.0 | 20.9 | na |
| **Government sector** [1] | *(In per cent of GDP)* | | | | | | |
| General government balance | 3.2 | 2.9 | 0.6 | 1.1 | 2.9 | 7.6 | na |
| General government expenditure | 33.7 | 34.6 | 37.0 | 35.6 | 33.6 | 35.6 | na |
| General government debt | 62.5 | 48.2 | 41.4 | 32.4 | 25.9 | 17.7 | na |
| **Monetary sector** | *(Percentage change)* | | | | | | |
| Broad money (M2, end-year) | 62.4 | 40.9 | 32.4 | 50.5 | 35.8 | 39.0 | na |
| Domestic credit (end-year) | 12.1 | 27.0 | 26.5 | 26.5 | 18.9 | 13.5 | na |
| | *(In per cent of GDP)* | | | | | | |
| Broad money (M2, end-year) | 15.7 | 18.0 | 19.7 | 24.3 | 26.0 | 30.6 | na |
| **Interest and exchange rates** | *(In per cent per annum, end-year)* | | | | | | |
| Central Bank refinance rate (uncompounded) | 25.0 | 25.0 | 21.0 | 16.0 | 13.0 | 12.0 | na |
| Treasury bill rate (all maturities) | 18.2 | 14.7 | 15.0 | 4.5 | 4.5 | 3.9 | na |
| Deposit rate | 4.2 | 5.2 | 4.3 | 4.4 | 3.8 | 4.0 | na |
| Lending rate | 18.2 | 16.5 | 15.0 | 12.4 | 10.0 | 10.7 | na |
| | *(Roubles per US dollar)* | | | | | | |
| Exchange rate (end-year) | 28.2 | 30.1 | 31.8 | 29.5 | 27.9 | 28.4 | na |
| Exchange rate (annual average) | 28.1 | 29.2 | 31.3 | 30.7 | 28.8 | 28.2 | na |
| **External sector** | *(In millions of US dollars)* | | | | | | |
| Current account | 46,839 | 33,934 | 29,116 | 35,845 | 59,936 | 86,600 | na |
| Trade balance | 60,171 | 48,120 | 46,335 | 60,493 | 87,145 | 123,700 | na |
| Merchandise exports | 105,033 | 101,884 | 107,301 | 135,929 | 183,452 | 240,000 | na |
| Merchandise imports | 44,862 | 53,764 | 60,966 | 75,436 | 96,307 | 116,300 | na |
| Foreign direct investment, net | -463 | 216 | -72 | -1,769 | 2,132 | 7,000 | na |
| International reserves, excluding gold (end-year) | 24,264 | 32,542 | 44,054 | 73,175 | 120,809 | 182,200 | na |
| External debt stock | 160,027 | 152,491 | 147,541 | 175,270 | 192,966 | 180,783 | na |
| | *(In months of imports of goods and services)* | | | | | | |
| International reserves, excluding gold (end-year) | 4.8 | 5.3 | 6.3 | 8.6 | 11.2 | 14.4 | na |
| | *(In per cent of exports of goods and services)* | | | | | | |
| Public debt service due | 10.3 | 15.2 | 11.7 | 12.6 | 9.2 | 13.2 | na |
| Public debt service paid | 10.3 | 15.2 | 11.7 | 12.6 | 9.2 | 13.2 | na |
| **Memorandum items** | *(Denominations as indicated)* | | | | | | |
| Population (end-year, million) | 145.2 | 144.4 | 145.2 | 144.9 | 144.9 | 144.1 | na |
| GDP (in billions of roubles) | 7,306 | 8,944 | 10,831 | 13,243 | 16,752 | 19,838 | 23,126 |
| GDP per capita (in US dollars) | 1,789 | 2,123 | 2,380 | 2,978 | 4,012 | 4,874 | na |
| Share of industry in GDP (in per cent) | 38.6 | 36.5 | 34.8 | 34.9 | 36.0 | na | na |
| Share of agriculture in GDP (in per cent) | 6.4 | 6.8 | 5.7 | 5.4 | 5.0 | na | na |
| Current account/GDP (in per cent) | 18.0 | 11.1 | 8.4 | 8.3 | 10.3 | 12.3 | na |
| External debt - reserves (in US$ million) | 135,763 | 119,949 | 103,487 | 102,095 | 72,157 | -1,417 | na |
| External debt/GDP (in per cent) | 61.6 | 49.7 | 42.7 | 40.6 | 33.2 | 25.7 | na |
| External debt/exports of goods and services (in per cent) | 139.6 | 134.6 | 122.0 | 115.3 | 94.7 | 68.5 | na |

[1] General consolidated government includes the federal, regional and local
budgets and extra-budgetary funds, and excludes transfers.

# Serbia and Montenegro

## Economic performance and prospects

Growth remains strong but slowed slightly in 2005, while inflation (in Serbia) accelerated to worryingly high levels.

High public expenditure and the large current account deficit need to be addressed to ensure further development of the private sector.

## Real economy

The economy grew in 2005 by an estimated 5 per cent in real terms, below the rate in 2004 but above projections at the start of the year. Industrial production slowed significantly and agriculture declined relative to the previous year. However, other sectors such as transport, services and exports performed strongly. The improved business climate and rapid expansion of credit to the private sector are encouraging the development of small businesses.

## Economic policies

Macroeconomic policies in both republics have been guided by prudent fiscal and monetary policies. There are concerns, however, over high and rising inflation (in Serbia) and external imbalances. In Serbia annual inflation continued to rise during 2005, ending the year above 17 per cent. This prompted the central bank to raise reserve requirements on enterprise foreign exchange deposits several times, from 21 to 38 per cent. The exchange rate against the euro remained broadly stable in real terms, backed by comfortable levels of foreign reserves. Inflation was low in Montenegro where the euro remains the sole legal currency. On the fiscal side, both republics performed at or above target. In Serbia a revised budget for 2005 was passed by the parliament in July, envisaging a surplus for the full year of about 2 per cent of GDP. More recent estimates, however, suggest a slightly lower surplus. The IMF's three-year Extended Arrangement was completed in February 2006, fulfilling the condition for a further write-off of the country's debt to the Paris Club.

## External sector

The current account deficit declined in 2005. This reflected a much-improved performance of exports, which rose by an estimated 25 per cent in dollar terms. However, the deficit remains at an uncomfortably high level. On the capital account side, foreign direct investment rose to a record US$ 2.0 billion, including substantial investments in the Serbian banking sector and a couple of large privatisations in Montenegro. In July 2005 Serbia received an upgrade in its sovereign rating from Standard and Poor's, from B+ to BB–, putting it one level below Montenegro.

## Outlook and risks

The long-term future of the Serbian and Montenegrin economies looks bright, but the short to medium-term outlook is dampened by political uncertainty. The possibility of elections in Serbia, the forthcoming referendum in Montenegro on independence in May 2006, and talks over the future status of Kosovo may distract attention from urgent reforms to large enterprises and pension provision.

### Exports and industrial production growth year-on-year

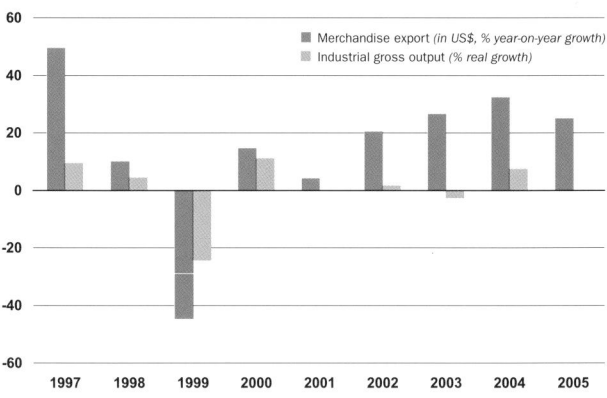

### Inflation, exchange rate developments and interest rates

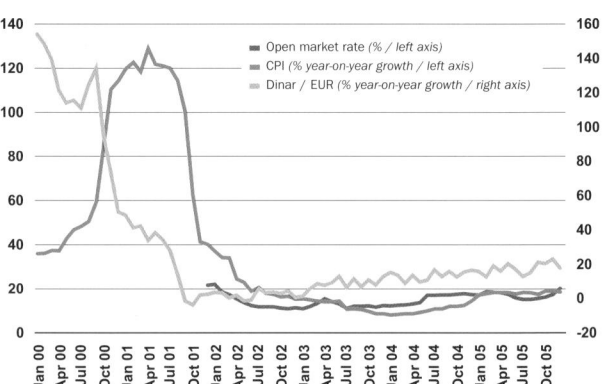

### Debt and fiscal balance

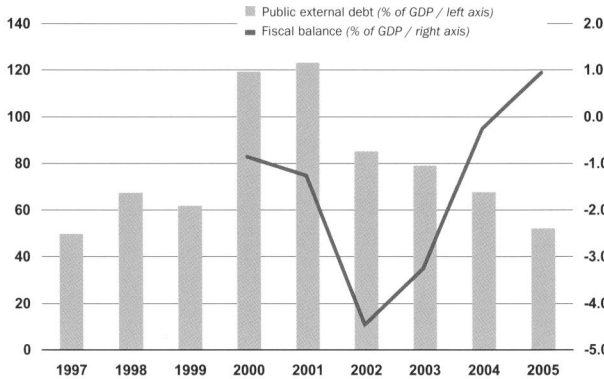

### Current account deficit and net FDI

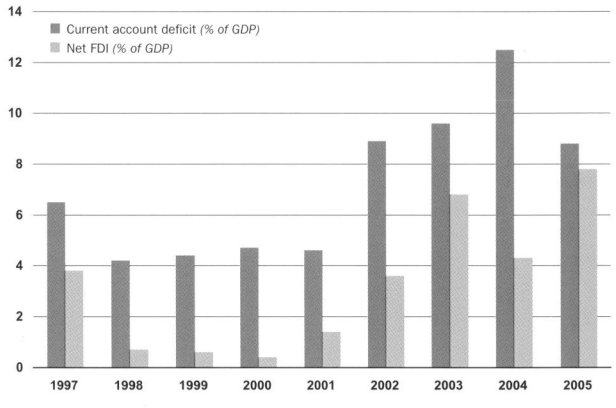

| | 2000 | 2001 | 2002 | 2003 | 2004 | 2005 Estimate | 2006 Projection |
|---|---|---|---|---|---|---|---|
| **Output and expenditure** | | | (Percentage change in real terms) | | | | |
| GDP | 5.0 | 5.5 | 3.8 | 2.7 | 7.2 | 5.0 | 5.0 |
| Industrial gross output | 11.1 | 0.0 | 1.7 | -2.7 | 7.5 | 0.0 | na |
| Agricultural gross output | -13.7 | 23.2 | 3.0 | -6.0 | 19.4 | na | na |
| **Employment** | | | (Percentage change) | | | | |
| Labour force (end-year) | -2.4 | 1.8 | 1.4 | 2.7 | -0.1 | na | na |
| Employment (end-year) | -2.6 | 0.2 | -1.7 | -1.3 | -0.1 | na | na |
| | | | (In per cent of labour force) | | | | |
| Unemployment (end-year) | 25.6 | 26.8 | 29.0 | 31.7 | 31.7 | na | na |
| **Prices and wages** | | | (Percentage change) | | | | |
| Consumer prices (annual average) | 60.4 | 91.1 | 21.2 | 11.3 | 9.5 | 17.2 | 11.4 |
| Consumer prices (end-year) | 113.5 | 39.0 | 14.2 | 7.6 | 13.4 | 17.5 | 10.9 |
| Producer prices (annual average) | 44.5 | na | na | na | na | na | na |
| Gross average monthly earnings in economy (annual average)[1] | 91.1 | 129.6 | 51.7 | 25.3 | 23.7 | 24.1 | na |
| **Government sector** | | | (In per cent of GDP) | | | | |
| General government balance | -0.9 | -1.3 | -4.5 | -3.3 | -0.3 | 0.9 | 2.3 |
| General government expenditure | 37.6 | 40.2 | 47.7 | 46.0 | 44.8 | 43.3 | na |
| **Monetary sector [2]** | | | (Percentage change) | | | | |
| Broad money (M2, end-year) | 58.5 | 67.6 | 73.4 | 26.7 | 30.3 | 32.8 | na |
| Domestic credit (end-year) | 58.2 | -54.3 | 48.6 | 6.4 | 61.9 | 41.7 | na |
| | | | (In per cent of GDP) | | | | |
| Broad money (M2, end-year) | 16.9 | 14.0 | 18.7 | 19.9 | 21.7 | 23.5 | na |
| **Interest and exchange rates** | | | (In per cent per annum, end-year) | | | | |
| Discount rate | 26.3 | 16.4 | 9.5 | 9.0 | 8.5 | 8.5 | na |
| Deposit rate | 8.3 | 4.1 | 2.6 | 2.7 | 3.6 | 3.7 | na |
| Lending rate (long-term) | 77.9 | 32.5 | 19.2 | 14.2 | 14.6 | 14.4 | na |
| | | | (Dinars per US dollar) | | | | |
| Exchange rate (official, end-year)[3] | 66.5 | 67.7 | 59.0 | 54.6 | 57.9 | 72.2 | na |
| Exchange rate (official, annual average) | 54.9 | 66.8 | 64.2 | 57.5 | 58.7 | 67.2 | na |
| **External sector** | | | (In millions of US dollars) | | | | |
| Current account | -327 | -528 | -1,384 | -1,996 | -3,016 | -2,275 | -2,913 |
| Trade balance | -1,788 | -2,834 | -3,908 | -4,887 | -7,344 | -6,422 | -6,730 |
| Merchandise exports | 1,923 | 2,003 | 2,412 | 3,054 | 4,044 | 5,055 | 6,082 |
| Merchandise imports | 3,711 | 4,837 | 6,320 | 7,941 | 11,388 | 11,477 | 12,812 |
| Foreign direct investment, net | 25 | 165 | 562 | 1,405 | 1,031 | 2,020 | 2,000 |
| Gross reserves, excluding gold (end-year) | 516 | 1,169 | 2,280 | 3,557 | 4,302 | 5,900 | na |
| External debt stock | 11,403 | 11,948 | 11,839 | 14,303 | 14,876 | 16,021 | na |
| | | | (In months of imports of goods and services) | | | | |
| Gross reserves, excluding gold (end-year) | 1.5 | 2.7 | 4.0 | 4.9 | 4.2 | 5.4 | na |
| | | | (In per cent of exports of goods and services) | | | | |
| Debt service | 2.2 | 3.9 | 5.6 | 10.8 | 17.1 | 24.4 | na |
| **Memorandum items** | | | (Denominations as indicated) | | | | |
| Population (end-year, million) | 8.3 | 8.3 | 8.3 | 8.3 | 8.3 | 8.3 | na |
| GDP (in billions of dinars) | 382 | 772 | 998 | 1,189 | 1,421 | 1,745 | 2,069 |
| GDP per capita (in US dollars) | 834 | 1,386 | 1,867 | 2,485 | 2,907 | 3,117 | na |
| Share of industry in GDP (in per cent) | na | na | na | na | na | na | na |
| Share of agriculture in GDP (in per cent) | na | na | na | na | na | na | na |
| Current account/GDP (in per cent) | -4.7 | -4.6 | -8.9 | -9.6 | -12.5 | -8.8 | -10.4 |
| External debt - reserves (in US$ million) | 10,887 | 10,779 | 9,559 | 10,746 | 10,574 | 10,121 | na |
| External debt/GDP (in per cent) | 164.0 | 103.5 | 76.1 | 69.1 | 61.4 | 61.7 | na |
| External debt/exports of goods and services (in per cent) | 447.7 | 435.6 | 365.3 | 341.8 | 261.4 | 227.5 | na |

[1]  Data refer to Serbia only.
[2]  Data refer to Serbia only.

[3]  The exchange rate regime was unified in December 2000. The unofficial rate in October 2000 was 30 dinars: 1 deutschmark (DM), compared with an official rate of 6 dinars: 1 DM.

# Slovak Republic

## Economic performance and prospects

■ Investment and household consumption continue
to support growth.

■ The immediate challenge is to reduce inflation and
the fiscal deficit to meet the EU Maastricht criteria.

## Real economy

Real GDP growth reached an estimated 6 per cent in 2005, even
higher than in 2004. Private consumption and fixed investment
strengthened appreciably throughout the year, and there was a
large rise in net exports in the second half of the year (following
the start of production at new automotive plants). Growth of
government consumption remained negligible.

## Economic policies

Fiscal performance in 2005 was better than expected, reflecting
high tax revenues and some expenditure savings. The general
government deficit, according to ESA95 methodology, was an
estimated 3.0 per cent of GDP in 2005 (excluding pension
costs). The cost of pension reform would add an extra 1 per cent
of GDP to the deficit. This will appear in the budget accounting
from 2007, following the conclusion of a transition period
granted by the EU. The Slovak Republic also aims to comply
with the Maastricht criteria at this time. These changes will
put pressure on the government to find alternative adjustment
measures to keep the fiscal deficit at the level required by the
Maastricht criteria.

The downward trend in inflation that resulted from strong
currency appreciation was partially reversed in late 2005
following increases in regulated prices in October. Inflation at
the end of the year was estimated at 3.4 per cent, compared
with 5.9 per cent at the end of 2004. Sound economic policies
enabled successful entry into the Exchange Rate Mechanism II
(ERM II) in November 2005. Adoption of the euro is planned for
January 2009.

## External sector

Despite a surge in exports at the end of the year, the current
account deficit reached an estimated 6 per cent of GDP in
2005, up from 3.5 per cent in 2004. This resulted from an
acceleration of private consumption and higher imports of
capital goods. However, net foreign direct investment (FDI)
inflows increased to an estimated US$ 1.7 billion in 2005
from US$ 1.3 billion in 2004. Net FDI inflows therefore covered
a large proportion of the current account deficit.

## Outlook and risks

Real growth is expected to stay at 5–6 per cent in 2006 and
over the medium term. However, pension costs and pending
elections during the year could pose some risks to the
government's fiscal adjustment strategy. Following accession to
the ERM II, the government's aim to join the eurozone in 2009
requires further fiscal consolidation and disinflation, as well as
structural reforms to increase the flexibility of the economy.

## Exports and industrial production growth year-on-year

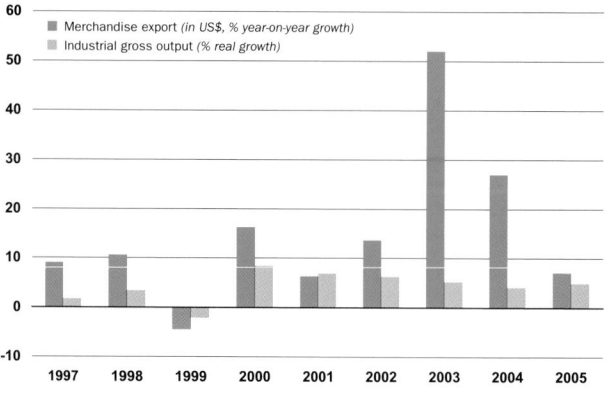

## Inflation, exchange rate developments and interest rates

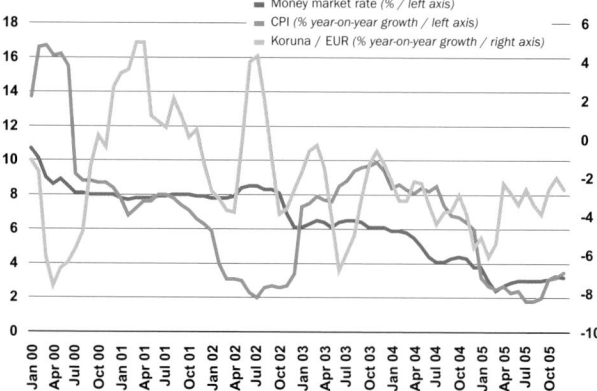

## Debt and fiscal balance

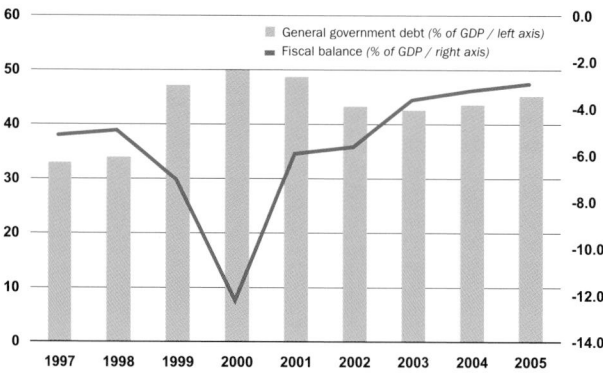

## Current account deficit and net FDI

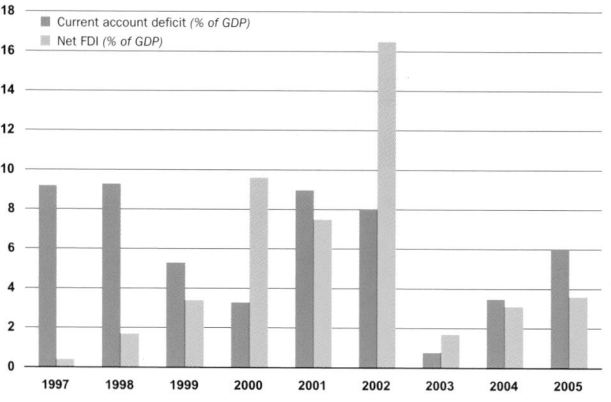

| | 2000 | 2001 | 2002 | 2003 | 2004 | 2005 Estimate | 2006 Projection |
|---|---|---|---|---|---|---|---|
| **Output and expenditure** | | | | *(Percentage change in real terms)* | | | |
| GDP | 2.0 | 3.8 | 4.6 | 4.5 | 5.5 | 6.0 | 6.0 |
| Private consumption | -0.8 | 4.7 | 5.5 | -0.8 | 3.5 | 5.8 | na |
| Public consumption | 1.6 | 4.6 | 4.9 | 2.7 | 1.2 | 2.0 | na |
| Gross fixed capital formation | -7.2 | 13.9 | -0.6 | -1.5 | 2.5 | 12.4 | na |
| Exports of goods and services | 13.7 | 6.3 | 5.6 | 22.5 | 11.4 | 10.9 | na |
| Imports of goods and services | 10.5 | 11.0 | 5.5 | 13.6 | 12.7 | 11.2 | na |
| Industrial gross output | 8.4 | 6.9 | 6.3 | 5.2 | 4.1 | 5.0 | na |
| Agricultural gross output | 3.2 | -4.0 | 10.9 | 4.4 | 1.2 | na | na |
| **Employment** | | | | *(Percentage change)* | | | |
| Labour force (end-year) | 2.0 | -10.6 | -0.5 | -0.1 | 1.9 | -0.7 | na |
| Employment (end-year) | -1.4 | -12.0 | 0.5 | 0.9 | 1.3 | 2.5 | na |
| | | | | *(In per cent of labour force)* | | | |
| Unemployment (end-year) | 17.9 | 19.2 | 18.5 | 17.5 | 17.9 | 15.3 | na |
| **Prices and wages** | | | | *(Percentage change)* | | | |
| Consumer prices (annual average) | 12.0 | 7.3 | 3.0 | 8.5 | 7.5 | 2.5 | 3.0 |
| Consumer prices (end-year) | 8.3 | 6.2 | 3.3 | 9.3 | 5.9 | 3.4 | 3.7 |
| Producer prices (annual average) | 9.8 | 6.6 | 2.1 | 8.3 | 2.6 | 5.3 | na |
| Producer prices (end-year) | 9.1 | 3.4 | 2.3 | 8.7 | 5.9 | 5.2 | na |
| Gross average monthly earnings in economy (annual average) | 6.5 | 8.2 | 9.3 | 6.3 | 10.2 | 9.2 | na |
| **Government sector** [1] | | | | *(In per cent of GDP)* | | | |
| General government balance [2] | -12.3 | -6.0 | -5.7 | -3.7 | -3.3 | -3.0 | -3.5 |
| General government expenditure | 59.9 | 51.5 | 50.9 | 39.2 | 48.0 | 37.3 | na |
| General government debt | 49.9 | 48.7 | 43.3 | 42.6 | 43.6 | 45.2 | na |
| **Monetary sector** | | | | *(Percentage change)* | | | |
| Broad money (M2, end-year) | 15.4 | 11.9 | 3.4 | 5.6 | 5.8 | 5.0 | na |
| Domestic credit (end-year) | 9.1 | 13.3 | -12.7 | 15.0 | 10.9 | 3.9 | na |
| | | | | *(In per cent of GDP)* | | | |
| Broad money (M2, end-year) | 61.3 | 72.1 | 64.0 | 61.8 | 59.3 | 57.3 | na |
| **Interest and exchange rates** | | | | *(In per cent per annum, end-year)* | | | |
| Refinancing rate | 8.0 | 7.8 | 6.5 | 6.0 | 4.0 | 3.0 | na |
| 3-month BRIBOR | 7.9 | 7.8 | 6.0 | 6.0 | 3.7 | na | na |
| Deposit rate [3] | 5.6 | 4.8 | 3.5 | 3.0 | 2.0 | na | na |
| Lending rate [3] | 10.8 | 9.8 | 8.8 | 7.2 | 7.4 | na | na |
| | | | | *(Korunas per US dollar)* | | | |
| Exchange rate (end-year) | 48.6 | 48.2 | 41.1 | 33.6 | 28.5 | 31.9 | na |
| Exchange rate (annual average) | 46.2 | 48.4 | 45.3 | 36.8 | 32.3 | 31.0 | na |
| **External sector** | | | | *(In millions of US dollars)* | | | |
| Current account | -713 | -1,756 | -1,939 | -276 | -1,447 | -2,780 | -1,750 |
| Trade balance | -917 | -2,135 | -2,131 | -637 | -1,456 | -1,700 | -2,000 |
| Merchandise exports | 11,870 | 12,632 | 14,365 | 21,843 | 27,754 | 29,750 | 38,000 |
| Merchandise imports | 12,786 | 14,766 | 16,497 | 22,480 | 29,210 | 31,450 | 40,000 |
| Foreign direct investment, net | 2,058 | 1,460 | 4,007 | 549 | 1,259 | 1,650 | 2,000 |
| Gross reserves, excluding gold (end-year) | 4,077 | 4,189 | 9,196 | 12,149 | 14,913 | 15,700 | na |
| External debt stock | 10,804 | 11,269 | 13,188 | 18,090 | 23,695 | 27,000 | na |
| | | | | *(In months of imports of goods and services)* | | | |
| Gross reserves, excluding gold (end-year) | 3.4 | 3.0 | 5.9 | 5.7 | 5.5 | 5.4 | na |
| | | | | *(In per cent of exports of goods and services)* | | | |
| Debt service due | 17.4 | 19.5 | 11.7 | 11.6 | 2.9 | 3.6 | na |
| **Memorandum items** | | | | *(Denominations as indicated)* | | | |
| Population (end-year, million) | 5.4 | 5.4 | 5.4 | 5.4 | 5.4 | 5.4 | na |
| GDP (in billions of korunas) | 992 | 944 | 1,099 | 1,201 | 1,325 | 1,440 | 1,573 |
| GDP per capita (in US dollars) | 3,974 | 3,615 | 4,506 | 6,073 | 7,639 | 8,632 | na |
| Share of industry in GDP (in per cent) | 25.9 | 26.0 | 25.9 | 26.0 | 27.0 | 27.5 | na |
| Share of agriculture in GDP (in per cent) | 5.2 | 4.8 | 5.1 | 4.1 | 4.7 | 5.0 | na |
| Current account/GDP (in per cent) | -3.3 | -9.0 | -8.0 | -0.8 | -3.5 | -6.0 | -3.4 |
| External debt - reserves (in US$ million) | 6,727 | 7,080 | 3,993 | 5,941 | 8,782 | 11,300 | na |
| External debt/GDP (in per cent) | 50.3 | 57.7 | 54.4 | 55.4 | 57.7 | 58.1 | na |
| External debt/exports of goods and services (in per cent) | 76.5 | 74.5 | 76.9 | 72.0 | 75.3 | 80.0 | na |

[1]  General government includes central government, municipalities and
    extra-budgetary funds.

[2]  The general government balance excludes privatisation revenues and is
    calculated according to Eurostat methodology (ESA95).

[3]  Weighted average over all maturities.

# Slovenia

## Economic performance and prospects

■ Growth is supported by sustained investment, household consumption and improving net exports.

■ Continued disinflation and fiscal restraint are necessary in the run-up to the planned adoption of the euro in January 2007.

## Real economy

Real GDP grew by an estimated 3.9 per cent in 2005, slightly lower than the rate of 4.2 per cent in 2004. This reflected sustained growth of domestic consumption, investment and exports. Private consumption increased by an estimated 3.6 per cent in 2005, compared with an estimated 2.5 per cent rise in public consumption.

## Economic policies

Macroeconomic policy remains focused on the planned adoption of the euro in early 2007. The Maastricht criteria for long-term interest rates, the fiscal deficit and debt ratios have already been met. The average inflation rate has continued to fall. This has been due mainly to the slow rate of currency depreciation, further (but limited) wage de-indexation in the public and private sectors, and lower oil prices at the end of 2005. Inflation converged with the Maastricht criteria in November 2005. The government is to introduce a "flat tax" system in 2007, subject to analysis and social consensus. The general government deficit remained stable in 2004–05 at around 2 per cent of GDP (using ESA95 methodology).

## External sector

Despite weak growth in the eurozone, export levels have been maintained in 2005. Merchandise exports (particularly road vehicles to the eurozone) grew in real terms by an estimated 8.6 per cent, compared with import growth of 1.4 per cent. Foreign direct investment inflows remained low in 2005, but may increase in 2006 if planned privatisations take place and attract foreign investors. Estimated external debt rose slightly to 66 per cent of GDP by the end of 2005. Other debt indicators, such as the net debt position and debt maturity ratios, suggest that this level of debt remains manageable.

## Outlook and risks

Slovenia is expected to maintain its real economic growth rate at around 4 per cent in 2006. Continued strong growth and employment creation are feasible over the medium term, but will require improved competitiveness through implementation of the government's ambitious new reform programme.

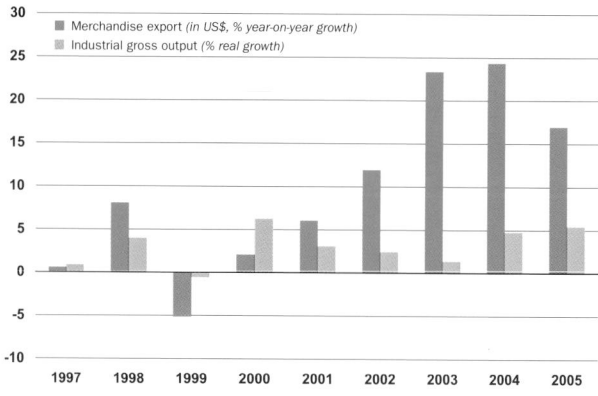

**Exports and industrial production growth year-on-year**

■ Merchandise export *(in US$, % year-on-year growth)*
■ Industrial gross output *(% real growth)*

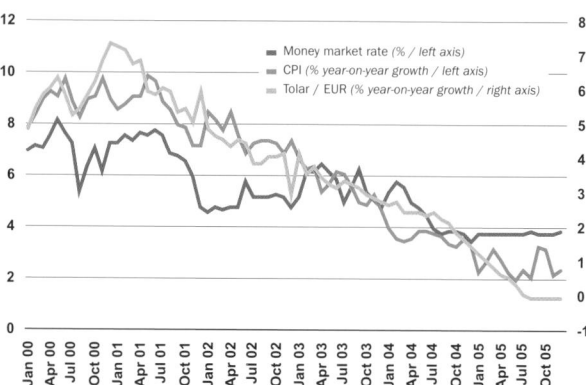

**Inflation, exchange rate developments and interest rates**

■ Money market rate *(% / left axis)*
■ CPI *(% year-on-year growth / left axis)*
■ Tolar / EUR *(% year-on-year growth / right axis)*

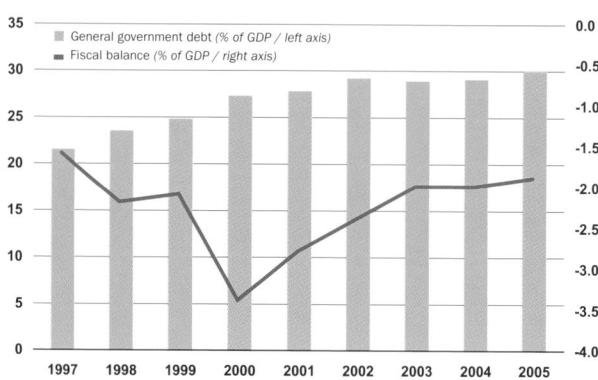

**Debt and fiscal balance**

■ General government debt *(% of GDP / left axis)*
■ Fiscal balance *(% of GDP / right axis)*

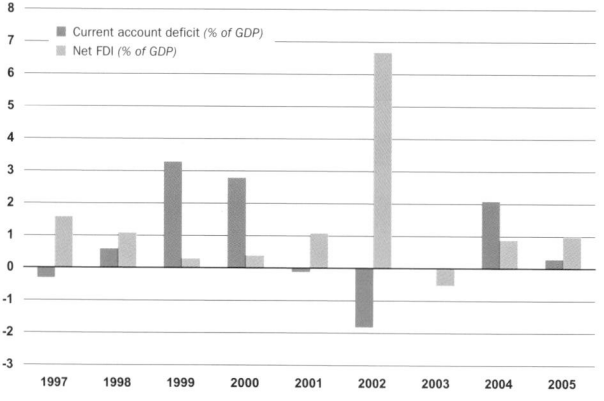

**Current account deficit and net FDI**

■ Current account deficit *(% of GDP)*
■ Net FDI *(% of GDP)*

| | 2000 | 2001 | 2002 | 2003 | 2004 | 2005 Estimate | 2006 Projection |
|---|---|---|---|---|---|---|---|
| **Output and expenditure** | *(Percentage change in real terms)* | | | | | | |
| GDP | 4.1 | 2.7 | 3.5 | 2.7 | 4.2 | 3.9 | 4.0 |
| Private consumption | 0.7 | 2.3 | 1.3 | 3.4 | 3.1 | 3.6 | na |
| Public consumption | 2.6 | 3.9 | 3.2 | 1.6 | 2.9 | 2.5 | na |
| Gross fixed capital formation | 1.8 | 0.4 | 0.9 | 7.1 | 5.9 | 4.0 | na |
| Exports of goods and services | 13.0 | 6.3 | 6.7 | 3.1 | 12.5 | 8.6 | na |
| Imports of goods and services | 7.6 | 1.7 | 1.1 | -2.0 | -0.4 | 1.5 | na |
| Industrial gross output | 6.3 | 3.1 | 2.5 | 1.4 | 4.8 | 5.5 | na |
| Agricultural gross output [1] | -1.0 | -2.5 | 1.1 | -8.2 | 2.3 | 1.5 | na |
| **Employment [2]** | *(Percentage change)* | | | | | | |
| Labour force (mid-year) | -5.8 | 0.1 | 0.3 | -1.3 | -0.1 | 1.6 | na |
| Employment (mid-year) | -10.3 | 0.7 | 0.4 | -1.0 | 0.7 | 1.4 | na |
| | *(In per cent of labour force)* | | | | | | |
| Unemployment (mid-year) | 7.6 | 6.3 | 6.4 | 7.3 | 6.8 | na | na |
| **Prices and wages** | *(Percentage change)* | | | | | | |
| Consumer prices (annual average) | 8.9 | 8.4 | 7.5 | 5.6 | 3.6 | 2.5 | 2.5 |
| Consumer prices (end-year) | 8.9 | 7.0 | 7.2 | 4.7 | 3.2 | 2.2 | 2.3 |
| Producer prices (annual average) | 7.6 | 9.0 | 5.1 | 2.5 | 4.3 | na | na |
| Producer prices (end-year) | 9.2 | 7.5 | 3.7 | 2.1 | 4.9 | na | na |
| Gross average monthly earnings in economy (annual average) [3] | 10.6 | 11.9 | 9.7 | 7.5 | 5.7 | na | na |
| **Government sector [4]** | *(In per cent of GDP)* | | | | | | |
| General government balance | -3.4 | -2.8 | -2.4 | -2.0 | -2.0 | -1.9 | -1.7 |
| General government expenditure | 47.6 | 47.5 | 47.7 | 47.6 | 47.3 | 46.9 | na |
| General government debt | 27.4 | 27.9 | 29.3 | 29.0 | 29.2 | 30.0 | na |
| **Monetary sector** | *(Percentage change)* | | | | | | |
| Broad money (M2, end-year) | 9.7 | 27.4 | 25.1 | 5.2 | 4.0 | 8.3 | na |
| Domestic credit (end-year) | 20.6 | 23.2 | 11.5 | 13.8 | 19.8 | 5.1 | na |
| | *(In per cent of GDP)* | | | | | | |
| Broad money (M2, end-year) | 37.6 | 42.9 | 48.1 | 46.6 | 45.1 | 45.9 | na |
| **Interest and exchange rates** | *(In per cent per annum, end-year)* | | | | | | |
| Discount rate | 10.0 | 11.0 | 10.0 | 6.0 | 4.0 | na | na |
| Interbank market rate (average) | 7.2 | 4.7 | 4.7 | 4.7 | 3.4 | na | na |
| Deposit rate (31-90 days) | 10.9 | 8.5 | 7.6 | 4.8 | 3.2 | na | na |
| Lending rate (short-term working capital) | 16.3 | 13.7 | 11.8 | 9.9 | 8.0 | na | na |
| | *(Tolars per US dollar)* | | | | | | |
| Exchange rate (end-year) | 235.6 | 250.9 | 226.2 | 189.4 | 176.2 | 197.2 | na |
| Exchange rate (annual average) | 222.7 | 243.0 | 240.2 | 207.1 | 192.4 | 192.8 | na |
| **External sector** | *(In millions of US dollars)* | | | | | | |
| Current account | -549 | 12 | 398 | 13 | -670 | -108 | -187 |
| Trade balance | -1,140 | -617 | -248 | -623 | -1,258 | -1,100 | na |
| Merchandise exports | 8,807 | 9,346 | 10,471 | 12,916 | 16,064 | 18,800 | 21,100 |
| Merchandise imports | 9,947 | 9,963 | 10,719 | 13,539 | 17,322 | 19,900 | 22,200 |
| Foreign direct investment, net | 71 | 226 | 1,489 | -139 | 277 | 346 | 470 |
| Gross reserves, excluding gold (end-year) | 4,376 | 5,747 | 8,168 | 9,629 | 10,189 | 10,466 | na |
| External debt stock | 8,516 | 9,283 | 11,694 | 16,572 | 20,783 | 22,988 | na |
| | *(In months of imports of goods and services)* | | | | | | |
| Gross reserves, excluding gold (end-year) | 4.6 | 6.0 | 7.9 | 7.4 | 6.1 | 5.5 | na |
| | *(In per cent of exports of goods and services)* | | | | | | |
| Debt service | 11.8 | 9.2 | 10.3 | 14.0 | 15.8 | 19.2 | na |
| **Memorandum items** | *(Denominations as indicated)* | | | | | | |
| Population (end-year, million) | 2.0 | 2.0 | 2.0 | 2.0 | 2.0 | 2.0 | na |
| GDP (in billions of tolars) | 4,300 | 4,800 | 5,355 | 5,814 | 6,251 | 6,652 | 7,074 |
| GDP per capita (in US dollar) | 9,704 | 9,984 | 11,174 | 14,105 | 16,329 | 17,337 | na |
| Share of industry in GDP (in per cent) | 26.9 | 27.5 | 27.9 | 28.1 | 28.2 | 28.4 | na |
| Share of agriculture in GDP (in per cent) | 2.8 | 2.4 | 2.7 | 2.2 | 2.3 | 2.3 | na |
| Current account/GDP (in per cent) | -2.8 | 0.1 | 1.8 | 0.0 | -2.1 | -0.3 | na |
| External debt - reserves (in US$ million) | 4,140 | 3,536 | 3,526 | 6,943 | 10,594 | 12,522 | na |
| External debt/GDP (in per cent) | 44.1 | 47.0 | 52.5 | 59.0 | 64.0 | 66.6 | na |
| External debt/exports of goods and services (in per cent) | 79.6 | 82.2 | 91.5 | 105.5 | 106.5 | 99.6 | na |

[1] Agricultural value-added.

[2] Data from labour force survey.

[3] Data refer to enterprises employing three or more persons.

[4] General government includes central government, municipalities and extra-budgetary funds. Data calculated according to Eurostat methodology (ESA95).

# Tajikistan

## Economic performance and prospects

- Although economic growth has slowed due to a reduction in cotton production and weaker electricity generation, it continues to be supported by higher incomes and remittances.

- Medium-term growth prospects are positive, given planned large-scale investments and capacity expansion in key industries. The economy remains, however, vulnerable to terms of trade shocks.

## Real economy

Real GDP grew by 6.7 per cent in 2005, following five consecutive years of more than 8 per cent growth. The slowdown resulted from weaker cotton and electricity production. Farm incomes were undermined by high fuel and low cotton prices. Nevertheless, domestic demand generally remained strong, fuelled by robust wage growth and increasing remittances.

## Economic policies

Fiscal policy has remained prudent, with the budget in near balance, and largely consistent with the objectives set out in Tajikistan's Poverty Reduction Strategy Paper (PRSP). On the revenue side, a new tax code in 2005 has simplified the tax structure, eliminated a number of distortions and exemptions, and raised overall revenues. However, the ratio of tax revenue to GDP remains one of the lowest in the CIS. Monetary policy has focused on achieving price stability. The annual average inflation rate in 2005 was moderate at 7 per cent, with some fluctuations during the year due to food and energy prices. The authorities are developing marketable government securities to broaden the range of available monetary instruments.

## External sector

Public external debt has been cut substantially. After a series of bilateral debt reduction agreements, the level declined to US$ 895 million by the end of 2005, or just under 40 per cent of GDP (from more than 80 per cent in 2002). Russia, the largest bilateral creditor, has written off US$ 306 million of debt, primarily as part of debt-equity swaps. Moreover, the IMF approved US$ 99 million in debt relief for Tajikistan under the Multilateral Debt Relief Initiative in December. The trade deficit increased in 2005 due to weaker cotton and aluminium prices during the first half of the year. However, this was largely offset by the growth in workers' remittances, which rose to US$ 247 million in 2005 from US$ 141 million in 2004.

## Outlook and risks

The economy is expected to return to high growth in the medium term. Large-scale investment commitments in the energy and aluminium sectors made by Russia and Iran should increase production capacity and provide opportunities for closer bilateral trade and business links. However, the country will remain dependent on a few key sectors – aluminium, cotton and power – which suffer from large price and demand fluctuations. The economy also remains vulnerable to terms of trade shocks, in particular from prices for foodstuffs and oil products.

**Exports and industrial production growth year-on-year**

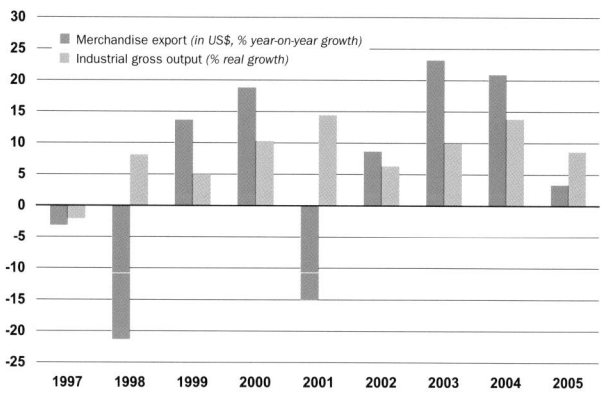

**Inflation, exchange rate developments and interest rates**

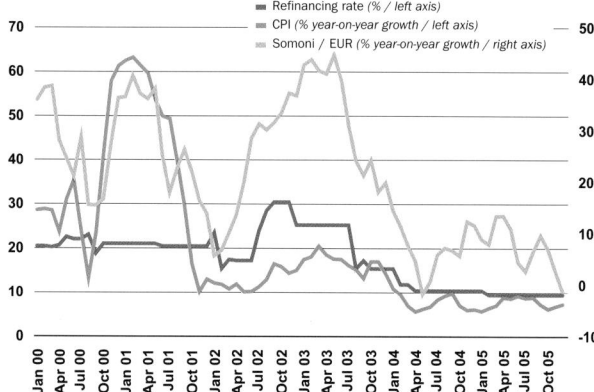

**Debt and fiscal balance**

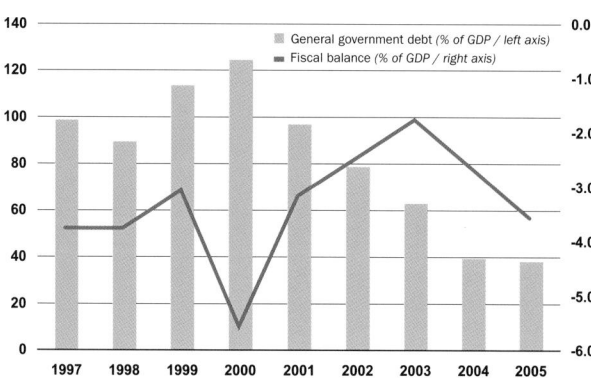

**Current account deficit and net FDI**

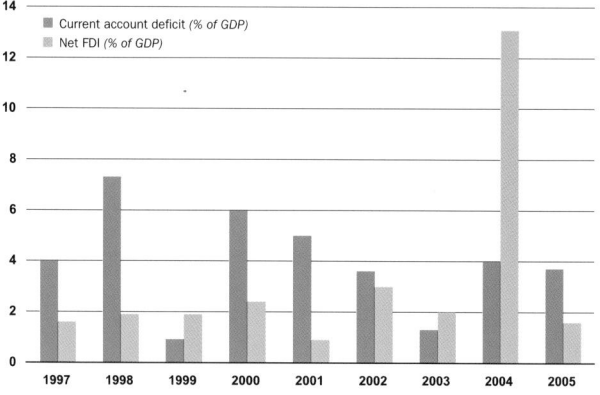

| | 2000 | 2001 | 2002 | 2003 | 2004 | 2005 Estimate | 2006 Projection |
|---|---|---|---|---|---|---|---|
| **Output and expenditure** | *(Percentage change in real terms)* | | | | | | |
| GDP | 8.3 | 10.2 | 9.1 | 10.2 | 10.6 | 6.7 | 7.0 |
| Industrial gross output | 10.3 | 14.4 | 6.3 | 9.9 | 13.8 | 8.6 | na |
| Agricultural gross output | 12.4 | 11.0 | 14.0 | 9.1 | 11.3 | 1.8 | na |
| **Employment** | *(Percentage change)* | | | | | | |
| Labour force (end-year) | 0.2 | 4.3 | 1.7 | 1.5 | -0.7 | 1.0 | na |
| Employment (end-year) | 0.4 | 4.8 | 1.5 | 1.7 | -0.7 | 0.9 | na |
| | *(In per cent of labour force)* | | | | | | |
| Unemployment (end-year) [1] | 2.7 | 2.3 | 2.5 | 2.2 | 2.2 | 2.3 | na |
| **Prices and wages** | *(Percentage change)* | | | | | | |
| Consumer prices (annual average) | 32.9 | 38.6 | 12.2 | 16.3 | 7.1 | 7.0 | 6.4 |
| Consumer prices (end-year) | 60.8 | 12.5 | 14.5 | 13.7 | 5.6 | 6.8 | 6.0 |
| Producer prices (annual average) | 43.5 | 28.7 | 10.1 | 15.0 | 17.1 | na | na |
| Producer prices (end-year) | 33.9 | 9.4 | 19.0 | 14.1 | 15.1 | na | na |
| Gross average monthly earnings in economy (annual average) | 25.8 | 50.6 | 38.6 | 36.9 | 36.3 | na | na |
| **Government sector** [2] | *(In per cent of GDP)* | | | | | | |
| General government balance | -5.6 | -3.2 | -2.5 | -1.8 | -2.7 | -3.6 | -3.5 |
| General government expenditure | 19.2 | 18.4 | 19.2 | 19.1 | 20.7 | 20.8 | na |
| General government debt | 124.5 | 97.0 | 78.8 | 63.0 | 39.4 | 38.2 | na |
| **Monetary sector** | *(Percentage change)* | | | | | | |
| Broad money (M2, end-year) | 70.1 | 40.0 | 39.7 | 29.3 | 14.3 | 18.4 | na |
| Domestic credit (end-year) | 14.5 | 95.0 | 14.0 | -6.5 | 32.2 | 5.8 | na |
| | *(In per cent of GDP)* | | | | | | |
| Broad money (M2, end-year) | 8.5 | 8.6 | 9.0 | 8.2 | 7.2 | 7.3 | na |
| **Interest and exchange rates** | *(In per cent per annum, end-year)* | | | | | | |
| Monetary policy rate | 20.6 | 23.4 | 21.0 | 15.0 | 10.0 | 9.0 | na |
| Deposit rate (up to 3 months) | 41.3 | 25.5 | 12.1 | 14.6 | 8.6 | 7.3 | na |
| Lending rate (up to 3 months) | 18.3 | 21.3 | 12.1 | 15.6 | 21.3 | 18.7 | na |
| | *(Tajik somoni per US dollar)* | | | | | | |
| Exchange rate (end-year) [3] | 2.2 | 2.5 | 3.0 | 2.9 | 3.0 | 3.2 | na |
| Exchange rate (annual average) [3] | 1.8 | 2.4 | 2.8 | 3.1 | 3.0 | 3.1 | na |
| **External sector** | *(In millions of US dollars)* | | | | | | |
| Current account | -60 | -52 | -43 | -20 | -83 | -86 | -118 |
| Trade balance | -43 | -104 | -94 | -103 | -151 | -279 | -351 |
| Merchandise exports | 791 | 673 | 730 | 900 | 1,088 | 1,124 | 1,188 |
| Merchandise imports | 834 | 777 | 824 | 1,003 | 1,239 | 1,403 | 1,539 |
| Foreign direct investment, net | 24 | 9 | 36 | 32 | 272 | 36 | 60 |
| Gross reserves, excluding gold (end-year) | 87 | 96 | 96 | 135 | 189 | 235 | na |
| External debt stock | 1,226 | 1,022 | 1,010 | 1,031 | 822 | 895 | na |
| | *(In months of imports of goods and services)* | | | | | | |
| Gross reserves, excluding gold (end-year) | 1.2 | 1.4 | 1.2 | 1.4 | 1.6 | 1.8 | na |
| | *(In per cent of exports of goods and services)* | | | | | | |
| Debt service | 9.2 | 16.1 | 14.1 | 6.0 | 6.1 | 5.8 | na |
| **Memorandum items** | *(Denominations as indicated)* | | | | | | |
| Population (end-year, million) | 6.2 | 6.3 | 6.4 | 6.5 | 6.5 | 6.5 | na |
| GDP (in billions of somoni) | 2 | 3 | 3 | 5 | 6 | 7 | 8 |
| GDP per capita (in US dollars) | 160 | 168 | 187 | 239 | 319 | 358 | na |
| Share of industry in GDP (in per cent) [4] | 23.9 | 22.7 | 22.1 | 20.9 | 19.6 | na | na |
| Share of agriculture in GDP (in per cent) [4] | 27.0 | 26.5 | 26.3 | 25.2 | 21.6 | na | na |
| Current account/GDP (in per cent) | -6.0 | -5.0 | -3.6 | -1.3 | -4.0 | -3.7 | -4.7 |
| External debt - reserves (in US$ million) | 1,139 | 926 | 914 | 896 | 633 | 660 | na |
| External debt/GDP (in per cent) | 124.5 | 97.0 | 84.0 | 66.3 | 39.7 | 38.5 | na |
| External debt/exports of goods and services (in per cent) | 142.9 | 138.6 | 126.2 | 105.6 | 70.9 | 74.3 | na |

[1] Officially registered unemployed. The World Bank estimates the true unemployment rate in 2000 was more than 30 per cent of the labour force.

[2] Includes externally financed public investment programmes.

[3] Tajik roubles (until October 2000) have been converted to somoni.

[4] Figures are based on current prices. Variations in the shares reflect changes in relative prices.

# Turkmenistan

## Economic performance and prospects

■ Strong economic growth continues, reflecting high hydrocarbon prices and public investments. The business environment for the private sector, however, remains difficult.

■ Economic prospects will depend largely on output growth and price increases in the hydrocarbon sector, which continues to be affected by production and pipeline capacity constraints.

## Real economy

According to official statistics (generally believed to be overstated) the economy grew by 20.7 per cent in 2005. The IMF estimates that the GDP growth rate was 9.6 per cent. The strong performance was supported in part by higher hydrocarbon prices and public investment programmes. The agriculture sector, however, continued to slow. Cotton production in 2005 stagnated at around 0.7 million tonnes (compared with 0.73 million tonnes in 2004), far below the target of 2.2 million tonnes.

## Economic policies

Inflation slightly increased to 10 per cent in 2005, from 9 per cent in 2004, due to higher food prices. Price increases have been in part offset by price and financial controls imposed by the authorities.

The approved balanced budget for 2006 envisages revenues and expenditures in line with the 2005 budget. Despite increases in tax revenues from the hydrocarbon sector, the benefits to the public finances have been eroded by reductions in the overall number of taxes and in the tax rates for the corporate sector. (These rates are in accordance with a new tax code introduced in November 2004.) The government stopped or reduced pension payments from February 2006, indicating serious problems in the fiscal situation.

## External sector

The trade surplus in 2005 reached US$1.3 billion, the highest since independence and equivalent to 15.6 per cent of GDP. This was due mainly to increased international energy prices and reduced imports. Accordingly, the current account surplus surged to an estimated 8.2 per cent of GDP in 2005, from 1.2 per cent in 2004. New contracts with Russia and Ukraine, which stipulate substantial rises in the gas price, are expected to lead to an additional US$500 million (or more) annually in export revenues. Meanwhile, foreign direct investment has remained limited at 3–5 per cent of GDP in recent years. This is in part due to the poor investment environment.

## Outlook and risks

The economic outlook is highly dependent on export volumes and prices in the hydrocarbon sector. This overdependence, combined with the lack of market-oriented reforms, leaves the economy vulnerable to external shocks and gas pipeline constraints. Moreover, as Turkmenistan faces increasing competition for gas exports and pipeline access from Kazakhstan and Uzbekistan, the country's competitive position could be weakened. Concerns over the level of its gas reserves could limit foreign investment in the gas sector.

### Exports and industrial production growth year-on-year

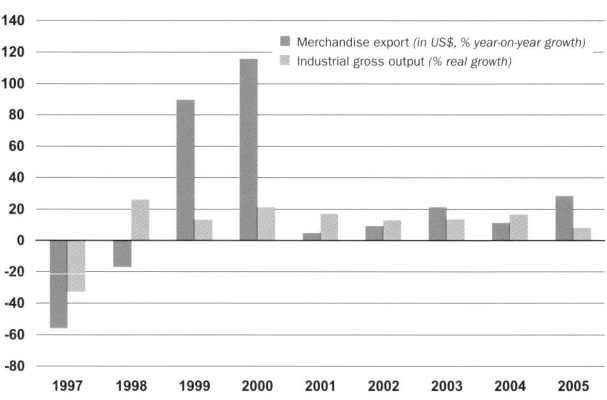

### Inflation, exchange rate developments and interest rates

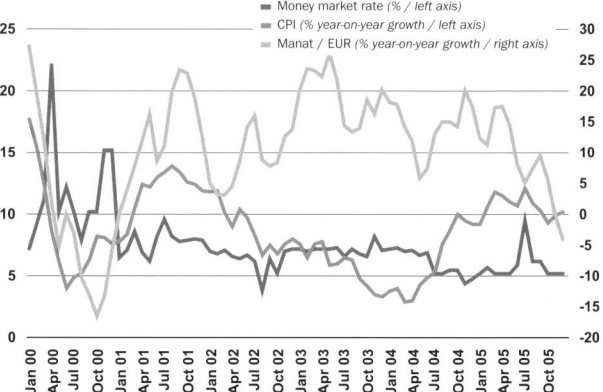

### Debt and fiscal balance

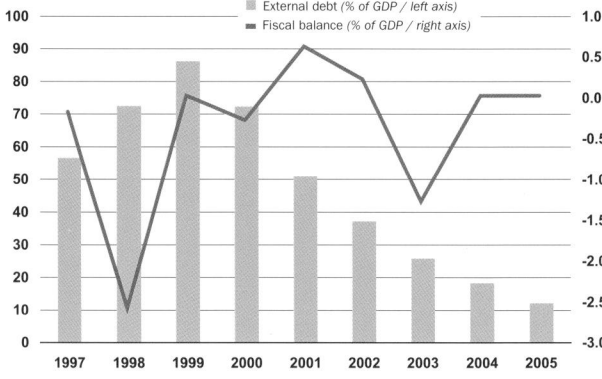

### Current account deficit and net FDI

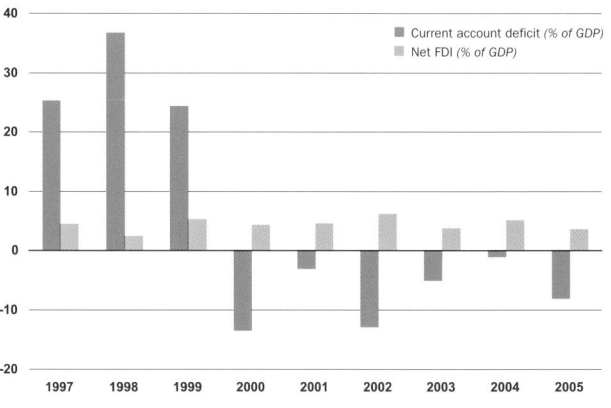

| | 2000 | 2001 | 2002 | 2003 | 2004 | 2005 Estimate | 2006 Projection |
|---|---|---|---|---|---|---|---|
| **Output and expenditure** | | | *(Percentage change in real terms)* | | | | |
| GDP | 18.6 | 20.4 | 15.8 | 17.1 | 17.2 | 9.6 | 10.6 |
| Private consumption | na | na | na | na | na | na | na |
| Public consumption | na | na | na | na | na | na | na |
| Gross fixed capital formation | na | na | na | na | na | na | na |
| Exports of goods and services | 92.6 | 4.8 | 13.0 | 4.0 | na | na | na |
| Imports of goods and services | 14.9 | 20.1 | -3.7 | 4.3 | na | na | na |
| Industrial gross output | 21.0 | 16.8 | 12.8 | 13.5 | 16.4 | 7.9 | na |
| Agricultural gross output | 17.0 | 23.0 | 9.5 | 9.5 | 13.0 | 4.0 | na |
| **Employment** | | | *(Percentage change)* | | | | |
| Labour force (end-year) | 3.1 | 3.2 | 3.2 | 3.0 | 3.0 | 0.0 | na |
| Employment (end-year) | 3.0 | 2.0 | 2.5 | 2.2 | na | na | na |
| | | | *(In per cent of labour force)* | | | | |
| Unemployment [1] | 27.9 | 28.8 | 29.3 | 29.8 | 30.2 | na | na |
| **Prices and wages** | | | *(Percentage change)* | | | | |
| Consumer prices (annual average) | 8.3 | 11.6 | 8.8 | 5.6 | 5.9 | 10.6 | 9.2 |
| Consumer prices (end-year) | 7.4 | 11.7 | 7.8 | 3.1 | 9.0 | 10.0 | 9.6 |
| Producer prices (annual average) | na | na | na | na | na | na | na |
| Producer prices (end-year) | na | na | na | na | na | na | na |
| Gross average monthly earnings in economy (annual average) | 80.4 | 47.1 | 8.2 | 84.2 | 5.7 | 21.6 | na |
| **Government sector [2]** | | | *(In per cent of GDP)* | | | | |
| General government balance | -0.3 | 0.6 | 0.2 | -1.3 | 0.0 | 0.0 | 0.0 |
| General government expenditure | 23.9 | 21.1 | 18.1 | 19.4 | 19.6 | 19.6 | 0.0 |
| General government debt | na | na | na | na | na | na | na |
| **Monetary sector** | | | *(Percentage change)* | | | | |
| Broad money (M3, end-year) | 94.6 | 16.7 | 1.5 | 40.9 | 13.4 | 26.3 | na |
| Domestic credit (end-year) | 24.4 | 7.7 | -2.9 | -0.6 | 3.6 | 0.6 | na |
| | | | *(In per cent of GDP)* | | | | |
| Broad money (M3, end-year) | 19.4 | 16.1 | 13.0 | 13.9 | 12.9 | 12.9 | na |
| **Interest and exchange rates** | | | *(In per cent per annum, end-year)* | | | | |
| Refinance rate | 20.0 | 12.0 | 12.0 | 10.0 | 5.0 | 5.0 | na |
| Interbank market rate | 15.0 | 7.7 | 7.0 | 6.9 | 4.6 | 5.0 | na |
| Deposit rate (up to 1 year) [3] | 22.8 | 16.9 | 17.8 | 15.4 | 11.3 | na | na |
| Lending rate (up to 1 year) [3] | 27.9 | 26.7 | 21.9 | 20.4 | 17.3 | na | na |
| | | | *(Manats per US dollar)* | | | | |
| Exchange rate (end-year) [4] | 9,790.0 | 10,060.0 | 10,150.0 | 10,390.0 | 10,540.0 | 10,870.0 | na |
| Exchange rate (annual average) | 8,478.6 | 9,827.9 | 10,097.5 | 10,033.5 | 10,375.0 | 11,015.2 | na |
| **External sector** | | | *(In millions of US dollars)* | | | | |
| Current account | 411 | 116 | 583 | 305 | 84 | 688 | 1,447 |
| Trade balance | 766 | 515 | 1,030 | 886 | 706 | 1,302 | 2,056 |
| Merchandise exports | 2,508 | 2,623 | 2,862 | 3,465 | 3,854 | 4,939 | 6,421 |
| Merchandise imports | 1,742 | 2,108 | 1,832 | 2,579 | 3,148 | 3,637 | 4,364 |
| Foreign direct investment, net | 131 | 170 | 276 | 226 | 354 | 300 | 308 |
| Gross reserves, excluding gold (end-year) [5] | 1,808 | 2,055 | 2,346 | 2,673 | 2,714 | 3,314 | na |
| External debt stock | 2,184 | 1,865 | 1,660 | 1,519 | 1,273 | 1,007 | na |
| | | | *(In months of imports of goods and services)* | | | | |
| Gross reserves, excluding gold (end-year) | 9.2 | 9.1 | 11.8 | 9.5 | 8.0 | 8.6 | na |
| | | | *(In per cent of exports of goods and services)* | | | | |
| Debt service [6] | 14.2 | 17.3 | 14.3 | 11.6 | 9.6 | 5.6 | na |
| **Memorandum items** | | | *(Denominations as indicated)* | | | | |
| Population (end-year, million) | 5.4 | 5.6 | 5.8 | 6.2 | 6.5 | 6.5 | na |
| GDP (in billions of manats) | 25,648 | 36,052 | 45,240 | 59,405 | 72,706 | 91,863 | 110,917 |
| GDP per capita (in US dollars) | 563 | 650 | 774 | 955 | 1,078 | 1,283 | na |
| Share of industry in GDP (in per cent) | 45.8 | 39.8 | 40.9 | 39.7 | 38.6 | na | na |
| Share of agriculture in GDP (in per cent) | 24.5 | 23.0 | 21.8 | 19.6 | 18.4 | na | na |
| Current account/GDP (in per cent) | 13.6 | 3.2 | 13.0 | 5.2 | 1.2 | 8.2 | 14.3 |
| External debt - reserves (in US$ million) | 376 | -190 | -686 | -1,154 | -1,441 | -2,307 | na |
| External debt/GDP (in per cent) | 72.2 | 50.8 | 37.1 | 25.7 | 18.2 | 12.1 | na |
| External debt/exports of goods and services (in per cent) | 78.7 | 64.8 | 53.9 | 40.8 | 30.2 | 18.9 | na |

[1] Officially registered unemployed.

[2] Significant off-budget expenditures occur through extra-budgetary funds and lending.

[3] Unweighted average deposit and lending rates for individuals (in local currency) of state commercial banks.

[4] Turkmenistan operates a dual exchange rate system. The series refers to a weighted average between the official exchange rate and the commercial rate (given as the black market rate). Weights are variable depending on official and shuttle trade.

[5] Includes foreign exchange reserves of the central bank plus the foreign exchange reserve fund.

[6] Excludes rescheduled amounts.

# Ukraine

## Economic performance and prospects

■ Poor export performance and a sharp slowdown in industrial and construction activities in 2005 led to a reversal of the fast growth recorded in 2004.

■ Higher gas import prices and weaker macroeconomic fundamentals are likely to dampen growth in the short term.

## Real economy

Real GDP growth slowed to 2.6 per cent in 2005 from 12.1 per cent in 2004. A sharp deceleration in exports and investment were the key factors behind the poor performance. On the demand side, growth was sustained by a boom in domestic consumption, fuelled by generous wage and pension increases. Industrial production rose by only 3.1 per cent in 2005, compared with 12.5 per cent in 2004. This reflected a contraction in metallurgy, coke and oil refining, which account for more than a third of output.

## Economic policies

Although the central bank raised the discount rate and the mandatory reserve requirement, inflation was 10.3 per cent at the end of 2005 and above the official forecast of 9.8 per cent. The exchange rate has been stable at around 5.1 hryvnia/US dollar since the 5 per cent nominal revaluation in April 2005.

Fiscal policy was tightened in 2005. The elimination of tax holidays and preferential tax treatments in special economic zones contributed to a substantial broadening of the tax base. Buoyant tax revenues and large privatisation inflows compensated for the significant increases in pensions, minimum wages and other social transfers. The 2006 budget law, approved by the parliament in December 2005, targets a consolidated budget deficit of 2.5 per cent of GDP. However, the 2006 budget is based on optimistic assumptions and may have to be revised after the March elections.

## External sector

Real exchange rate appreciation and a fall in metal export prices contributed to a deceleration in export growth in the first nine months of 2005. Fuelled by an increase in average real incomes, import demand grew faster than exports, causing the trade balance to swing into deficit. Record foreign direct investment inflows, estimated in the range of US$ 6.5 billion to US$ 7.5 billion, contributed to the rise in gross foreign reserves, which peaked at US$ 19.4 billion (more than five months of import coverage) by the end of 2005. In October the Ministry of Finance successfully placed a 10-year eurobond of € 600 million at an annual yield of 4.95 per cent.

## Outlook and risks

The sharp increase in natural gas import prices in early 2006, coupled with double-digit annual inflation, a fall in investment and a deceleration in external demand for Ukraine's metals, is likely to further constrain GDP growth in the short term. In the long term, the convergence of gas import prices towards international levels may act as a catalyst for the restructuring of the industrial sector and promote energy efficiency measures.

### Exports and industrial production growth year-on-year

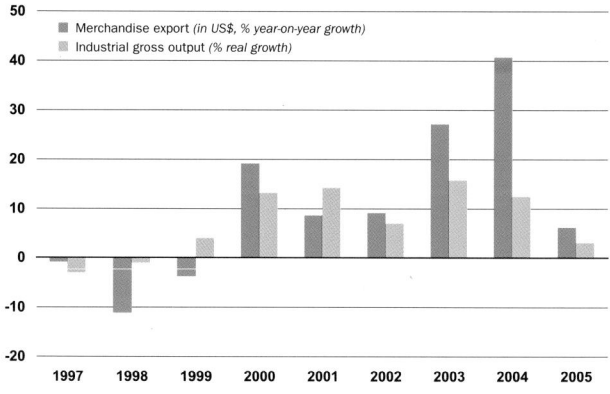

### Inflation, exchange rate developments and interest rates

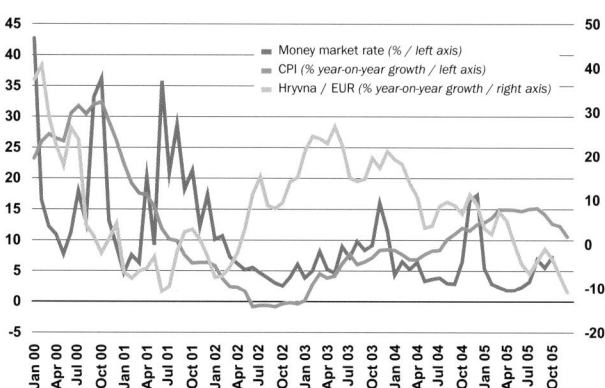

### Debt and fiscal balance

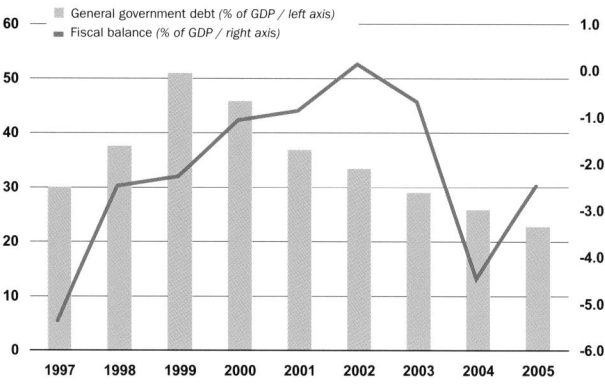

### Current account deficit and net FDI

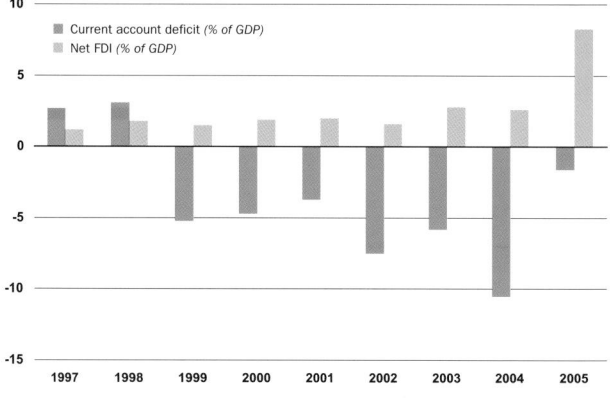

| | 2000 | 2001 | 2002 | 2003 | 2004 | 2005 Estimate | 2006 Projection |
|---|---|---|---|---|---|---|---|
| **Output and expenditure** | | | *(Percentage change in real terms)* | | | | |
| GDP | 5.9 | 9.2 | 5.2 | 9.4 | 12.1 | 2.6 | 1.2 |
| Private consumption | 2.3 | 9.0 | 9.0 | 12.1 | 14.5 | 8.0 | na |
| Public consumption | 1.0 | 10.4 | -6.7 | 14.8 | 5.4 | 4.0 | na |
| Gross fixed capital formation | 12.4 | 6.2 | 3.4 | 15.8 | 10.0 | 2.0 | na |
| Exports of goods and services | 21.5 | 3.5 | 7.4 | 10.3 | 10.0 | 5.0 | na |
| Imports of goods and services | 23.8 | 6.0 | 3.3 | 16.4 | 9.5 | 11.0 | na |
| Industrial gross output | 13.2 | 14.2 | 7.0 | 15.8 | 12.5 | 3.1 | na |
| Agricultural gross output | 9.8 | 10.2 | 1.2 | -9.9 | 19.1 | 0.0 | na |
| **Employment** | | | *(Percentage change)* | | | | |
| Labour force (end-year) | 0.3 | -0.1 | 0.5 | 0.3 | 0.0 | na | na |
| Employment (end-year) | -1.2 | 1.7 | 0.3 | -6.0 | 0.7 | na | na |
| | | | *(In per cent of labour force)* | | | | |
| Unemployment (end-year) | 4.2 | 3.7 | 3.8 | 3.6 | 3.5 | 2.9 | na |
| **Prices and wages** | | | *(Percentage change)* | | | | |
| Consumer prices (annual average) | 28.2 | 12.0 | 0.8 | 5.2 | 9.0 | 13.5 | 11.3 |
| Consumer prices (end-year) | 25.8 | 6.1 | -0.6 | 8.2 | 12.3 | 10.3 | 12.3 |
| Producer prices (annual average) | 20.8 | 8.7 | 3.0 | 7.6 | 20.4 | 16.8 | na |
| Producer prices (end-year) | 20.6 | 0.9 | 5.7 | 11.1 | 24.1 | 9.5 | na |
| Gross average monthly earnings in economy (annual average) | 29.2 | 35.2 | 20.9 | 22.9 | 27.9 | 36.4 | na |
| **Government sector** [1] | | | *(In per cent of GDP)* | | | | |
| General government balance | -1.1 | -0.9 | 0.1 | -0.7 | -4.5 | -2.5 | -3.4 |
| General government expenditure | 34.5 | 34.4 | 35.6 | 37.2 | 40.0 | 42.7 | na |
| General government debt | 45.9 | 36.9 | 33.5 | 29.0 | 25.9 | 22.8 | na |
| **Monetary sector** | | | *(Percentage change)* | | | | |
| Broad money (M2, end-year) | 45.3 | 43.2 | 42.3 | 46.9 | 32.8 | 39.4 | na |
| Domestic credit (end-year) | 23.1 | 18.7 | 28.9 | 39.6 | 22.8 | 30.8 | na |
| | | | *(In per cent of GDP)* | | | | |
| Broad money (M2, end-year) | 18.5 | 22.1 | 28.5 | 35.3 | 36.3 | 43.4 | na |
| **Interest and exchange rates** | | | *(In per cent per annum, end-year)* | | | | |
| Refinancing rate | 27.0 | 12.5 | 7.0 | 7.0 | 9.0 | 9.5 | na |
| Deposit rate [2] | 13.7 | 11.0 | 7.9 | 7.0 | 7.8 | 8.5 | na |
| Lending rate [2] | 41.5 | 32.3 | 25.4 | 17.9 | 17.4 | 16.2 | na |
| | | | *(Hryvnias per US dollar)* | | | | |
| Exchange rate (end-year) | 5.4 | 5.3 | 5.3 | 5.3 | 5.3 | 5.1 | na |
| Exchange rate (annual average) | 5.4 | 5.4 | 5.3 | 5.3 | 5.3 | 5.1 | na |
| **External sector** | | | *(In millions of US dollars)* | | | | |
| Current account | 1,481 | 1,402 | 3,173 | 2,891 | 6,804 | 1,247 | -1,594 |
| Trade balance | 779 | 198 | 710 | -269 | 3,741 | -1,576 | -6,094 |
| Merchandise exports | 15,722 | 17,091 | 18,669 | 23,739 | 33,432 | 35,538 | 39,500 |
| Merchandise imports | 14,943 | 16,893 | 17,959 | 24,008 | 29,691 | 37,114 | 45,594 |
| Foreign direct investment, net | 594 | 769 | 698 | 1,411 | 1,711 | 6,500 | 1,800 |
| Gross reserves, excluding gold (end-year) | 1,353 | 2,955 | 4,241 | 6,731 | 9,302 | 19,413 | na |
| External debt stock [3] | 11,819 | 12,098 | 12,771 | 14,578 | 20,157 | 23,298 | na |
| | | | *(In months of imports of goods and services)* | | | | |
| Gross reserves, excluding gold (end-year) | 0.9 | 1.7 | 2.4 | 2.9 | 3.2 | 5.4 | na |
| | | | *(In per cent of exports of goods and services)* | | | | |
| Debt service [4] | 10.4 | 8.7 | 5.7 | 6.3 | 4.8 | 4.9 | na |
| **Memorandum items** | | | *(Denominations as indicated)* | | | | |
| Population (end-year, million) | 48.9 | 48.5 | 48.0 | 47.6 | 47.3 | 47.1 | na |
| GDP (in billions of hryvnias) | 170 | 204 | 226 | 267 | 346 | 403 | 454 |
| GDP per capita (in US dollar) | 639 | 785 | 883 | 1,053 | 1,374 | 1,671 | na |
| Share of industry in GDP (in per cent) | 26.7 | 27.1 | 30.5 | 31.0 | 30.0 | na | na |
| Share of agriculture in GDP (in per cent) | 14.4 | 14.4 | 13.4 | 13.0 | 13.5 | na | na |
| Current account/GDP (in per cent) | 4.7 | 3.7 | 7.5 | 5.8 | 10.5 | 1.6 | -1.7 |
| External debt - reserves (in US$ million) | 10,466 | 9,143 | 8,530 | 7,847 | 10,855 | 3,885 | na |
| External debt/GDP (in per cent) | 37.8 | 31.8 | 30.1 | 29.1 | 31.0 | 29.6 | na |
| External debt/exports of goods and services (in per cent) | 60.5 | 57.4 | 54.7 | 50.4 | 50.7 | 54.5 | na |

[1] General government includes the state, municipalities and extra-budgetary funds.

[2] Weighted average over all maturities.

[3] Includes public and publicly guaranteed debt and an estimate of the stock of private debt (in both cases medium and long-term debt only).

[4] Refers to payments on official debt only.

# Uzbekistan

## Economic performance and prospects

■ Growth has picked up, fiscal reforms are advancing and the balance of payments position is favourable, but inflation is high and state interference is pervasive.

■ Private investment and sustained economic growth can occur only if there is a revival of financial intermediation and a commitment to market-oriented reforms.

## Real economy

According to official statistics, real GDP grew by 7.2 per cent in the year up to September 2005. Preliminary estimates indicate growth of 7 per cent for the year as a whole, underpinned by the agricultural and natural resource sectors and certain state-owned industries, and driven by net exports. Growth is largely dependent on commodity prices and demand in Russia, and is unlikely to be self-sustaining in the absence of economic reforms. Household incomes and demand were flat in 2005, although there were reports of improved rural incomes, and growing workers' remittances from Kazakhstan and Russia.

## Economic policies

The government has maintained a fairly disciplined fiscal policy. The budget for 2006 targets a deficit of 1.5 per cent. The expansion of domestic money supply, in contrast, has been too loose despite the rationing of cash in circulation. The central bank has continued to target a gradual depreciation of the nominal currency rate. In 2005 there was a substantial reserve accumulation of over US$ 0.5 billion to US$ 2.6 billion by the end of the year, equivalent to over six months of imports. This was reflected in a substantial expansion of broad money (about 40 per cent) and put pressure on prices. (Independent estimates for inflation are considerably higher than the official figure.)

## External sector

High export growth supported a current account surplus of about 9 per cent of GDP in 2005. Despite some substantial medium-term commitments by foreign investors in the resources sector, foreign direct investment has remained low relative to the size of the economy. Through stringent control over external public and publicly guaranteed borrowing, the external debt-to-GDP ratio declined to about 32 per cent at the end of 2005.

## Outlook and risks

The fairly benign macroeconomic situation is unlikely to be sustainable in the medium-term, as the government continues to rule out fundamental market-oriented reform. A second year of strong growth in the industrial sector was again underpinned by state-directed credit, tax preferences and prohibitive external tariffs. The distorted allocation of resources is likely to be reflected in a substantial bad loan problem in the large state-owned banks. The solvency of these banks and their access to external credit is increasingly at risk. Serious inflationary pressures and the re-emergence of a parallel market in foreign exchange will need to be addressed urgently.

### Exports and industrial production growth year-on-year

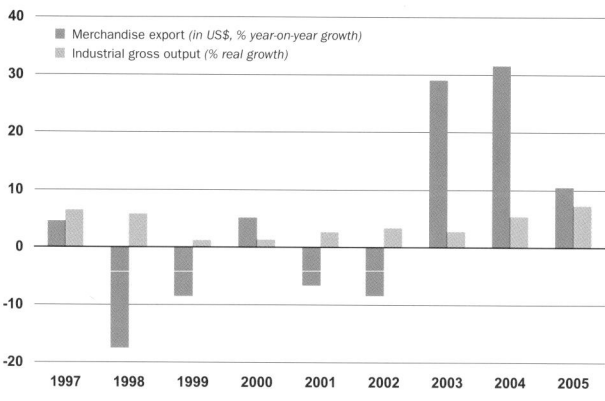

### Inflation, exchange rate developments and interest rates

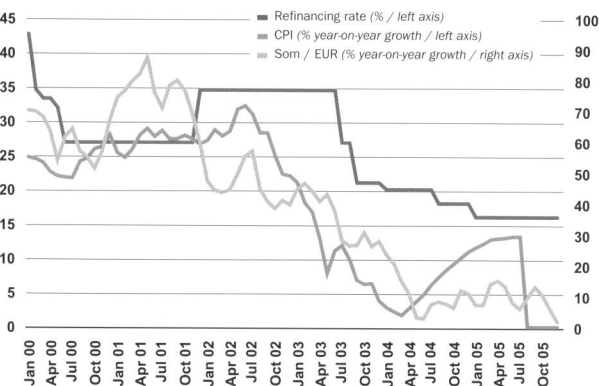

### Debt and fiscal balance

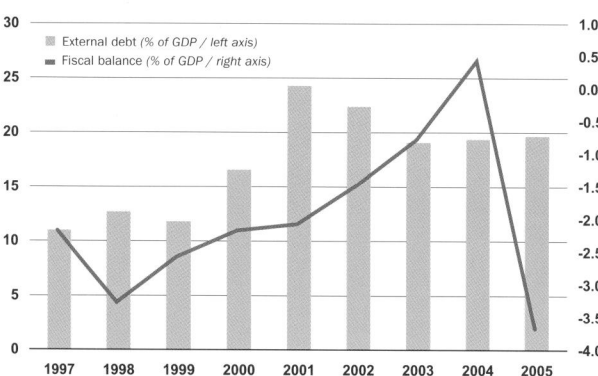

### Current account deficit and net FDI

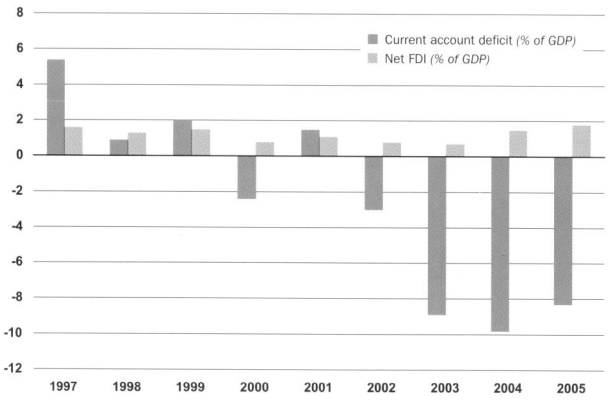

| | 2000 | 2001 | 2002 | 2003 | 2004 | 2005 Estimate | 2006 Projection |
|---|---|---|---|---|---|---|---|
| **Output and expenditure** | *(Percentage change in real terms)* | | | | | | |
| GDP [1] | 3.8 | 4.1 | 3.1 | 1.5 | 7.4 | 7.0 | 4.0 |
|   Private consumption | na | na | na | na | na | na | na |
|   Public consumption | na | na | na | na | na | na | na |
|   Gross fixed capital formation | na | na | na | na | na | na | na |
|   Exports of goods and services | na | na | na | na | na | na | na |
|   Imports of goods and services | na | na | na | na | na | na | na |
| Industrial gross output | 1.3 | 2.7 | 3.4 | 2.8 | 5.4 | na | na |
| Agricultural gross output | 3.2 | 4.1 | 6.0 | 5.9 | 10.1 | na | na |
| **Employment** | *(Percentage change)* | | | | | | |
| Labour force (end-year) | 1.1 | 1.5 | 3.1 | 3.1 | 3.1 | na | na |
| Employment (end-year) | 1.1 | 1.5 | 2.4 | 2.7 | 3.4 | na | na |
| | *(In per cent of labour force)* | | | | | | |
| Unemployment (end-year) [2] | 0.4 | 0.4 | 0.4 | 0.3 | 0.3 | na | na |
| **Prices and wages** | *(Percentage change)* | | | | | | |
| Consumer prices (annual average) [3] | 49.2 | 47.5 | 44.3 | 14.8 | 8.8 | 7.0 | 17.5 |
| Consumer prices (end-year) | 28.2 | 26.4 | 24.4 | 7.7 | 15.5 | 7.0 | 18.0 |
| Producer prices (annual average) | 61.1 | 42.2 | na | na | na | na | na |
| Producer prices (end-year) | 70.2 | 44.0 | 12.2 | 8.0 | 6.5 | na | na |
| Gross average monthly earnings in economy (annual average) | 47.4 | 58.2 | 111.8 | 28.2 | 39.7 | 22.0 | na |
| **Government sector** [4] | *(In per cent of GDP)* | | | | | | |
| General government balance | -2.2 | -2.1 | -1.5 | -0.8 | 0.4 | -3.7 | na |
| General government expenditure | 30.2 | 36.0 | 37.2 | 33.9 | 32.0 | 34.7 | na |
| General government debt | 16.6 | 24.3 | 22.4 | 19.1 | 19.4 | 19.7 | na |
| **Monetary sector** | *(Percentage change)* | | | | | | |
| Broad money (M3, end-year) | 37.1 | 54.3 | 29.7 | 27.2 | 47.8 | 30.4 | na |
| Domestic credit (end-year) | 88.8 | 90.8 | 40.9 | 3.9 | 6.8 | 6.1 | na |
| | *(In per cent of GDP)* | | | | | | |
| Broad money (M3, end-year) | 12.2 | 12.4 | 10.6 | 10.3 | 12.2 | 13.2 | na |
| **Interest and exchange rates** | *(In per cent per annum, end-year)* | | | | | | |
| Refinancing rate | 26.8 | 26.8 | 34.5 | 20.0 | 20.0 | na | na |
| Treasury bill rate (3-month maturity) | 17.1 | 17.1 | 17.1 | na | na | na | na |
| Deposit rate (1 year) | 18.8 | 21.2 | 26.0 | na | na | na | na |
| Lending rate (1 year) | 27.6 | 27.6 | 33.4 | na | na | na | na |
| | *(Sums per US dollar)* | | | | | | |
| Exchange rate (end-year) [5] | 631.3 | 937.6 | 1,068.3 | 979.0 | 1,056.6 | 1,140.0 | na |
| Exchange rate (annual average) [5] | 360.7 | 646.3 | 885.0 | 995.5 | 999.2 | 1,071.1 | na |
| **External sector** | *(In millions of US dollars)* | | | | | | |
| Current account | 218 | -113 | 252 | 882 | 1,193 | 1,137 | 972 |
| Trade balance | 494 | 186 | 324 | 836 | 1,202 | 1,189 | 1,036 |
|   Merchandise exports | 2,935 | 2,740 | 2,510 | 3,240 | 4,263 | 4,709 | 4,678 |
|   Merchandise imports | 2,441 | 2,554 | 2,186 | 2,404 | 3,061 | 3,520 | 3,642 |
| Foreign direct investment, net | 75 | 83 | 65 | 70 | 187 | 250 | 300 |
| Gross reserves, excluding gold (end-year) | 684 | 1,212 | 1,215 | 1,659 | 2,147 | 2,372 | na |
| External debt stock | 4,418 | 4,279 | 4,260 | 4,426 | 4,498 | 4,606 | na |
| | *(In months of imports of goods and services)* | | | | | | |
| Gross reserves, excluding gold (end-year) | 2.8 | 4.6 | 5.4 | 6.4 | 6.5 | 6.3 | na |
| | *(In per cent of exports of goods and services)* | | | | | | |
| Debt service | 25.5 | 26.2 | 23.3 | 22.5 | 17.4 | 14.6 | na |
| **Memorandum items** | *(Denominations as indicated)* | | | | | | |
| Population (end-year, million) | 24.7 | 24.9 | 25.6 | 26.0 | 26.0 | 26.0 | na |
| GDP (in billions of sums) | 3,256 | 4,925 | 7,450 | 9,838 | 12,190 | 14,704 | na |
| GDP per capita (in US dollars) [6] | 366 | 306 | 329 | 380 | 470 | 528 | na |
| Share of industry in GDP (in per cent) | 14.2 | 14.1 | 14.5 | 15.0 | 17.0 | na | na |
| Share of agriculture in GDP (in per cent) | 30.1 | 30.0 | 30.1 | 28.8 | 27.0 | na | na |
| Current account/GDP (in per cent) | 2.4 | -1.5 | 3.0 | 8.9 | 9.8 | 8.3 | na |
| External debt - reserves (in US$ million) | 3,734 | 3,067 | 3,045 | 2,767 | 2,351 | 2,234 | na |
| External debt/GDP (in per cent) | 48.9 | 56.2 | 50.6 | 44.8 | 36.9 | 33.6 | na |
| External debt/exports of goods and services (in per cent) | 131.4 | 133.7 | 142.7 | 117.2 | 93.0 | 86.6 | na |

[1] EBRD estimate. Official figures are considerably higher.

[2] Officially registered unemployed. No labour force survey estimates were available.

[3] Unofficial estimates; official figures are lower.

[4] Includes extra-budgetary funds, but excludes local government.

[5] Dual exchange rates were in operation until October 2003. Data show a weighted average of the official, bank and parallel market rates.

[6] Calculated at the weighted exchange rate for periods in which dual exchange rates were in effect.

# Abbreviations

| | | | | |
|---|---|---|---|---|
| The Bank, EBRD | European Bank for Reconstruction and Development | | IMF | International Monetary Fund |
| BEEPS | Business Environment and Enterprise Performance Survey | | na | not available |
| | | | PPP | purchasing power parity |
| BTC | Baku-Tbilisi-Ceyhan | | PRSP | Poverty Reduction Strategy Paper |
| CEB | central eastern Europe and the Baltic states (see map inside front cover) | | PRGF | Poverty Reduction and Growth Facility |
| | | | RPI | retail price index |
| CIS | Commonwealth of Independent States (see map inside front cover) | | SBA | Stand-By Arrangement |
| CPI | consumer price index | | SEE | south-eastern Europe (see map inside front cover) |
| EMU | Economic and Monetary Union | | | |
| ERM | Exchange Rate Mechanism | | SEE-3 | Bulgaria, Croatia, Romania |
| EU | European Union | | SEE-4 | Albania, Bosnia and Herzegovina, FYR Macedonia, Serbia and Montenegro |
| FDI | foreign direct investment | | UN | United Nations |
| FYR | Former Yugoslav Republic | | VAT | value added tax |
| GDP | gross domestic product | | WTO | World Trade Organization |
| ILO | International Labour Organization | | | |